THE ARCHEOLOGY OF
WORLD RELIGIONS

To aid readers making comparative studies of the archeological backgrounds of the ten religions contained in the casebound edition of *The Archeology of World Religions*, the publishers have retained the original page, chapter, and illustration numbers, and have included in each of the three paperbound volumes the complete index to all ten religions that appeared in the original edition.

Volume I
Primitivism, Zoroastrianism,
Hinduism, Jainism

Volume II
Buddhism, Confucianism, Taoism

THE ARCHEOLOGY OF
WORLD RELIGIONS

Shinto
Islam
Sikhism

BY JACK FINEGAN

PRINCETON, NEW JERSEY

PRINCETON UNIVERSITY PRESS

Preface

THERE are many living religions in the world today. In addition to the more prominent systems of belief and practice cherished by groups which have long recorded histories or political or numerical importance, there are the numerous forms of faith found among preliterate peoples in various parts of the earth. If the latter may be dealt with collectively under the heading of "primitivism" the major religions of the present world are at least twelve. They are Buddhism, Christianity, Confucianism, Hinduism, Islam, Jainism, Judaism, Primitivism, Shinto, Sikhism, Taoism, and Zoroastrianism.

The archeological background of the Hebrew and Christian faiths was the subject of my *Light from the Ancient Past* (Princeton University Press, 1946), and it is the purpose of the present book to give a similar account relative to the ten others.

In a study primarily archeological it is clear that the chief concern will be with the early history of the religions, rather than with their recent and contemporary aspects. A beginning of the entire inquiry will be made with Primitivism. Pertaining as the adjective primitive does to that which is earliest in time, this subject directs our attention to the first discernible evidences of religion, back in the mists of man's prehistory; but synonymous as the same adjective is with aboriginal, it also points to the faiths of native peoples still on earth today. Many of these may have been in existence for a very long time and even have had a history as long as that of men of literate cultures, but the facts that this history has not been recorded in writing and that these people have lived in relative isolation from advancing civilization, suggest that among them religion may be at least relatively simple and archaic. It will not be assumed in advance that the contemporary beliefs of such folks correspond with those of prehistoric men, but if similarities are actually observed they will be pointed out. Thus two glimpses will be had of Primitivism, one in prehistoric times, the other in the life of present-day preliterate peoples.

We shall then deal with the other religions, in an order suggested by both geographical and chronological considerations. As far as geography is concerned, the study will take us eastward from Iran to India, China and Japan, then westward to Arabia and back once more to India. Each of these lands will be described briefly when we first come to it. In regard to chronology, it is of course often difficult or impossible to assign exact dates to the lives of the founders of religions or to crucial events in the history of religions. Evidence will be presented on such questions, however, and the order in which the various religions are considered will reflect at least to some extent the relative times of their emergence in world history. In each major geographical area the rise of human culture will be traced from the earliest times; in each religion the history of the faith will be followed from its origin to the point where its most distinctive emphases have come into view. Considerations of space as well as the archeological interest preclude any attempt to carry the history farther than such point as this. Inevitably the limitation means that a great many developments cannot be touched at all. In the case of Buddhism, for example, a relatively full story is told of its rise in India but to its later spread through many other lands only very brief references are made.

The archeological interest also determines the fact that attention is focused throughout upon the ancient monuments and documents of the various religions. The actual objects and manuscripts which archeology brings to light provide materials of tangible and fascinating sort for understanding the nature of the religions which produced them. Through the ancient writings and the monuments which are often far older than any written records, the religion speaks with its own authentic voice.

In order to make these fundamental materials known in as direct a way as possible, extensive quotations are given from the texts, and many of the monuments are reproduced in photographs. The work is based upon my own travel around the world, gathering of material from museums, libraries and other sources in Asia, Europe and America, and consultation of the literature cited. Except for books appearing in the List of Abbreviations, each work is listed fully upon its first mention.

I wish to express deep appreciation to various members of the staff of Princeton University Press, and especially to Miss Margot Cutter, Fine Arts Editor, for many courtesies.

JACK FINEGAN

Pacific School of Religion
Berkeley, California

Acknowledgments

Sources of photographs and quotations are given in the List of Illustrations and in the footnotes. In addition to these acknowledgments, appreciation is also expressed to the following for permission to make reproductions of pictures: to the American Council of Learned Societies, Washington, for Fig. 133; to the Director General of Archaeology in India, New Delhi, for Figs. 54, 61 and 65; to Ludwig Bachhofer for Figs. 89, 91, 92, 93, 94, 95, 96, 97, 99, 100 and 101; to Ernest Benn Limited, London, for Fig. 59; to the Bobbs Merrill Company, Indianapolis, for Fig. 187; to the Trustees of the British Museum, London, for Fig. 33; to W. Norman Brown for Figs. 82, 83, 84, 85, 86 and 87; to Avery Brundage for Fig. 141; to the Syndics of the Cambridge University Press for Fig. 115; to the Carnegie Institution of Washington for Fig. 46; to the Chicago Natural History Museum for Fig. 149; to the Clarendon Press, Oxford, for Fig. 238; to the Columbia University Library, New York, for Fig. 220; to Mrs. A. K. Coomaraswamy for Figs. 55, 56, 57, 62, 63, 64, 67, 72 and 114; to the John Day Company, Inc., New York, for Fig. 143; to Faber and Faber Limited, London, for Fig. 16; to the Freer Gallery of Art, Washington, for Figs. 82 and 83; to Librairie Orientaliste Paul Geuthner, Paris, for Figs. 154, 158, 159, 162, 211 and 219; to George G. Harrap and Company Limited, London, for Fig. 183; to Harvard University Press, Cambridge, for Fig. 129; to the late Ernst E. Herzfeld for Figs. 23, 32, 41 and 42; to the High Commissioner for India, London, for Fig. 128; to the Institut de Paleontologie Humaine, Paris, for Figs. 11, 12 and 13; to the Macmillan Company, New York, for Fig. 136; to the Matson Photo Service, Jerusalem, for Fig. 227; to the Museum of Navajo Ceremonial Art, Santa Fe, for Fig. 19; to the National Geological Survey of China, Nanking, for Figs. 137 and 138; to the National Museum, Stockholm, for Figs. 180, 184, 185 and 186; to the New York Public Library for Fig. 208; to Martinus Nijhoff, The Hague, for Figs. 124, 125 and 126; to Oxford University Press, London, for Figs. 37, 39, 40, 44, 45, 243, 244 and 250; to Oxford University Press, New York, for Fig. 23; to Pantheon Books Inc., New York, for Figs. 148 and 176; to Arthur Upham Pope for Figs. 37, 39, 40, 44, 45, 243, 244 and 250; to Presses Universitaires de France, Paris, for Fig. 237; to Princeton University Press, Princeton, for Fig. 131; to Routledge and Kegan Paul Ltd., London, for Fig. 136; to the Society of Antiquaries of London for Figs. 209 and 210; to the Society for Promoting Christian Knowledge, London, for Fig. 164; and to Van Oest, Les Editions d'Art et d'Histoire, Paris, for Figs. 110, 118, 167, 202, 205 and 206.

Certain material reproduced in this book, namely, seven pictures, three figures, two plates, and the reproduction of the first page of a preface of a work (in Japanese), which material is specifically identified in the acknowledgments in the List of Illustrations, was taken from six German works and two Japanese works, originally published in Germany and Japan, respectively. The German and Japanese interests in the United States copyrights in these works were vested in the Attorney General of the United States in 1950, pursuant to law. The works involved and the particular material taken therefrom are listed below. The use of this material in the present book is by permission of the Attorney General of the United States under License No. JA-1482.

1. William Cohn, *Buddha in der Kunst des Ostens.* Leipzig: Klinkhardt & Biermann, 1925. "Copyright 1924 by Klinkhardt & Biermann, Leipzig."
   (1) Picture on page 5, with title on page 4 (for my Fig. 102)
   (2) Picture on page 101, with title on page 100 (for my Fig. 132)
2. Ernst Diez, *Die Kunst Indiens.* Wildpark-Potsdam: Akademische Verlagsgesellschaft Athenaion M.B.H., 1925.
   (1) Figure 136, on page 115 (for my Fig. 105)
3. P. Andreas Eckardt, *Geschichte der koreanischen Kunst.* Leipzig: Karl W. Hiersemann, 1929. "Copyright 1929 by Karl W. Hiersemann, Leipzig."
   (1) Figure 178 on Plate LXII (for my Fig. 130)
4. Otto Fischer, *Die Kunst Indiens, Chinas und Japans.* Propyläen-Kunstgeschichte, IV. 2d ed. Berlin: Propyläen-Verlag, 1928. "Copyright 1928 by Propyläen-Verlag, G.M.B.H., in Berlin."
   (1) Picture on page 168 (for my Fig. 104)
   (2) Picture on page 247 (for my Fig. 77)
5. Helmuth von Glasenapp, *Die Literaturen Indiens von ihren Anfängen bis zur Gegenwart.* In Oskar Walzel, ed., Handbuch der Literatur-Wissenschaft. Wildpark-Potsdam: Akademische Verlagsgesellschaft Athenaion M.B.H., 1929. "Copyright 1929 by

Akademische Verlagsgesellschaft Athenaion M.B.H., Wildpark-Potsdam."

(1) Figure 26 on page 51 (for my Fig. 50)

6. Heinrich Glück and Ernst Diez, *Die Kunst des Islam.* Propyläen-Kunstgeschichte, v. 3d ed. Berlin: Propyläen-Verlag, 1925. "Copyright 1925 by Der Propyläen-Verlag G.M.B.H., Berlin."

(1) Picture on page 186 (for my Fig. 241)

(2) Picture between pages 188 and 189 (for my Fig. 242)

(3) Picture on page 338 (for my Fig. 252)

7. Mizoguchi, Teijiro and Eikyu Matsuoka, eds., *Nihon Emakimono Shusei.* Tokyo: Yuzankaku, 1929.

(1) Vol. III, Plate 64 (for my Fig. 193)

(2) Vol. IV, Plate 10 (for my Fig. 192)

8. Uematsu, Yasushi and Tatso Otsuka, annotators, *Kojiki Zenshaku.* Tokyo: Fukyusha-shoten, 1935.

(1) Facsimile in Japanese language of first page of Preface (for my Fig. 188)

Contents

[xi]

X. SIKHISM

List of Illustrations

LIST OF ILLUSTRATIONS

LIST OF MAPS

AJA   *American Journal of Archaeology.*

ARAB   Daniel D. Luckenbill, *Ancient Records of Assyria and Babylonia.* 2 vols. 1926-27.

ARE   James H. Breasted, *Ancient Records of Egypt.* 5 vols. 1906-07.

BASOR   *Bulletin* of the American Schools of Oriental Research.

BEIS   Ludwig Bachhofer, *Early Indian Sculpture.* 2 vols. 1929.

CAH   J. B. Bury, S. A. Cook, F. E. Adcock, M. P. Charlesworth and N. H. Baynes, eds., *The Cambridge Ancient History.* 12 vols. and 5 vols. of plates. 1923-39.

CBC   Herrlee G. Creel, *The Birth of China, A Study of the Formative Period of Chinese Civilization.* 1937.

CEMA   K. A. C. Creswell, *Early Muslim Architecture, Umayyads, Early ʿAbbāsids and Ṭūlūnids.* Part I, *Umayyads*, A.D. 622-750 (1932); Part II, *Early ʿAbbāsids, Umayyads of Cordova, Aghlabids, Ṭūlūnids, and Samānids*, A.D. 751-905 (1940).

CHI   E. J. Rapson, Wolseley Haig, Richard Burn and H. H. Dodwell, *The Cambridge History of India.* 6 vols. 1922-37.

CHIIA   Ananda K. Coomaraswamy, *History of Indian and Indonesian Art.* 1927.

CRW   Carl Clemen and others, *Religions of the World, Their Nature and Their History.* tr. A. K. Dallas. 1931.

CSECC   Herrlee G. Creel, *Studies in Early Chinese Culture*, First Series (American Council of Learned Societies Studies in Chinese and Related Civilizations, 3). 1937.

CSHI   H. H. Dodwell, ed., *The Cambridge Shorter History of India.* 1934.

EB   *The Encyclopaedia Britannica.* 14th ed. 24 vols. 1929.

EI   M. Th. Houtsma and others, eds., *The Encyclopaedia of Islām, A Dictionary of the Geography, Ethnography and Biography of the Muhammadan Peoples.* 5 vols. 1913-38.

FAH   Nabih Amin Faris, ed., *The Arab Heritage.* 1944.

FHCP   Fung Yu-lan, *A History of Chinese Philosophy*, I, *The Period of the Philosophers (From the Beginnings to circa 100 B.C.).* tr. Derk Bodde. 1937.

FLP   Jack Finegan, *Light from the Ancient Past, The Archeological Background of the Hebrew-Christian Religion.* 1946.

GCBD   Herbert A. Giles, *A Chinese Biographical Dictionary.* 1898.

GCE   René Grousset, *The Civilizations of the East.* tr.

[xx]

Catherine A. Phillips. I, *The Near and Middle East*. 1931; II, *India*. 1931; III, *China*. 1934; IV, *Japan*. 1934.

GJ Helmuth von Glasenapp, *Der Jainismus, Eine indische Erlösungsreligion* (Kultur und Weltanschauung, Eine Sammlung von Einzeldarstellungen). 1925.

HERE James Hastings, ed., *Encyclopaedia of Religion and Ethics*. 12 vols. 1910-22.

HHA Philip K. Hitti, *History of the Arabs*. 2d ed. 1940.

JAOS *Journal of the American Oriental Society*.

JGRMW Edward J. Jurji, ed., *The Great Religions of the Modern World, Confucianism, Taoism, Hinduism, Buddhism, Shintoism, Islam, Judaism, Eastern Orthodoxy, Roman Catholicism, Protestantism*. 1946.

JNES *Journal of Near Eastern Studies*.

LCL *The Loeb Classical Library*.

MASI *Memoirs of the Archaeological Survey of India*.

MHR George Foot Moore, *History of Religions* (International Theological Library). I, *China, Japan, Egypt, Babylonia, Assyria, India, Persia, Greece,* *Rome*. rev. ed. 1920; II, *Judaism, Christianity, Mohammedanism*. 1919.

MPEW Charles A. Moore, ed., *Philosophy—East and West*. 1946.

OIC *Oriental Institute Communications*.

PSPA Arthur Upham Pope, ed., *A Survey of Persian Art from Prehistoric Times to the Present*. 6 vols. 1938-39.

REJH *Early Japanese History* (c.40 B.C.-A.D. 1167). 2 vols. Part A by Robert K. Reischauer; Part B by Jean Reischauer and Robert K. Reischauer. (Princeton University: School of Public and International Affairs). 1937.

SAOC *Studies in Ancient Oriental Civilization*. Oriental Institute.

SBE F. Max Müller, ed., *The Sacred Books of the East Translated by Various Oriental Scholars*. 50 vols. 1885-1910.

SJSCH G. B. Sansom, *Japan, A Short Cultural History*. rev. ed. 1943.

SLR Alfred Bertholet and Edvard Lehmann, eds., *Lehrbuch der Religionsgeschichte, begründet von Chantepie de la Saussaye*. 2 vols. 4th ed. 1925.

THE ARCHEOLOGY OF

WORLD RELIGIONS

CHAPTER VIII

Shinto

THE Japanese islands form an arc off the coast of northeast Asia. Four main islands, named Hokkaido, Honshu, Shikoku and Kyushu, together with many smaller ones, constitute Japan proper, while to the north and the south respectively extend the Kurile and the Ryukyu groups. The area of the central archipelago is approximately 150,000 square miles, or slightly less than that of the State of California.

Some seventy-five per cent of the country is mountainous, and only about fifteen per cent of the total area of the land is under cultivation. The highest peak is the symmetrical volcanic cone of Mount Fuji, which reaches an elevation of 12,461 feet. If the Kurile and Ryukyu Islands are included, there are more than five hundred volcanoes within the land. Not far off the eastern coast of Japan the ocean bed descends to depths of twenty and thirty thousand feet below sea level, thus making a difference in elevation between the high peaks and the ocean depths of seven or eight miles. The geological stresses set up by this enormous differential are believed responsible for the frequent earthquakes which are felt throughout the area. There is snow and relatively cold weather in Japan in the winter, and rain and heat in the summer.

The largest approximately level region is the Kwanto Plain around modern Tokyo, most of which has been built up as an alluvial fan by the numerous rivers which flow down out of the mountains. Central Honshu, whence these rivers descend, is the most mountainous region in all Japan. Northern Honshu is also rugged, and has a more severe climate, as does also the northernmost island of Hokkaido. Western Honshu is hilly rather than mountainous, and facing on the island-dotted Inland Sea is perhaps the most beautiful part of the entire picturesque land. Shikoku is the smallest of the main islands and the least important; Kyushu, by virtue of its location, has long served as a connecting link with China and the South Seas.[1]

---

[1] For the geography of Japan see Glenn T. Trewartha, *Japan, A Physical, Cultural and Regional Geography.* 1945; George B. Cressey, *Asia's Lands and Peoples, A Geography of One-Third the Earth and Two-Thirds Its People.* 1944, pp.170-252.

1. PREHISTORIC JAPAN

THE ANCESTRAL AINUS

As FAR as is now known there was no Paleolithic culture in Japan, and the earliest inhabitants belonged to the Neolithic Age. This epoch probably began in Japan in the third millennium B.C. and lasted until near the end of the pre-Christian era.[2] The most ancient people of this period lived primarily by hunting and fishing, and are known to us chiefly from the thousands of shell mounds, or kitchen middens, which they left around the coasts of the islands.[3] Mixed in with the discarded shells in these refuse heaps are animal bones, stone implements and weapons, and broken pottery. The stone objects include picks, axes, scrapers, knives, and heads for arrows and spears. The pottery fragments are from all sorts of vessels such as jars, pots, bowls, cups and bottles. The manufacture of the pottery was by hand, and it was relatively coarse in material but ornate in decoration. Much of it was of the "rope-pattern" type, so-called because it was built up by coiling strips of clay or was ornamented with the coil as a conventional design.

It is thought that the people represented by this Neolithic culture were not indigenous to the islands but had come from elsewhere in several successive waves of immigration. Their racial origin is not certainly known, but it is surmised that they were of Caucasoid affinity. There seems little doubt that the Ainus, an aboriginal people now living on the northern island of Hokkaido, are their modern descendants; hence the ancient Neolithic people may conveniently be called the ancestral Ainus.[4]

The religion of the present-day Ainus probably has much in common with that of their prehistoric ancestors, and a few words concerning it may cast light upon the kind of beliefs which prevailed in the Neolithic Age. This religion is characterized by animism and nature worship. Almost every object in the universe, whether ani-

[2] Menghin, *Weltgeschichte der Steinzeit,* pp.81,297-302.

[3] Neil G. Munro, *Prehistoric Japan.* 1908, pp.44f. This book is still, despite its date, the only comprehensive study of the period. See Hugh Borton, Serge Elisséeff, and Edwin O. Reischauer, *A Selected List of Books and Articles on Japan in English, French and German.* 1940, p.18.

[4] H. Matsumoto in *American Anthropologist, New Series, Organ of the American Anthropological Association, The Anthropological Society of Washington, and the American Ethnological Society of New York.* 23 (1921), pp.50-76; Carl W. Bishop in *Annual Report of the Board of Regents of the Smithsonian Institution, Showing the Operations, Expenditures, and Condition of the Institution for the Year Ending June 30, 1925* (Publication 2836). 1926, pp.550f.; sjsch pp.1-5.

mate or inanimate, organic or inorganic, is supposed to be the seat of personal, intelligent life. In the skies the highest deity is the sun, while on earth the chief deity is of related character, namely, fire. The spirit of fire, which is worshiped on every pagan hearth, is regarded as a goddess and is commonly called Fuji, meaning "ancestress." Since the same Ainu word is the name of Japan's highest mountain, it may be supposed that this famous volcano was an object of worship to the prehistoric Ainus. Other nature deities include spirits of stars, clouds, seas and vegetation. Over against the beneficent spirits are many demons of air and land, the exorcism of which is a part of their religious practice.[5]

THE YAMATO CONQUEST

In the last centuries B.C. and the first centuries A.D. other people made their way into the islands and began to push the Ainus before them. These invaders probably came for the most part from the Asiatic mainland by way of Korea, and are believed to have been of Mongoloid stock with perhaps an admixture of a proto-Malay element from the tropical South.[6] It is at this time that Japan begins to figure in Chinese writings. The earliest reference is in an ancient treatise on geography called the Shan-hai-ching, where it is stated that the northern and southern Wo are tributary to the Chinese state of Yen. Since Yen ceased to exist as an independent state about 226 B.C., this statement must have to do with a time in the third or even fourth century B.C. Again we are told of the Ta Wo Wang or Great King of the Wo who ruled in the region of Ye-ma-t'ai south of Korea. This place must have been on the island of Kyushu, and the name Ye-ma-t'ai is evidently the same as Yamato, by which the Japanese people have ever afterward designated themselves.[7]

Since Yamato is also the name later applied to a province in central Honshu, we may assume that from an original stronghold on Kyushu the Yamato people pushed gradually forward onto the larger island. The region of Yamato is near Lake Biwa, and the establishment of this as their center shows that the Yamato people had made large gains against the Ainus. Another independent kingdom, closely related to the kingdom of Silla in Korea, also came into existence in western Honshu.

[5] J. Batchelor in HERE I, pp.239-252; Carl Etter, *Ainu Folklore, Traditions and Culture of the Vanishing Aborigines of Japan.* 1949, pp.51f.
[6] Katsuro Hara, *An Introduction to the History of Japan.* 1920, pp.39-49.
[7] Bishop in *Annual Report of the . . . Smithsonian Institution . . . 1925*, pp.554f.

HOKKAIDO

N

O F

A N

H

U

S

O

A

N

P

Nikko•

Tokyo
• Kamagawa
•Yokohama
•Kamakura

+ Fuji

Kyoto• •Adzuchi
Yamato
Osaka• •Nara
•Asuka
Ise•

A

MAP 8

JAPAN

0   50   100   150

Scale of miles

The invaders of whom we have been telling had a culture much more advanced than that of the Ainus. Whereas the latter were still a people of the Stone Age, the Yamato enjoyed all the advantages of the use of iron. Since relatively few bronze remains have been found in Japan, it is supposed that with the arrival of the newcomers the land witnessed a transition from the Neolithic Age to the Iron Age with scarcely any intervening Bronze Age at all. Among the numerous objects of iron now found, are not only axes, chisels, swords and daggers, but also bits and stirrups which give us the important additional information that the horse was introduced and ridden. As a matter of fact it was doubtless the practice of fighting on horseback as well as with weapons of iron which gave the conquerors their superiority over the Ainus. The possession of domesticated animals also made possible the practice of true agriculture in distinction from such hoe culture as may have prevailed previously.

One other mark of this time was the practice of burying important deceased persons in dolmens. These tombs were megalithic structures built out of huge rough boulders, covered with mounds of earth and surrounded by moats. Iron objects of the kind already mentioned were found in these burial places, and also wheelmade pottery and interesting terra cotta figures technically called *haniwa*. The last are generally in the form of cylinders surmounted by a bust of a man or woman. Sometimes it is a soldier in armor who is represented, and occasionally it is a horse or even a house. These figures were probably set up around the edges of the tomb terraces, and may have been substitutes for living beings who were buried with the deceased in earlier times. A group of such *haniwa* is shown in Fig. 187.[8]

While exact dates are not available for the times of which we have been speaking, it may be safely affirmed that the culture just described was flourishing in Japan in the second century A.D. It is also known that the dolmen type of burial prevailed until in the seventh or eighth century, and that by that time the Ainus had been pushed northward to a line approximately corresponding to the thirty-seventh parallel of latitude. Not until the tenth century was the subjugation of the Ainus completed on Honshu, and by then there was a considerable admixture of Ainu blood in the Japanese race. Meanwhile, in the fifth and sixth centuries respectively, the art of writing

[8] Otto Kümmel, *Die Kunst Chinas, Japans und Koreas* (Handbuch der Kunstwissenschaft). 1929, p.103; Mary A. Nourse, *Kodo, The Way of the Emperor, A Short History of the Japanese.* 1940, pp.30f., Fig. facing p.31,upper.

and the faith of Buddhism were introduced into Japan from Korea and China.[9]

ANCIENT TIMES ACCORDING TO THE OLDEST WRITTEN RECORDS

Thus far our account has been based primarily upon archeological studies, and while lacking in many details concerning which we would like to be informed, has the relative dependability of a grounding upon tangible remains of the past. Japanese myths, legends and chronicles also reach back into these same ancient times, and supply a great many details which are extremely vivid but unfortunately do not always have the same kind of dependability.

The two earliest written sources we have are the Kojiki or "Record of Ancient Things" and the Nihongi (also called Nihon-shoki) or "Chronicles of Japan," which were compiled respectively in A.D. 712 and 720. A facsimile of the first page of the Preface to the Kojiki is reproduced in Fig. 188.

THE KOJIKI[10]

In the preface of the Kojiki it is related that the Emperor Temmu (A.D. 673-686) was concerned over the inaccuracies to be found in the official records then existing, and that he therefore issued the following decree: "I hear that the chronicles of the emperors and likewise the original words in the possession of the various families deviate from exact truth, and are mostly amplified by empty falsehoods. If at the present time these imperfections be not amended, ere many years shall have elapsed, the purport of this, the great basis of the country, the grand foundation of the monarchy, will be destroyed. So now I desire to have the chronicles of the emperors selected and recorded, and the old words examined and ascertained, falsehoods being erased and the truth determined, in order to transmit [the latter] to after ages."[11]

At that time, it is further narrated, there was a retainer named Hiyeda no Are who had such a remarkable memory that he could repeat anything he ever read and remember anything he ever heard. This man was therefore commanded to memorize the genealogies of the emperors and the "words of former ages." Meanwhile, how-

[9] Bishop in *Annual Report of the . . . Smithsonian Institution . . . 1925*, pp.559, 561f.,566f.
[10] tr. Basil H. Chamberlain, *"Ko-ji-ki,"* or *"Records of Ancient Matters"* (Transactions of the Asiatic Society of Japan, Supplement to Vol. x). 1882; 2d ed. with annotations by W. G. Aston, 1932. The references here are to the original edition.
[11] tr. Chamberlain, p.9.

ever, Emperor Temmu died and no further progress was made on the matter until under the Empress Gemmyo (A.D. 708-721). Then a court official named Yasumaro was commissioned to put into written form the materials which had been preserved in the memory of Are for the past twenty-five years. Coming to this event in his preface, Yasumaro says, referring to the Empress: "She, on the eighteenth day of the ninth moon of the fourth year of Wa do,[12] commanded me Yasumaro to select and record the old words learnt by heart by Hiyeda no Are according to the Imperial Decree, and dutifully to lift them up to her."[13]

As completed, the work written by Yasumaro covered events from the mythological beginnings of heaven and earth to the end of the reign of the Empress Suiko (A.D. 593-628), and was laid before Empress Gemmyo in three volumes only a little more than five months after it was first commissioned. This is stated by the writer in the conclusion of his preface: "All together the things recorded commence with the separation of Heaven and Earth, and conclude with the august reign at Woharida.[14] So from the Deity Master-of-the-August-Center-of-Heaven down to His Augustness Prince-Wave-Limit-Brave-Cormorant-Thatch-Meeting-Incompletely makes the First Volume; from the Heavenly Sovereign Kamu-yamato-ihare-biko down to the august reign of Homuda makes the Second Volume; from the Emperor Oho-Sazaki down to the great palace of Woharida makes the Third Volume. All together I have written Three Volumes, which I reverently and respectfully present. I Yasumaro, with true trembling and true fear, bow my head, bow my head.

"Reverently presented by the Court Noble Futo no Yasumaro, an Officer of the Upper Division of the First Class of the Fifth Rank and of the Fifth Order of Merit, on the twenty-eighth day of the first moon of the fifth year of Wa do."[15]

As Yasumaro indicated in his preface, the Kojiki opens with the beginning of heaven and earth. At this time numerous deities began to come into existence, of whom the first one was mentioned in the preface, namely the Deity Master-of-the-August-Center-of-Heaven

---

[12] Wa do is the name of a Japanese "year-period" which extended from A.D. 708 to 714, and the date indicated corresponds to November 3, 711. For a list of these "year-periods," see Ernest W. Clement in *Transactions of the Asiatic Society of Japan.* 30 (1902), pp.57-60; and, for detailed tables, Supplement of Vol. 37 (1910) of the same *Transactions* (for Wa do, pp.54f.).

[13] tr. Chamberlain, p.11.

[14] Woharida was the residence of Empress Suiko.

[15] tr. Chamberlain, pp.12f. The last date is equivalent to March 10, 712.

(Ame-no-mi-naka-nushi-no-kami). Here is the si tc
in the first two sentences of the Kojiki: "The name c
were born [literally, that became] in the Plain of H
the Heaven and Earth began were the Deity Maste
Center-of-Heaven, next the High-August-Producing
ity, next the Divine-Producing-Wondrous-Deity. Thes
were all deities born alone, and hid their persons."[16]

These words evidently mean that three gods came int
of nothing at the same time that the heaven and the earth
existence. The "Plain of High Heaven" was presumably t
some mythical place in it, and so it may be supposed that th
sky gods. The statement that they "hid their persons" would s
indicate that they made themselves invisible to human sight.
fact that the Deity Master-of-the-August-Center-of-Heaven is
mentioned again after this first appearance, while the High-
gust-Producing-Wondrous-Deity and the Divine-Producing-Wc
drous-Deity are active in the events which follow, has been inte
preted as showing that the first god was comparatively lofty and
transcendent.[18]

The next two deities "were born . . . from a thing that sprouted up
like unto a reed-shoot when the earth, young and like unto floating
oil, drifted about medusa-like," and were named Pleasant-Reed-
Shoot-Prince-Elder-Deity and Heavenly-Eternally-Standing-Deity.
After these, a dozen more gods and goddesses came into being, with
translated names such as Deity Mud-Earth-Lord, Deity Oh-Awful-
Lady, Deity the Male-Who-Invites, and Deity the Female-Who-Invites. The last two are often referred to by their Japanese names,
Izanagi-no-kami and Izanami-no-kami, or simply Izanagi and Izanami.

After this the Kojiki proceeds to relate how through Izanagi and
Izanami the Japanese islands came into being. "Hereupon all the
Heavenly Deities commanded the two Deities His Augustness[19] the
Male-Who-Invites and Her Augustness the Female-Who-Invites, or-
dering them to 'make, consolidate, and give birth to this drifting
land.' Granting to them a heavenly jeweled spear, they [thus] deigned

[16] I, 1. tr. Chamberlain, p.15.
[17] I. Dooman in *Transactions of the Asiatic Society of Japan.* 25 (1897), pp.67f.
[18] Genchi Kato in *Transactions of the Asiatic Society of Japan.* 36 (1908), pp.137-162; and in *Annales du Musée Guimet, Bibliothèque de vulgarisation.* 50 (1931), pp.68-72.
[19] The Japanese title is Mikoto.

charge them. So the two deities, standing upon the Floating Bridge
Heaven, pushed down the jeweled spear and stirred with it,
hereupon, when they had stirred the brine till it went curdle-
urdle,[20] and drew [the spear] up, the brine that dripped down from
the end of the spear was piled up and became an island. This is the
island of Onogoro [i.e. Self-Curdling]."[21]

Izanagi and Izanami then descended upon the island just created
and there became the parents of the other Japanese islands and also
of a host of additional deities. Not a few of these deities were produced upon an occasion when Izanagi was performing a ceremonial
purification. As he divested himself of his garments a new god came
into being with each item of apparel removed, and the same thing
happened at each new stage in the washing of himself. Of these
deities we are particularly concerned with the one who is said to
have been born as Izanagi "washed his left august eye." This was
the goddess Ama-terasu-o-mi-kami or the Heaven-Shining-Great-
August-Deity.

Reading on a little ways farther we find that Izanagi bestowed upon
Amaterasu the rule of the Plain of High Heaven, that is of the sky,
and signalized this event by giving her the string of jewels which
had been about his own neck. These jewels, incidentally, were turned
into more deities a little later. Thus, according to mythology, did
Amaterasu attain the position of sun goddess in which she has always
been so prominent for Japanese religion.

Some time after this, the brother of Amaterasu, named His Brave-
Swift-Impetuous-Male-Augustness (Take-haya-susa-no-wo-no-mikoto), did a number of things which caused grave offence and fright
to the sun goddess. For example he caused damage to be done to
the rice-fields, and he also flayed backward a "heavenly piebald
horse" and flung it through the roof of the hall where Amaterasu
was weaving garments for the gods. The sun goddess thereupon retired into the Rock-Cave of Heaven and made fast the door. "Then
the whole Plain of High Heaven was obscured and all the Central
Land of Reed-Plains darkened."

The darkness caused by the withdrawal of the sun goddess was a
matter of much concern to the "eight hundred myriad" deities, and
they assembled at the Tranquil River of Heaven to devise a plan for
coping with the situation. Under the inspiration of the Thought-

[20] This is an onomatopoeic expression in the Japanese.
[21] I, 3. tr. Chamberlain, pp.18f.

Combining-Deity, they proceeded as follows. They gathered "long-singing birds of eternal night" and set them singing. They made a long string of brilliant jewels and a large and beautiful mirror. They obtained a Sakaki tree[22] from the Heavenly Mount Kagu,[23] and hung the jewels on its upper branches, the mirror on its middle branches, and gifts of cloth on its lower branches. After that they recited a grand liturgy together, and Her Augustness Heavenly-Alarming-Female performed a dance in front of the door of the Rock-Cave of Heaven.

"Then," continues the Kojiki, "the Plain of High Heaven shook, and the eight hundred myriad deities laughed together. Hereupon the Heaven-Shining-Great-August-Deity was amazed, and, slightly opening the door of the Heavenly Rock-Dwelling, spoke thus from the inside: 'Methought that owing to my retirement the Plain of Heaven would be dark, and likewise the Central Land of Reed-Plains would all be dark: how then is it that the Heavenly-Alarming-Female makes merry, and that likewise the eight hundred myriad deities all laugh?' Then the Heavenly-Alarming-Female spoke, saying: 'We rejoice and are glad because there is a deity more illustrious than Thine Augustness.' While she was thus speaking, His Augustness Heavenly-Beckoning-Ancestor-Lord and his Augustness Grand-Jewel pushed forward the mirror and respectfully showed it to the Heaven-Shining-Great-August-Deity, whereupon the Heaven-Shining-Great-August-Deity, more and more astonished, gradually came forth from the door and gazed upon it, whereupon the Heavenly-Hand-Strength-Male-Deity, who was standing hidden, took her august hand and drew her out, and then His Augustness Grand-Jewel drew the bottom-tied rope along at her august back, and spoke, saying: 'Thou must not go back further in than this!' So when the Heaven-Shining-Great-August-Deity had come forth, both the Plain of High Heaven and the Central-Land-of-Reed-Plains of course again became light."[24]

The sequel to the foregoing events was the expulsion from heaven of His Brave-Swift-Impetuous-Male-Augustness for having caused all the trouble. This deity thereupon descended to the Land of Izumo where he found that certain earthly deities were terrorized by an eight-forked serpent. His Brave-Swift-Impetuous-Male-Augustness

---

[22] Identified as the *cleyera japonica*, and still a sacred tree in the Shinto religion.

[23] Kagu was a mountain in Yamato, and is here thought of as having a counterpart in heaven.

[24] I, 16. tr. Chamberlain, pp.58f.

slew this serpent and in its middle tail found a sword which is the Herb-Quelling Great Sword (Kusa-nagi-no-tachi). Although he informed Amaterasu of his exploit and perhaps presented her with the sword, His Brave-Swift-Impetuous-Male-Augustness seems not to have been readmitted to heaven, since afterward we find him building a palace for himself in the Land of Izumo.

Numerous earthly deities seem to have been dwelling on the Japanese islands, and things in general there were in a great state of tumult. Amaterasu resolved to send her son, His Augustness Truly-Conqueror-I-Conquer-Conquering-Swift-Heavenly-Great-Great-Ears (Masa-ka-a-katsu-kachi-hayabi-ame-no-oshi-ho-mimi-no-mikoto),[25] to be the ruler there, but when he went and looked down from the Floating Bridge of Heaven he saw so much violence that he turned back. A long process of pacifying the land then ensued, and by the time it was completed His Augustness Heavenly-Great-Great-Ears (as we may call him for short) was himself the father of a son named His Augustness Heaven-Plenty-Earth-Plenty-Heaven's-Sun-Height-Prince-Rice-ear-Ruddy-Plenty (Ame-nigishi-kuni-nigishi-ama-tsu-hi-daka-hiko-ho-no-ni-nigi-no-mikoto). The father now proposed that the son be sent, and so Prince-Rice-ear-Ruddy-Plenty was commissioned with these words: "This Luxuriant Reed-Plain-Land-of-Fresh-Rice-ears is the land over which thou shalt rule."[26]

Prince-Rice-ear-Ruddy-Plenty was given as marks of his authority the jewels and mirror which had been on the tree in front of Amaterasu's heavenly rock-cave, and the sword which had come from the tail of the eight-forked serpent. The mirror in particular was to symbolize the spirit of the sun goddess, Amaterasu. "Regard this mirror," he was told, "exactly as if it were our august spirit, and reverence it as if reverencing us." Also certain of the heavenly deities were appointed to accompany him. When all was ready, Prince-Rice-ear-Ruddy-Plenty made his great descent and came down upon a mountain peak on the island of Tsukushi, which is modern Kyushu.

There he married Princess Blossoming-Brilliantly-Like-the-Flow-

[25] The word *mimi* or "ears" is a part of many ancient Japanese names. Large ears were considered lucky in Japan as well as in China and Korea. Chamberlain, *op.cit.*, p.48 n.18.

[26] I, 33. tr. Chamberlain, p.107. In the Nihongi, of which we will tell in the next section, the commission reads more fully: "Then she [Amaterasu] commanded her August Grandchild, saying:—'This Reed-plain-1500-autumns-fair-rice-ear Land is the region which my descendants shall be lords of. Do thou, my August Grandchild, proceed thither and govern it. Go! and may prosperity attend thy dynasty and may it, like Heaven and Earth, endure for ever'" (II, 16. tr. Aston, I, p.77).

ers-of-the-Trees, daughter of the Deity Great-Mountain-Possessor, and became the father of three sons known as Fire-Shine, Fire-Climax and Fire-Subside. His Augustness Fire-Shine was a skillful fisherman, and His Augustness Fire-Subside, also known as His Augustness Heaven's-Sun-Height-Prince-Great-Rice-ears-Lord-Ears (Ama-tsu-hi-daka-hiko-ho-ho-de-mi-no-mikoto), was a mighty hunter. One day they exchanged occupations, but His Augustness Fire-Subside lost his elder brother's fishhook and had to go on a long journey to the realm of the Deity Ocean-Possessor to recover it. There he married this monarch's daughter, Luxuriant-Jewel-Princess, and obtained certain wonderful jewels by virtue of which, upon his return home, he became master over his elder brother.

His Augustness Fire-Subside and Her Augustness Luxuriant-Jewel-Princess had a son named His Augustness Heaven's-Sun-Height-Prince-Wave-limit-Brave-Cormorant-Thatch-Meeting-Incompletely (Ama-tsu-hi-daka-hiko-nagisa-take-u-gaya-fuki-ahezu-no-mikoto). He in turn married his mother's younger sister, Her Augustness Jewel-Good-Princess (Tamayori-hime-no-mikoto), and had four sons. They were named His Augustness Five-Reaches, His Augustness Boiled-Rice, His Augustness August-Food-Master, and His Augustness Young-August-Food-Master, or His Augustness Divine-Yamato-Ihare-Prince.

Volume I of the Kojiki closes with the crossing over of His Augustness August-Food-Master to the Eternal Land, and the departure of His Augustness Boiled-Rice for the Sea-Plain which was the land of his deceased mother. This left two brothers out of the four, namely the youngest one, His Augustness Divine-Yamato-Ihare-Prince or Kamu-yamato-ihare-biko-no-mikoto, and the oldest one, His Augustness Five-Reaches or Itsu-se-no-mikoto, and Volume II of the work opens with the account of a conference which these two held as to their future plans. At the time they were still living in a palace at the mountain where Prince-Rice-ear-Ruddy-Plenty had first descended upon Kyushu, and the question they raised was: "By dwelling in what place shall we [most] quietly carry on the government of the Empire?" Their conclusion was: "It were probably best to go east."

The progress to the east was a matter of military campaigns extending from Kyushu on to Honshu and lasting over many years. Defeats as well as successes are recorded, and in one battle Itsu-se was wounded and later died. Kamu-yamato-ihare-biko was ultimately

[431]

successful, however, and we read that "having thus subdued and pacified the savage deities, and extirpated the unsubmissive people, [he] dwelt at the palace of Kashibara near Unebi, and ruled the Empire."[27] The place indicated was probably in Yamato in central Honshu.

Although the work of Kamu-yamato-ihare-biko is filled with much that is fabulous and fantastic, it is probable that here at last we have a reflection of actual happenings even if in a highly legendary form. The military campaigns pushing eastward from Kyushu and resulting in the establishment of rule in central Honshu sound very much like what we may suppose to have been the actual progress of the Yamato people earlier discussed, and Kamu-yamato-ihare-biko may have been an actual leader of theirs. All the later Japanese histories consider him to have been the first emperor of Japan. In the eighth century A.D. it became customary to bestow a "canonical name" upon each emperor after his death, and at that time such "canonical names" were also selected for the sovereigns who had reigned previously. Kamu-yamato-ihare-biko, the first of these, received the name Jimmu. To this is ordinarily added Tenno, meaning sovereign, and thus it is that we are most familiar with the legendary original potentate of Japan as Jimmu Tenno.

THE NIHONGI

We now leave the Kojiki and turn to the Nihongi,[28] the second oldest Japanese chronicle. Unlike the Kojiki, the Nihongi has no preface to tell about its authorship. A series of commentaries was soon written on it, however, and several of these, known as Shiki or "private notes," are preserved in the thirteenth century Shaku-nihongi. Of these the Konin Shiki, ascribed to the "year period" A.D. 810-823, informs us that the Nihongi was compiled by Prince Toneri and Yasumaro Futo no Ason and laid before the Empress Gemmyo in A.D. 720. The Yasumaro here mentioned was the same as the one who took down the Kojiki from the lips of Are, but the Kojiki is not mentioned in the Nihongi nor does much use seem to have been made of it.[29]

The Nihongi is composed of thirty books, and there was also orig-

[27] II, 50. tr. Chamberlain, p.145.
[28] tr. W. G. Aston, *Nihongi, Chronicles of Japan from the Earliest Times to A.D. 697, Translated from the Original Chinese and Japanese* (Transactions and Proceedings of the Japan Society, London, Supplement I). 2 vols. 1896.
[29] *ibid.*, pp.xiii,xix.

inally a book of genealogies of the emperors which is no longer extant. In size the Nihongi is perhaps twice as large as the Kojiki, and it carries the history somewhat further, closing with the year A.D. 697. As far as the early mythology is concerned, the Kojiki is fuller, but the Nihongi presents some interesting variants. In the later history, the Nihongi is more detailed and therefore perhaps more useful.

The Nihongi also provides a complete chronology with dates as far back as the beginning of the reign of Jimmu Tenno, which is placed in 660 B.C. Unfortunately these dates do not prove dependable until about the beginning of the sixth century A.D. As a matter of fact it was not until about A.D. 603 that a calendar was adopted for the first time in Japan,[30] and it is now supposed that the chronologists of the seventh century arrived at the beginning date of 660 B.C. quite arbitrarily. The theory is that they used the Chinese idea of a cycle of 1,260 years from one event of world-shaking importance to another, and counting back from A.D. 601 when, under Empress Suiko, the Prince-Regent Shotoku Taishi was working on important governmental reforms, came to 660 B.C. as the date of Jimmu's coronation. Modern studies have introduced a large revision, and it is now thought that Jimmu's rule may have started around 40 B.C. We append below a list of all the emperors of Japan with their traditional accession dates, and show also in parentheses the critically revised dates for the first twenty-seven sovereigns after which the usual dates seem to be accurate within one year.[31]

(1) Jimmu, 660 B.C. (c.40 B.C.)	(14) Chuai, 192 (c.356);
(2) Suizei, 581 B.C. (c.10 B.C.)	Jingo Kogo, Regent, 201
(3) Annei, 548 B.C. (A.D. c.20)	(c.363)
(4) Itoku, 510 B.C. (A.D. c.50)	(15) Ojin, 270 (c.380)
(5) Kosho, 475 B.C. (A.D. c.80)	(16) Nintoku, 313 (c.395)
(6) Koan, 392 B.C. (A.D. c.110)	(17) Richu, 400 (c.428)
(7) Korei, 290 B.C. (A.D. c.140)	(18) Hanzei or Hansho, 406 (c.433)
(8) Kogen, 214 B.C. (A.D. c.170)	(19) Ingyo, 412 (c.438)
(9) Kaika, 157 B.C. (A.D. c.200)	(20) Anko, 454 (c.455)
(10) Sujin, 97 B.C. (A.D. c.230)	(21) Yuryaku, 457 (c.457)
(11) Suinin, 29 B.C. (A.D. c.259)	(22) Seinei, 480 (c.490)
(12) Keiko, A.D. 71 (A.D. c.291)	(23) Kenso, 485 (c.495)
(13) Seimu, 131 (c.323)	(24) Ninken, 488 (c.498)

[30] N. Sakuma in *Transactions of the Asiatic Society of Japan.* 30 (1902), p.72.
[31] Herbert H. Gowen, *An Outline History of Japan.* 1927, pp.xvii-xviii; REJH I, pp.13f.,77-84; Émile Gaspardone in *Journal asiatique, Recueil trimestriel de mémoires et de notices relatifs aux études orientales, publié par la Société Asiatique.* 230 (1938), pp.240f.

(25) Buretsu, 499 (c.504)
(26) Keitai, 507 (c.510)
(27) Ankan, 534 (c.527)
(28) Senka, 536
(29) Kimmei, 540
(30) Bidatsu, 572
(31) Yomei, 586
(32) Sushun, 588
(33) Suiko, Empress, 593
(34) Jomei, 629
(35) Kokyoku, Empress, 642
(36) Kotoku, 645
(37) Saimei, 655
(38) Tenchi, 661
(39) Kobun, 672
(40) Temmu, 673
(41) Jito, Empress, 687
(42) Mommu, 697
(43) Gemmyo, Empress, 708
(44) Gensho, Empress, 715
(45) Shomu, 724
(46) Koken, Empress, 749
(47) Junnin, 759
(48) Shotoku, 765
(49) Konin, 770
(50) Kammu, 782
(51) Heijo, 806
(52) Saga, 810
(53) Junna, 824
(54) Nimmyo, 834
(55) Montoku, 851
(56) Seiwa, 859
(57) Yozei, 877
(58) Koko, 885
(59) Uda, 888
(60) Daigo, 898
(61) Suzaku, 931
(62) Murakami, 947
(63) Reizei, 968
(64) Enyu, 970
(65) Kazan, 985
(66) Ichijo, 987
(67) Sanjo, 1012
(68) Go-Ichijo, 1017
(69) Go-Suzaku, 1037
(70) Go-Reizei, 1046
(71) Go-Sanjo 1069

(72) Shirakawa, 1073
(73) Horikawa, 1087
(74) Toba, 1108
(75) Sutoku, 1124
(76) Konoe, 1142
(77) Go-Shirakawa, 1156
(78) Nijo, 1159
(79) Rokujo, 1166
(80) Takakura, 1169
(81) Antoku, 1181
(82) Go-Toba, 1186
(83) Tsuchi-mikado, 1199
(84) Juntoku, 1211
(85) Chukyo, 1222
(86) Go-Horikawa, 1231
(87) Yojo, 1232
(88) Go-Saga, 1242
(89) Go-Fukakusa, 1246
(90) Kameyama, 1259
(91) Go-Uda, 1274
(92) Fushimi, 1288
(93) Go-Fushimi, 1298
(94) Go-Nijyo, 1301
(95) Hanazono, 1308
(96) Go-Daigo, 1318
(97) Go-Murakami, 1339
(98) Go-Kameyama, 1373
(99) Go-Komatsu, 1382
(100) Shoko, 1414
(101) Go-Hanazono, 1429
(102) Go-Tsuchi-mikado, 1465
(103) Go-Kashiwabara, 1521
(104) Go-Nara, 1536
(105) Ogimachi, 1560
(106) Go-Yojo, 1586
(107) Go-Mizuo, 1611
(108) Myosho, Empress, 1630
(109) Go-Komyo, 1643
(110) Go-Nishio, 1656
(111) Reigen, 1663
(112) Higashiyama, 1687
(113) Naka-mikado, 1710
(114) Sakuramachi, 1720
(115) Momozono, 1747
(116) Go-Sakuramachi, Empress, 1763
(117) Go-Momozono, 1771

[434]

(118) Kokaku, 1780
(119) Jinko, 1817
(120) Komei, 1847

(121) Meiji, 1868
(122) Taisho, 1912
(123) Hirohito, 1925.

In general it may be said of the Nihongi, that while it deals with the early Emperors in a very legendary manner, the narrative becomes more realistic as it proceeds, and from around the beginning of the sixth century A.D. on, appears to be a trustworthy record.

2. THE ASUKA PERIOD, A.D. 552-645

IN WHAT has been said thus far it has become evident that real history, in distinction from the earlier mythological and legendary periods, only begins in Japan in about the sixth century A.D. This was also, it will be remembered (p.312) the time when Buddhism was introduced under Kimmei Tenno. This sovereign reigned from A.D. 540 to 571, and it was in the thirteenth year of his reign, A.D. 552, that Buddhism came. This year may be taken as the opening date of the first historical period in Japan, a time that extended from A.D. 552 to 645.

In order to obtain a name for this and succeeding periods, it is not possible to refer to successive dynasties since there was only one house of rulers throughout all Japanese history, and therefore another system must be utilized. That which is most customary is to designate the periods by the names of the places from which the supreme authority was exercised at the time. In this earliest period of which we are now speaking, however, the capital was moved with the accession of each new ruler, and hence we simply take the most prominent single place and use its name to mark the whole time. This was Asuka. Actually the various early capitals were all quite close together in the region of Yamato, and also the later and more famous capitals like Nara and Kyoto were located in the same district.[32]

It is in the reign of Kimmei's second successor, Yomei Tenno (A.D. 586-587), that we first encounter the actual term Shinto. Concerning this ruler we read in the Nihongi, "The Emperor believed in the Law of Buddha and reverenced the Way of the Gods (Shinto)."[33] The phrase, "the Way of the Gods," is a literal translation of "Shinto," *shin* (Chinese, *shen*) meaning "gods," and *to* (Chinese, *tao*), "way." Since *to* already means "way" or "doctrine," it is not necessary to add "ism" to form the proper name of this religion. The equivalent in pure Japanese of the basically Chinese name Shinto, is Kami no Michi.

The fact that the name Shinto appears now for the first time does not mean that the religion arose only at this time. Actually this was the ancient, long-known religion of Japan, and not a few of its basic

[32] For detailed maps of the region and the capitals, see REJH II, pp.27-36; for tables of the periods, SJSCH p.xviii; Soper, *The Evolution of Buddhist Architecture in Japan*, pp.xv-xvi.
[33] XXI, 1. tr. Aston, II, p.106.

ideas, particularly in the realm of nature worship, prevailed already among the ancestral Ainus. What happened here in the sixth century was simply that with the introduction of Buddhism it became necessary for the first time to have a term by which to distinguish the ancient faith of the land from the newly imported religion. The foreign teaching was Butsudo, "the Way of the Buddha"; the indigenous cult was Shinto, "the Way of the Gods."[34]

SHINTO SHRINES

The place of worship characteristic of Shinto is the shrine (*jinja*). At the outset, objects of nature such as rocks and trees were doubtless worshiped directly; after that, it is thought, sacred areas were marked out for worship with rows of evergreen branches. When the mirror and the jewels and the sword, of which we have heard in the myths, became divine symbols, a house was necessary in which to keep them. This was constructed in the same fashion as an ordinary dwelling, being little more than a wooden hut with a thatched roof. Large size was not even necessary, because there was no congregational worship, and the individual visitor simply stood outside to make obeisance or present some supplication.[35]

After the introduction of Buddhism, Shinto architecture was strongly influenced by the Chinese habits incorporated in Buddhist temple design: complex symmetrical plans, southward orientation, surrounding walls and colonnades and gate buildings, painting, gilding, sculptural decoration, curving roof lines. Nevertheless, the typical Shinto shrine remained always relatively simple and presented a comparatively austere appearance.

In the literary traditions, shrines are mentioned from time to time. In noting several of these references, we may begin with the account in the Nihongi relating to the reign of Sujin Tenno (97-30 B.C. by the traditional chronology; A.D. c.230-c.258 by the revised). It seems that at this time there was a great plague. Hitherto both the goddess Amaterasu and the god Yamato-no-o-kuni-dama (The Spirit of the Great Land of Yamato) had been worshiped in the palace of the emperor, but the latter now felt a sense of fear at having these two powerful beings so close to him. Accordingly separate shrines were established for them elsewhere. That of Amaterasu, in which we are specially interested, was placed at the village of Kasanuhi some distance northeast of Asuka, and the emperor's own daughter Toyo-

[34] MHR I, p.93.   [35] SJSCH pp.57f.

suki-iri-hime-no-mikoto was installed there as high priestess. The mirror which was the symbol of the sun goddess, and the legendary sword, Kusa-nagi, were both put in the new shrine.

The Nihongi makes reference to this event in these words: "Before this the two gods Ama-terasu-o-mi-kami and Yamato-no-o-kuni-dama were worshiped together within the Emperor's Great Hall. He dreaded, however, the power of these gods, and did not feel secure in their dwelling together. Therefore he entrusted Ama-terasu-o-mi-kami to Toyo-suki-iri-hime-no-mikoto to be worshiped at the village of Kasanuhi in Yamato, where he established the sacred enclosure of Shiki. Moreover, he entrusted Yamato-o-kuni-dama-no-kami to Nunaki-iri-hime-no-mikoto to be worshiped. But Nunaki-iri-hime-no-mikoto was bald and lean, and therefore unfit to perform the rites of worship."[36]

In the reign of the next emperor, Suinin Tenno (29 B.C.-A.D. 70; or A.D. c.259-c.290), the shrine of Amaterasu was established at Ise, where it remained permanently thereafter. The daughter of Suinin Tenno, named Yamato-hime-no-mikoto, was priestess of the shrine, and it was to her that the command of the sun goddess came for the transferal. As the Nihongi records: "Now Ama-terasu-o-mi-kami instructed Yamato-hime-no-mikoto, saying:—'The province of Ise, of the divine wind, is the land whither repair the waves from the eternal world, the successive waves. It is a secluded and pleasant land. In this land I wish to dwell.' In compliance, therefore, with the instruction of the Great Goddess, a shrine was erected to her in the province of Ise."[37]

Yamato-hime-no-mikoto was still serving as high priestess of the shrine at Ise when her brother, Keiko Tenno, was on the throne (A.D. 71-130; or c.291-c.322). At this time we get an interesting glimpse of the custom of repairing to the shrine before proceeding on an important mission. Yamato-dake-no-mikoto, son of Keiko Tenno, was ordered to subdue the Eastern Barbarians, and as he set out upon his journey he went first to notify the sun goddess. "He turned aside from his way," records the Nihongi, "to worship at the shrine of Ise. Here he took leave of Yamato-hime-no-mikoto, saying:—'By order of the Emperor, I am now proceeding on an expedition against the East to put to death the rebels, therefore I am taking leave of thee.'" Since the expedition was of great importance, the high priestess gave him the famous sword, of which we have already heard, to

36 v, 3f. tr. Aston, I, pp.151f.   37 vi, 16. tr. Aston, I, p.176.

use. "Hereupon Yamato-hime-no-mikoto took the sword Kusa-nagi and gave it to Yamato-dake-no-mikoto, saying:—'Be cautious, and yet not remiss.' "[38]

While the foregoing quotations have dealt chiefly with the central sanctuary of Amaterasu at Ise, there were many other shrines throughout the land. The earliest statistical record is from the eighth century, and from this we learn that in A.D. 737 there were more than three thousand shrines which were officially recognized, and that about one-fourth of these were supported at government expense.[39]

Being made of wood, the shrines were not of great durability and had to be rebuilt frequently. In comparatively recent times it has been the custom to rebuild the Ise shrine every twenty years. In such reconstructions, however, care was expended to make the new shrine a replica of its predecessor, and thus the essential forms of antiquity were long preserved.

THE IZUMO SHRINE

The most primitive type of sanctuary still existing is represented by the Great Shrine of Izumo, known in Japanese as the Izumo-no-oyashiro. It is second only to the Shrine at Ise in national popularity, and like that sanctuary also has connections with the earliest mythology.

It will be remembered that after Take-haya-susa-no-wo-no-mikoto was expelled from heaven for offending Amaterasu, he made his way to the land of Izumo. There he had numerous descendants, among whom the most important was a son of perhaps the sixth generation,[40] named Oho-kuni-nushi-no-kami or Deity Master-of-the-Great-Land.[41] When the heavenly deities were pacifying the Japanese islands in preparation for the inauguration of the rule of the grandson of Amaterasu, Oho-kuni-nushi-no-kami abdicated his throne and surrendered his territory to the emissary of the sun goddess.[42] Remembered particularly for this act, Oho-kuni-nushi-no-kami was the chief deity worshiped at Izumo-no-oyashiro.

When the Great Shrine was first erected we cannot tell, but it must have been at an early time. It certainly was in existence in the third century, for we know that in the reign of Sujin Tenno

[38] VII, 23. tr. Aston, I, p.205.   [39] SJSCH p.58.
[40] See the genealogical table in REJH II, p.39.
[41] Kojiki. I, 20. tr. Chamberlain, p.67.
[42] Kojiki. I, 32. tr. Chamberlain, pp.99-105.

(A.D. c.230-258 by the revised chronology) a certain Izumo Furone (d. A.D. c.255) was in charge of the sacred treasures of the shrine.[43]

The Great Shrine[44] is shown in Fig. 189. It is surrounded by a small veranda, and approached by a steep stairway. The building is entered from the end, through a doorway to the right of the central vertical pillar. Inside, there is a single pillar in the center, and a partition separating the rear of the room from the front. The style of construction is called Oyashiro-zukuri.

On top of the building near either end of the roof ridge is seen a pair of crossed timbers (*chigi*). These are regarded as sacred symbols, and probably survive from an earlier method of building in which the roof was supported by beams reaching from the ground and crossing at the top. The short round pieces of wood (*katsuogi*) laid horizontally across the roof ridge are likewise inseparable attachments of a Shinto shrine, and probably are remnants of the timbers which were employed in earlier times to hold down the straw-thatched roof.

THE ISE SHRINE

We return now to the shrine of Amaterasu at Ise, a number of references to the history of which have already been given. There are two sacred areas at Ise, that of the Outer Shrine occupying two hundred acres, and that of the Inner Shrine, three and one-half miles away, extending over one hundred and seventy-five acres. The grounds of the Inner Shrine are approached by a bridge over the Isuzu River, back of which rises a heavily wooded mountain, Mount Kamiji. The Inner Shrine itself is located within a rectangular fenced space known as Omiyanoin. The measurement around this area is 1,386 feet. There are four entrances, one in each direction of the compass, the southern being the principal. Ascending broad, gently sloping steps (Fig. 191), the visitor to the shrine passes under a plain torii, a post and lintel construction commonly found at all Shinto shrines,[45] and enters through a gateway. Within, there are yet other fences and gates. In an innermost precinct, flanked by other structures, stands the Seiden or main building. It is shown from a distance, seen through the trees, in Fig. 190. Architecturally, the chief difference from the Izumo Shrine consists in the fact that here the

[43] REJH I, p.117.
[44] W. L. Schwartz in *Transactions of the Asiatic Society of Japan*. 41 (1913), pp.491-681; Aisaburo Akiyama, *Shintô and Its Architecture*. 1936, pp.59,62f.
[45] Akiyama, *Shintô and Its Architecture*, pp.82-86.

main building has been turned around and the entrance placed at the center of the long side. This change made the Ise design fit into general Far Eastern practice; perhaps it was due to Chinese influence filtering in through Korea along with new ideas in building palaces. Except for this difference the general appearance of the shrine is much the same as that of the structure at Izumo. The *chigi* and the *katsuogi* of course appear upon the roof. In technical terminology the advanced architectural style exemplified here at Ise is known as the Shimmei-zukuri.[46]

In summary, then, the Asuka Period, when Buddhist art unfolded in monumental architecture and rich sculpture, only serves to throw into sharp relief the essential simplicity of Shinto. The centers of the faith then, as before and since, were relatively crude wooden structures in the richest of which there were no more impressive treasures than the symbolic mirror, jewels and sword.

[46] *ibid.*, pp.66f.; Seichi Taki, *Japanese Fine Art.* tr. Kazutomo Takahashi. 1931, pp.45f.; Tokugoro Nakamura, *Kotaijingu Shi* (The History of the Grand Imperial Shrine). 1921, pp.407-417.

3. THE NARA PERIOD, A.D. 645-794

THE next division in Japanese history may be called the Nara Period. The capital of the country was not actually established at Nara until A.D. 710, but even so the years from 645 to 710 are often looked upon as preparatory and called "Early Nara" or "Proto-Nara"; hence for our purposes it will be simplest to apply the one name to the entire period.

The most important event in the political situation was doubtless the Great Reform of A.D. 645. Some forty-five years before, the Prince-Regent Shotoku Taishi had done much to improve the government of Japan, but the growing power of the Soga family, which he had favored and which had grown more and more grasping of power after his death, seemed an ever increasing menace. It will be remembered (p.312) that this was the family which had welcomed Buddhism upon its first arrival; and as for Shotoku Taishi, so strong was his support of that faith that he has been called the Constantine of Japanese Buddhism. Of the two families which had stood against the acceptance of Buddhism, the Mononobe clan had lost prestige because of defeat in the struggle, but the Nakatomi family was still a force to be reckoned with. It was from the latter clan that the leader of the Great Reform arose.

This leader was Kamatari. Although his family had long been devoted to Shinto, Kamatari took up an intensive study of the Chinese classics and from these sources derived his ideal of government. The details do not concern us here, suffice it to say that the net result of his work was the transformation of Japan from a tribal confederation into a centralized bureaucracy patterned after the government of China. In the process the dominance of the Soga clan was destroyed, and the Nakatomi family, henceforth known as Fujiwara, achieved the position of great power which it occupied for the next four or five centuries.

In the edict embodying these reforms and published in the first month of A.D. 646, one provision called for the imperial capital to be "regulated."[47] Up to this time the capital had been moved with the accession of each new ruler, a thing that was not too difficult to do since the palaces were probably like the Shinto shrines hitherto described, simple structures of wood thatched with straw or reeds. Now with the increased complexity of government, larger and more dur-

[47] REJH I, p.147.

[442]

able buildings were needed, and such transferals would be less easy. Furthermore, knowledge was now had of the magnificent T'ang capital at Ch'ang-an, and along with the imitation of things Chinese in general, came the desire to have a similar fine center of rule. Such were some of the factors which led in A.D. 710 to the building of Nara, Japan's capital for the next seventy-five years.

Nara was located on a level plain nearly surrounded by mountains. The city was rectangular in plan, like its Chinese model. As compared with preceding capitals, it was large and elaborate. Perhaps the most beautiful buildings were the many temples and shrines. Of these, the most numerous and of course the most ornate were the Buddhist. On the mountain eastward above the city, however, there was a relatively large and important Shinto shrine, the Kasuga-no-jinja, which deserves special mention.

THE KASUGA SHRINE

As already indicated, the Fujiwara clan had long been devoted to the Shinto faith. Indeed, the family traced its descent from no less a personage than Ame-no-koyane-no-mikoto (His Augustness Heavenly-Beckoning-Ancestor-Lord), who had played a prominent part in the mythological episode of enticing Amaterasu forth from the Rock-Cave of Heaven. The wife of Ame-no-koyane-no-mikoto, and Takemikazuchi-no-kami and Futsunushi-no-kami who had led in the pacification of the Japanese islands prior to the descent of the grandson of Amaterasu, were the other deities worshiped by the Fujiwara, and it was to these four deities that the Kasuga Shrine was dedicated.[48]

A fourteenth century picture scroll called the Kasuga Gongenrei Kenki[49] contains pictures of worship at the Kasuga Shrine. From this source we show two scenes, identified according to legends in the scroll. In the first (Fig. 192) a priest is ordering the stopping of the drum music; in the second (Fig. 193) people are praying in seclusion at the shrine.

In the sixteenth century, the Jesuit missionary, Luis Alameida, visited Nara (1565) and wrote an extended description of the Kasuga Shrine. According to this source, the shrine was set in the midst of a dense forest and approached by an avenue lined with cedars and

[48] REJH II, p.161.
[49] *Nihon Emakimono Shusei.* 1929, IV, Fig. 10; III, Fig. 64; cf. Kenji Toda, *Japanese Scroll Painting.* 1935, pp.108-110.

pines. The missionary expressed the opinion that he had never seen such fine trees in all his life. The avenue had also a double row of stone pillars in which were set lanterns made of black wood. These were lighted throughout every night, for when such a lantern was set up it was required that the donor provide a sufficient yearly endowment for this purpose. At the end of the avenue stood a house in which dwelt the lady bonzes, whose chief duty was to give tea to drink to the numerous pilgrims who came to the shrine. From this house a covered alley led up to the temple itself. Beyond the alley no one was allowed to go except certain men who were dedicated to the service of the idol, the Jesuit said. He also told of seeing some of these priests, who were robed in silk gowns and wore tall caps. They collected the alms which the people threw onto the veranda of the temple.[50]

Approaching the Kasuga Shrine today, one passes along an avenue lined with cryptomeria trees and stone lanterns. There are four main buildings, similar to each other in appearance and dedicated to the four deities previously mentioned, as well as numerous other structures which were added later. The architectural style is essentially similar to that with which we have already become familiar. One important development, however, is the employment of curved lines. Furthermore, the buildings are painted red like contemporary Buddhist temples and Chinese architecture generally; this is a significant change from the natural wood surface seen earlier.[51] A photograph of the shrine is reproduced in Fig. 194.

RYOBU SHINTO

The strong influence of Buddhism in the Nara Period led in some instances to outright amalgamation between that faith and Shinto. An interesting evidence of this trend appeared in the year 715 when for the first time a Buddhist temple annex was established at a Shinto shrine.[52] Again, in A.D. 750, the Shinto war god, Hachiman-no-kami,[53] was brought from his shrine at Usa on Kyushu to the Todai-ji Tem-

[50] George Schurhammer, *Shin-tō, The Way of the Gods in Japan, According to the Printed and Unprinted Reports of the Japanese Jesuit Missionaries in the 16th and 17th Centuries.* 1923, pp.61-63.

[51] Akiyama, *Shintō and Its Architecture*, pp.68f.; Garrett C. Pier, *Temple Treasures of Japan.* 1914, pp.92-95; *Handbook of the Old Shrines and Temples and Their Treasures in Japan* (Bureau of Religions). 1920, pp.87f.

[52] REJH I, p.174.

[53] According to some legends, this god was the deified Emperor Ojin, son of the warrior queen, Jingo Kogo, conqueror of Korea. W. G. Aston, *Shinto (The Way of the Gods).* 1905, pp.178f.

ple in Nara to pay his respects to the Great Statue of the Buddha (Daibutsu); and there he remained in a specially built shrine as the guarding spirit of the temple.[54]

The process of intermixture between Shinto and Buddhism was also advanced by an event which took place in A.D. 735. In that year a terrible epidemic of smallpox which had started in Kyushu reached the capital. Under the impact of this calamity it was deemed necessary to placate the divine forces, under whatever name known. The common people turned to the old gods for help; the Emperor Shomu resolved to erect a new and colossal statue of the Buddha (the Daibutsu at Nara). At this juncture the Buddhist patriarch Gyogi was sent to the Shrine at Ise to seek the blessing of the sun goddess for the emperor's project. The oracle was favorable, and the succeeding night the emperor himself experienced a dream in which Amaterasu declared herself identical with Vairocana, a great Buddha of the Mahayana. From here on it was easy to identify every native Japanese deity with some Buddha or Bodhisattva, and thus a theological basis was provided for a thoroughgoing syncretism. The mixture of Shinto and Buddhism which thus arose in the eighth and ninth centuries, and prevailed for a thousand years, is called Ryobu Shinto, the Twofold Way of the Gods.[55]

THE NORITO

Important as Ryobu Shinto became, "pure" Shinto also lived on. An interesting glimpse of its primitive character is obtainable in the *norito* or ancient Shinto rituals.[56] In the performance of a Shinto rite, for example the presentation of an offering to a god, it was customary to read a sort of liturgy in which the grounds of the worship were stated and the offerings enumerated. This liturgy is called a *norito*. It may be composed for a single special occasion, or the same formulation may be used repeatedly.

An example of the *norito* is a ritual called Praying for Harvest which comes probably from the reign of Konin (A.D. 770-782) and thus from the period of which we are here speaking.

The reader of the liturgy is supposed to be giving the words of none other than the emperor, to whom the introductory formula, "He says," refers. Beginning with a salutation to the assembled priests and to the gods, the text continues:

[54] REJH I, p.193.   [55] MHR I, pp.94,118f.
[56] tr. Ernest Satow in *Transactions of the Asiatic Society of Japan.* 7 (1879), pp.97-132,393-434; 9 (1881), pp.183-211; Karl Florenz, *ibid.*, 27 (1900), pp.1-112.

He says: "I declare in the presence of the sovereign gods of the harvest. If the sovereign gods will bestow in many-bundled ears and in luxuriant ears the late-ripening harvest which they will bestow, ... then I will fulfill their praises by setting-up the first fruits in a thousand ears and many hundred ears. . . ."

He says: "Parting the words,[57] I declare in the presence of the Heaven-Shining-Great-Deity who sits in Ise. Because the sovereign great deity bestows on him the countries of the four quarters over which her glance extends, as far as the limit where heaven stands up like a wall, as far as the bounds where the blue clouds lie flat, as far as the bounds where the white clouds lie fallen; the blue-sea-plain as far as the limit whither come the prows of the ships without letting their poles or paddles be dry, the ships which continuously crowd on the great-sea-plain; the road which men go by land, as far as the limit whither come the horses' hoofs, with the baggage-cords tied tightly, treading the uneven rocks and tree-roots and standing up continuously in a long path without a break; making the narrow countries wide and the hilly countries plane, and as it were drawing together the distant countries by throwing many tens of ropes over them, [because she does all this,] he will pile up the first-fruits like a range of hills in the great presence of the sovereign great deity, and will tranquilly take to himself the remainder."[58]

[57] i.e., taking up a fresh theme.
[58] tr. Satow, *op.cit.*, 7 (1879), pp.113-116.

4. THE HEIAN PERIOD, A.D. 794-1185

IN A.D. 794 the capital of Japan was established at Heian-kyo ("the capital of peace and tranquility"), later called simply Kyoto, meaning "the capital." If Nara had been a relatively permanent center in contrast with the frequent changes of the seat of government before that time, the new capital endured amazingly longer still. Kyoto was the capital for over a thousand years, or until the reformation of 1868 ushered in the modern period. Counting from the establishment of the city, the first four centuries, approximately, constitute the so-called Heian Period.

Like Nara, Heian-kyo was patterned after Ch'ang-an. It occupied a rectangle three and one-third miles from north to south and three miles from east to west. An enclosure in the north central part contained the Greater Imperial Palace and the chief government buildings. Not far away were other offices and institutions, and near the southern gate was the large and important university. All the buildings, of course, were of wood.[59]

SHRINES AT HEIAN-KYO

Several shrines already existed at the site before Heian-kyo was built, and gained added prestige with the coming of the capital. Two of these were the Kamo-no-mioya-no-jinja or Shimo-kamo-no-jinja, and the Kamo-no-wakiikatsuchi-no-jinja or Kami-kamo-no-jinja, which are also known collectively as the Kamo-no-jinja. The deities worshiped there are the Kamo-no-kami, and include Takemikazuchi-no-kami who was also mentioned in connection with the Kasuga-no-jinja. The architectural style is called "Nagare," meaning a stream, or flowing. This has reference particularly to the smooth-flowing lines of the roof, the front of which is carried far out over the front porch.[60]

Another shrine existent before the building of the capital was the Yasaka-no-jinja or Gion-no-yashiro, dedicated to Take-haya-susa-no-wo-no-mikoto, built in the "Gion" style with a gabled roof, and serving as the center for a great annual Shinto festival (Gion-no-go-ryo-e).[61]

Other Shinto shrines and also many Buddhist temples were erected

[59] SJSCH pp.191-194.
[60] REJH II, pp.157f.; Akiyama, *Shintô and Its Architecture*, p.70f.; *Handbook of the Old Shrines and Temples and Their Treasures in Japan*, pp.56-58.
[61] Akiyama, *Shintô and Its Architecture*, p.75; *Handbook of the Old Shrines and Temples and Their Treasures in Japan*, pp.52f.

after the founding of the capital. These spread over the plain on which the city stood, and also were placed on the surrounding hills. Indeed, so numerous were the sanctuaries becoming throughout the country, and so extensive were the lands which were becoming the tax-free properties of the temples, that Kammu (A.D. 782-806), the first emperor to rule at Heian-kyo, was constrained to issue an edict in which he said, "If this continues, in a few years there will be no land which is not temple property." He therefore forbade the selling or donating of land to religious institutions, and established limitations to the building of temples and the admission of persons to the priesthood.[62]

One of the later shrines at Heian-kyo was the Kitano-no-jinja, where Sugawara Michizane was worshiped. Sugawara Michizane was a scholar and statesman who taught at the university and then held the very highest governmental posts under the Emperors Uda (A.D. 888-898) and Daigo (898-930). His advancement was in opposition to the Fujiwara family, and when the final test of strength came, they prevailed. Michizane was sent away to a minor position in distant Kyushu, and thus virtually banished. There in exile he died in A.D. 903.

Prior to his departure from home, Michizane wrote this poem to a plum tree in his garden:

> When the east wind blows,
> Emit thy perfume
> Oh thou plum blossom;
> Forget not the spring,
> Because thy master is away.

According to legend, a branch of this tree broke off of its own accord and went with him into banishment. Other marvels transpired before his death, it is said, and after that event his ghost began to take vengeance on his enemies and to disturb the nation. Finally in A.D. 947 a six-year-old boy transmitted the following oracle from Michizane: "All the thunder-gods and demons to the number of 168,000 have become my servants. If any one does evil I have him trampled to death by them. Pestilence, eruptive diseases, and other calamities have been placed in my hands by the Supreme Lord of Heaven, and no kami, however powerful, can control me. But I will give help to those who piously express their sorrow." In order to placate this

[62] SJSCH p.192.

dangerous spirit, therefore, the Kitano Shrine was forthwith erected to him in Heian-kyo. His spirit was called Temmangu, and was supposed to preside over affairs of learning and literature. As it stands, the architecture of the Kitano Shrine is late in plan and ornament. It combines Shinto and Buddhist influences, and exemplifies the Yatsu-mune ("eight-roofed") style, which features a complicated and elegant system of roofs. A photograph of the Kitano Shrine is reproduced in Fig. 195.[63]

SHINTO AND BUDDHISM

A famous Buddhist priest named Kobo Daishi, who lived in the early Heian Period, did much to further the process of assimilation which was going on between Shinto and Buddhism. Returning from residence in China in A.D. 806, Kobo Daishi founded the Shingon sect of Buddhism. Following the formula already introduced by Gyogi, Kobo taught that the various aboriginal deities of Japan were in reality Buddhas and Bodhisattvas which had anciently visited the land in the guise of Kami to bring blessing to the people. In Buddhism the deeper nature of these beings was made known, and thus that faith appeared as only an unfolding of the hidden meaning of Shinto itself. The common man could be a Shintoist and a Buddhist at the same time, without contradiction.[64]

Due to Buddhist influence, the Shinto religion which had originally been content with such symbols as the mirror, jewels and sword, now had images of the deities similar to those so long used by the Indian faith. For illustration we may turn to the Matsuno-o-no-jinja, a Shinto shrine of national prominence not far west of Kyoto. There we find the striking and powerful wooden statues of a Shinto god and a Shinto goddess pictured in Figs. 196 and 197. They were carved probably in the ninth century A.D. Only the garb distinguishes them from cult statues of the Buddhists.[65]

Again, in the Yakushi-ji Temple at Nara there are the two wooden statues shown in Figs. 198 and 199. They also belong to the ninth century. The first portrays the war god Hachiman in a fully Buddhist guise; the second shows his wife, Nakatsu-hime. Not only are these images actually in a Buddhist temple they are supposed to have

[63] Aston, Shinto, pp.179-183; Noritake Tsuda, Handbook of Japanese Art. 1935, pp.391-394; Akiyama, Shintô and Its Architecture, p.79.

[64] MHR I, pp.119f.

[65] Japanese Temples and Their Treasures, 1910, II, Pls. 283,284; Kümmel, Die Kunst Chinas, Japans und Koreas, p.128.

been carved by a Buddhist priest named Eisho who lived during the era A.D. 889-898.[66] Thus the role of Buddhism in the development of such representations of Shinto deities is clearly demonstrated.

[66] *Japanese Temples and Their Treasures,* 1910, ii, Pls. 298,299; Pier, *Temple Treasures of Japan,* p.47.

5. THE KAMAKURA PERIOD, A.D. 1185-1392

IN THE later part of the Heian Period, extravagance and luxury became more common, the power of the Fujiwara weakened, and general disorder spread. Two great families, the Taira and the Minamoto, then struggled for dominance, and the Minamoto emerged victorious. No more than the Fujiwara, would the Minamoto have thought of abolishing the divinely-descended imperial house of Japan. The emperors simply continued to reign in name, while the feudal lords exercised authority in fact.

The leader of the Minamoto was Yoritomo, and this remarkable leader now devoted himself to building up a powerful military society. He himself was the shogun or military governor; under him were his lords, each with his retainers or samurai. The residence of Yoritomo and the center of the shogunate were established at Kamakura, two hundred and fifty miles east of Kyoto. This explains the name applied to the period now under discussion.

The code of moral principles which prevailed in the military system of the time is known as Bushido, the Way of the Warrior. This was developed out of elements from all three of the major teachings then known in Japan. The political and ethical precepts of Confucianism, calling for a careful ordering of all the relationships of society and favorable toward aristocracy and conservatism, provided the chief basis for the code. Buddhism gave a sense of calm submission to the inevitable; and Shinto contributed a strong emphasis on patriotism and loyalty.[67]

Two Shinto deities whom we have already met were of particular prominence at the time. They were Sugawara Michizane or Temmangu, who served as god of literature and of civil affairs in general; and Hachiman, who was god of war. Hachiman had been closely connected with the Minamoto family from the beginning, and as a deity of battles was understandably important in a military society. In A.D. 1191 Yoritomo erected a great shrine to Hachiman in Kamakura. This sanctuary is approached by an avenue lined with pines and spanned by three torii. In the court is the Wakamiya Shrine,[68] dedicated to a son of the war god, and beyond it is the Shirahata Shrine, consecrated to Yoritomo himself. The Hachiman Shrine

[67] Inazo Nitobé, *Bushido, The Soul of Japan.* rev. ed. 1905, pp.11-22.
[68] Wakamiya means a branch shrine. It is usually one for the son of the deity, or for a second relic of the deity, who is worshiped in the main shrine. REJH II, p.242.

proper is accessible by a flight of steps, and is surrounded by an open colonnade. In its style of architecture both Shinto and Buddhist influences are blended.[69] A photograph of this shrine is reproduced in Fig. 200.

The ability of the god of war was soon put to the test. In A.D. 1274 and again in 1281, Kublai Khan attempted to invade Japan. On both occasions great storms broke and drove back the ships of the enemy with heavy losses. The worshipers who had thronged to the shrines of Hachiman and the other deities to plead for help believed that their prayers had been answered, and the myth of a divinely guarded and impregnable nation was much furthered.[70]

Despite the military aspect of the times, the arts were promoted and indeed manifested a new vitality in the Kamakura Period. Both sculpture and painting flourished. Here we show two examples of such work in this period. The statue in Fig. 201 is a representation of the Shinto goddess, Tamayori-hime-no-mikoto, legendary mother of Jimmu Tenno. She is portrayed in the garb of a court lady of the time. The figure is made of wood, painted, and is dated A.D. 1251. It is in the Shinto shrine, Yoshino-take-mikumari-jinja near Nara.[71] The portrait in Fig. 202 is of the scholar-statesman-deity, Sugawara Michizane. Although not signed, the work is attributed to Tosa Tsunetaka, around A.D. 1240. It is in the collection of Ulrich Odin.[72]

[69] Wilhelm Gundert, *Japanische Religionsgeschichte, Die Religionen der Japaner und Koreaner in geschichtlichem Abriss dargestellt.* 1935, pp.52,110f.; Pier, *Temple Treasures of Japan*, pp.117-119.

[70] Mary A. Nourse, *Kodo, The Way of the Emperor.* 1940, pp.107-113.

[71] *Japanese Temples and Their Treasures*, III, Pl. 425; Fischer, *Die Kunst Indiens, Chinas und Japans*, pp.117,615.

[72] *Peintures chinoises et japonaises de la collection Ulrich Odin, avec une introduction et des notices de M. Ulrich Odin et un avant-propos de M. Sylvain Lévi* (Ars Asiatica, XIV). 1929, p.29, Pl. XII.

6. THE MUROMACHI PERIOD, A.D. 1392-1568

EVEN though Japan was wonderfully delivered from the invasions of Kublai Khan, the wars of that time brought an aftermath of economic troubles and general disorder. In the struggles which followed, Kamakura was destroyed by fire (A.D. 1333), Kyoto became once more the seat of government, and the Ashikaga family gradually secured the chief power in the land. By 1392 the Ashikaga shogunate was fully established, and this date is taken as the beginning of a fresh period in Japanese history. The name of the period, Muromachi, is that of the Ashikaga residence at Kyoto.[73]

The new shogunate was not as powerful or centralized as that at Kamakura, and the entire period was one of almost continual civil war. Kyoto itself was burned in 1467, but afterward rebuilt with lavish expenditure by the shoguns. Despite much warfare, the arts flourished and the period was by no means lacking in brilliance.

Shinto was much overshadowed by Buddhism, yet due to its compromises with that faith, lived on. The ancestral deities of the land were never forgotten, and the custom of pilgrimage to the Shrine of the Sun Goddess at Ise grew in popularity. Religious dances which had doubtless long been performed in front of the Shinto shrines, developed into the form of lyric drama known as No. A Shinto priest named Kwanami (A.D. 1333-1384) and his son Seami (1363-1444) perfected the No, and in their dramatic work enjoyed the patronage of the third Ashikaga shogun, Yoshimitsu (1368-1393).[74]

The finest artistic work was doubtless that done in painting, and here the chief subject matter was now sought in nature. It is generally recognized that the master painters of the time were much influenced by Zen Buddhism, which was introduced into Japan from China in A.D. 1191.[75] This form of Buddhism had become to some extent amalgamated with the temper of Taoist quietism in China, and agreed with that religion in a love of nature and a desire to attain through contemplation a tranquil sense of identity with the universe. Hence we can understand how Zen Buddhism helped to inspire in Japan paintings strongly reminiscent of the slightly earlier Sung paintings in China (pp.415f.). At the same time we should not forget that an appreciation of the beauty of nature was native to the Japanese people, and had been fostered in the Shinto religion from the

[73] SJSCH pp.325f. [74] ibid., pp.384-488.
[75] K. Florenz in SLR I, pp.373-381; Anesaki, History of Japanese Religion, pp.206-214.

earliest times. Hence the paintings of the period are not irrelevant to our present concern with Shinto.

Perhaps the greatest painter of the time was Sesshu, himself a Buddhist priest. He lived from 1420 to 1506, and spent a period of two years in study in China. He painted in ink, and produced landscapes scarcely excelled in all East Asia. For a single example, we show in Fig. 203 his Winter Landscape, which is in the Manjuin Temple in Kyoto.[76]

[76] Jon Carter Covell, *Under the Seal of Sesshū.* 1941.

7. THE MOMOYAMA (A.D. 1568-1615) AND YEDO (A.D. 1615-1867) PERIODS

AFTER centuries of civil war, three dictators began to forge the unity of modern Japan. The first was Oda Nobunaga (A.D. 1534-1582), a descendant of the illustrious family of Taira (p.451). Forming a powerful feudal army, he set out upon campaigns which brought half of Japan into his control. Among the obstacles to a unified country were the very powerful Buddhist temples and monasteries, and many of these were reduced by his troops. On the other hand, the Spanish Jesuit missionary Francis Xavier, who arrived in Japan in 1549, was looked upon with favor. The headquarters of Nobunaga were at the powerful castle of Adzuchi which he built on the shore of Lake Biwa.

The second man of conquest was Toyotomi Hideyoshi, who had been a general in the army of Nobunaga. Upon the assassination of the latter, Hideyoshi took power and continued the program already begun. So successful was he that by 1590 all Japan had submitted to his mastery. His ambition was not yet satisfied, however, and he planned an Asiatic empire which should also include Korea, China, India and Persia. Wars intended to accomplish this purpose were begun in Korea, but ended in disaster, and Japan's attempt at foreign conquest was abandoned, at least for three hundred years. Like his predecessor, Hideyoshi at first was favorable to Christianity, but becoming suspicious of the imperialistic intentions of the Spaniards, he issued an edict of persecution in 1597. A colossal, moated, granite castle at Osaka was the stronghold of Hideyoshi; and at a suburb of Kyoto called Momoyama he built an ornate palace for his residence. The latter place gives its name to the period (A.D. 1568-1615) of which we are now speaking.

The third of the dictators was Tokugawa Ieyasu. He worked in unity with Hideyoshi, and ruled in the Kwanto Plain where he had a fortress at Yedo (or Edo, now Tokyo). Upon the death of Hideyoshi (1598), Ieyasu had to struggle with rivals but eventually (1615) succeeded in claiming the mastery of all Japan.

Through the work of Ieyasu, the Tokugawa family was established in a supremacy which it maintained for over two hundred years. The emperors were in virtual seclusion at Kyoto, restricted to the performance of little but ceremonial functions. The shogunate wielded the real power, and its seat, Yedo, was practically the capital of the

[455]

country. Hence, to use the same kind of terminology hitherto employed, this epoch of Tokugawa dominance may be called the Yedo Period (A.D. 1615-1867).

NIKKO

Ieyasu died in A.D. 1616, having expressed the wish to be buried at Nikko. This is an extremely picturesque place in the hills ninety miles north of Tokyo. Its antiquity as a religious center goes far back of the time of Ieyasu. When the first Shinto shrine was erected there we do not know, but the first Buddhist temple is said to have been built in A.D. 767. This was done by Shodo Shonin (735-817), a pioneer of Buddhism among the mountains and a man possibly also influenced by Taoism.[77]

The wish of Ieyasu was carried out by his son and successor, Hidetada. A mausoleum was erected at Nikko, and the remains of Ieyasu buried there with much ceremony in the year 1617. This mausoleum was rebuilt in its present form by the third Tokugawa shogun, the grandson of Ieyasu, Iyemitsu, the work being completed in 1626. Iyemitsu himself was slain upon a visit to this tomb in 1651, and his sepulcher is also at Nikko.

The mausoleum of Ieyasu comprises an extensive complex of buildings which are known collectively as the Toshogu Shrine. A gigantic granite torii spans the approach avenue, which leads on past various structures. These include the Honji-do Temple, dedicated to Yakushi, a god of healing who was worshiped by Ieyasu as his tutelary Buddha. At last one stands before the Yomei-mon. This is probably the finest architecture of the entire shrine, and is a notable example of the "divine gate" (shim-mon) which was now a characteristic feature in many Shinto shrines.[78] As the photograph in Fig. 204 shows, the Yomei Gate is built in two stories and is everywhere covered with intricate carvings. What is not shown in a black and white picture is the resplendent polychrome decoration of the whole, which stands out brilliantly against the surrounding forest. On the ceiling of the first story there are monochrome dragons and various heavenly beings in color, which were executed by Tanyu (A.D. 1602-1674), one of the famous Kano family of artists.[79]

Beyond the Yomei-mon is the smaller Kara-mon, and beyond that are the Hall for Prayers (Hai-den), the Stone-floored Chamber (Ishi-

---

[77] Anesaki, History of Japanese Religion, p.92 n.4.
[78] Akiyama, Shintô and Its Architecture, p.109.
[79] Handbook of the Old Shrines and Temples and Their Treasures in Japan, p.20.

no-ma), and the Main Shrine (Hon-den). The Main Shrine, deco-rated in exquisite detail, is built in the Gongen style, which is similar to the Yatsu-mune style and like it combines Shinto and Buddhist motifs.[80]

The tomb of Ieyasu is a little distance away on a high mound. The path which leads to it passes beneath another gate made famous by a carved cat springing out of a peony plant, the work of the notable sculptor, Hidari Jingoro (A.D. 1594-1634). The tomb is in the form of a bronze stupa standing upon a platform of steps, with a tall bronze candlestick of stork design in front of it.[81]

The Shrine of Iyemitsu, known as the Daiyu-in, is in a separate quarter west of the Toshogu. It was begun in 1651 and completed in 1653. This shrine is on the whole comparable to that of Ieyasu, but on a somewhat less grand scale. Whereas the Shinto element was strong in the Toshogu, the Buddhistic influence is stronger here.[82]

In addition to the two Tokugawa shrines, there are numerous other buildings at Nikko. These include the Shinto shrine, Futa-ara-jinja, and the Buddhist temple, Rinnoji, the existence of which at the same sacred site further emphasizes the thorough interrelatedness of the two faiths at this time.

THE WARONGO

An important literary expression of Ryobu Shinto appeared at about this time. This is the Warongo or Japanese Analects,[83] pub-lished in ten volumes in 1669. While the names of various compilers are given in the text, ranging in date from the Kamakura Period to the early Tokugawa shogunate, it has been shown that the entire work was probably in actuality the product of one author, Sawada Gennai, otherwise known as Sasaki Ujisato, who lived in the middle of the seventeenth century.

The Warongo consists in the main of a collection of oracles of various Shinto deities together with sayings of certain princes, priests and others. Strongly Japanese as the work is, the Shinto it expresses is a syncretistic religion in which both Buddhist and Confucian ele-ments are prominent. Thus in the Oracle of the Sea God, Watatsumi Daimyojin, it is said:

[80] Akiyama, *Shintô and Its Architecture*, p.78.
[81] Pier, *Temple Treasures of Japan*, pp.298f.
[82] *Handbook of the Old Shrines and Temples and Their Treasures in Japan*, pp.22f.
[83] tr. Genchi Kato in *Transactions of the Asiatic Society of Japan*. 45 (1917), pp.1-138.

Not only in Japan doth one and the same Japanese God of Heaven manifest himself in different forms but also in many other lands.

In India he was born as the Buddha Gautama, the Supremely Enlightened One. . . . In China the three sages, K'ung-fu-tzu, Lao-tzu, and Yen Hui, were neither more nor less than our own kami.

You may ask: Why does one and the same God assume such varied forms? It is simply because, being one and the same God, he desires to preach the selfsame truth, and therefore he takes forms differing only in appearance from each other, so that he may best adapt his teaching to the understanding of every man.[84]

Similarly in a saying ascribed to Fujiwara Kanetomo (A.D. 1435-1511) it is concluded: "Thus viewed, the introduction of Confucianism and Buddhism in olden days is not to·be understood as something utterly new and foreign imported then for the first time into Japan, but as the revival of the ancient Shinto teachings disguised in the form of Buddhism and Confucianism which, having penetrated into foreign lands [India and China] from their original home in Japan, had returned hither in a quickened form."[85]

PAINTING

In the earlier discussion of the Nikko shrines were introduced the names of two of the foremost artists of those days, Hidari Jingoro the sculptor, and Kano Tanyu the painter. An additional word about painting will enlarge our conception of the artistic work then being done. It was the Kano family, to which Tanyu belonged, which provided the continuity of tradition from the Muromachi Period into the Momoyama and Yedo Periods. The founder of their school of painting was Kano Masanobu, who had lived about 1453 to 1490 and been a personal friend of the great Sesshu. To illustrate the work which this school produced in the later times we can do nothing better than show one of the paintings of Kano Tanyu (1602-1674) himself. This is a picture in the collection of Ulrich Odin, and is known as Moon Upon the Snow (Fig. 205).[86]

Another great painter was Maruyama Okyo (1753-1795), whose landscapes breathe a sense of reverie and mystery. For one example of his work we present a painting dated in 1772, showing Mount Fuji among the clouds (Fig. 206).[87] Yet a final name may be men-

[84] *ibid.*, p.75.   [85] *ibid.*, p.77.
[86] *Peintures chinoises et japonaises de la collection Ulrich Odin*, p.42, Pl. xxxvi.
[87] *ibid.*, pp.48f., Pl. xlviii.

tioned here, that of Katsushika Hokusai (1760-1849),[88] who devoted to the same sacred mountain of Japan a series of thirty-six paintings. In them he has grouped around the peak almost every aspect of the Japanese life and land. One of the series is reproduced in Fig. 207. Here Fuji is seen across the sea from near Kamagawa, dramatically framed by a breaking wave, and with boats tossing on the waters. The waves are animated by a mysterious power, an almost divine life, the force of which is infinitely greater than man.[89]

Perhaps it is not without significance that here in the last of the periods covered in our survey, we have come upon a fresh interest in that sacred mountain to which also the most primitive people of Japan had directed their worship, and upon a sense of a divine power permeating the natural world which was also shared in their own way by those same early ancestors.

MOTOORI

At all events in this same Yedo Period there was a distinct revival of interest in the ancestral faith and philosophy of the land. After all the years of ready acceptance of the doctrines of Buddhism and Confucianism, there was now a distinct movement calling for the repudiation of Chinese teachings and for a return to the inspiration of the ancient Japanese literature, and for a reestablishment of "pure" Shinto.

The leader of this movement who is of most significance for us was Motoori (A.D. 1730-1801). He was born in the province of Ise, home of the shrine of the sun goddess, and as a man he devoted himself to intensive studies of the ancient writings of the land. His greatest work was a thoroughgoing commentary on the Kojiki, known as the Kojiki-den.[90]

One fateful result of such studies was a renewed sense of the divine dignity of the imperial dynasty of Japan, and there was a growth of feeling against the shogunate through which the emperors had been pushed so much into the background.

The ultimate outcome, to which of course many other factors also contributed, was the revolution of 1868 in which the shogunate was abolished and the emperor "restored" as actual ruler of Japan. In the period following World War II, "state" Shinto was officially abol-

---

[88] W. Boller in *Mitteilungen der schweizerischen Gesellschaft der Freunde ostasiatischer Kultur.* 7 (1945), pp.39-59.
[89] GCE IV, p.246.
[90] Anesaki, *History of Japanese Religion*, p.308; Aston, *Shinto*, p.373.

ished and the Emperor Hirohito issued a formal denial of his own divinity as monarch. "Sectarian" Shinto survived, and in 1945 the number of its adherents was estimated at over twenty million.

CHAPTER IX

Islam

THE religion of Islam originated in Arabia, and now has more than 250,000,000 believers throughout the world, mostly in the Eastern Hemisphere. In the land where it began, of the nine million inhabitants at least ninety-nine per cent are numbered among the faithful.[1]

Arabia is the world's largest peninsula. Projecting 1,500 miles southeastward from the mainland of Asia, it has an area of 1,000,000 square miles, as much as that of the United States east of the Mississippi. On each of its three seacoast sides there are lowlands backed by mountain ranges. The mountains paralleling the western coast are the highest, Jebel al-Maqla in the north being over 9,500 feet in elevation, and Jebel Hadhur in the south over 12,000 feet. Near the eastern coast, Jebel Sham is 9,900 feet high. Between the western ramparts and the eastern, the land may be described in general as a vast plateau, sloping gently eastward.

In the entire land there is not a single permanent river, but a network of wadis carries off the occasional rainfall. Deserts and steppes comprise the greater part of the country, but there are also many oases where springs exist or the subterranean waters are not too far beneath the surface of the ground. At the oases and also around the edges of the peninsula where the rainfall is slightly more, permanent habitations are possible. Actually the bulk of the population is found in the settlements, and the Bedouins who follow a truly nomadic life number perhaps only around one million.

Of the various regions which may be distinguished in the country, that in the west where the important cities of Mecca and Medina are, is called the Hejaz. The central tableland is the Nejd, to the north, east and south of which are the Nefud, Dahana and Rab' al-Khali deserts. In the southwest are the highlands of Yemen, in the southeast those of Oman, and in between the Aden Protectorate and the region of Hadhramaut. In the extreme northeast is Kuwait. Yemen, Oman and Kuwait have long been independent countries, and

[1] Samuel M. Zwemer, *A Factual Survey of the Moslem World with Maps and Statistical Tables.* 1946, pp.10-15.

Aden belongs to Great Britain, but otherwise the bulk of the peninsula is included in the Kingdom of Saudi Arabia, named after the royal house of Saud. The capital of Saudi Arabia is at Riyadh.

The Greek and Roman writers of classical antiquity divided the land into three main parts, and spoke of Arabia Deserta, the "desert" region of the north; Arabia Felix, the "happy" area with more water in the south; and Arabia Petraea, the "rocky" portion in the northwest including Sinai[2] and much of what is now Transjordan.

Due to its isolation and forbidding character, Arabia has remained less well known to the outside world than most of the lands with which we have dealt. Indeed it has been said that prior to World War I there was nowhere else on earth except in the polar areas so large an unexplored and unmapped region as here.[3] Archeological exploration is likewise not far advanced, nevertheless considerable information is already available concerning the period before Muhammad as well as after.

The earliest evidences of the existence of man on the Arabian peninsula are flints of the Paleolithic Age, such as have been found for example in Wadi Hadhramaut, where prehistoric hunters gathered to manufacture their primitive implements and weapons.[4]

In historical times, Arabia, projecting as it does between Asia and Africa, was an object of interest to the neighboring peoples including the Egyptians, Assyrians, Hebrews, Greeks and Romans. The records of these peoples contain many references which relate to Arabian history, the general nature of which it will be helpful to indicate at this point.

The Egyptians prized both the minerals of Sinai and the frankincense of South Arabia. Probably as early as in the First Dynasty, King Semerkhet carried on mining operations in the Wadi Maghara and, as later Pharaohs also did, left there a memorial in the form of an inscription and a relief showing himself smiting a Bedouin.[5] In the Fifth Dynasty King Sahure, like many a later ruler including the famous Queen Hatshepsut, sent a sea expedition to Punt to get incense and ointment and recorded the same in his inscriptions.[6] The

---

[2] For Sinai as a part of Arabia, cf. Galatians 4:25.

[3] Cressey, *Asia's Lands and Peoples*, p.397.

[4] G. Caton Thompson, *The Tombs and Moon Temple of Hureidha* (*Hadhramaut*) (Reports of the Research Committee of the Society of Antiquaries of London, XIII). 1944, pp.3f.

[5] James H. Breasted, *A History of Egypt from the Earliest Times to the Persian Conquest*. 1905, p.48 and Fig. 28; ARE I, §168f.

[6] *ibid.*, pp.127,274-278; ARE I, §161; II, §246-295.

name Punt probably referred to what is now Somaliland, and may have also included portions of Arabia across the Straits of Bab el-Mandeb, whence similar products were to be obtained.[7]

The Assyrians came into military conflict with the people of the peninsula to the south of them, and the "Monolith Inscription" of Shalmaneser III (858-824 B.C.) provides the first explicit reference to the "Arabians." This is the inscription which in a list of conquered enemy forces contains the name of Ahab, the Israelite. A little farther on in the same list we encounter "Gindibu', the Arabian," and find that he is described, appropriately enough for a desert leader, as commanding a force of one thousand camels.[8] Tiglath-pileser III (744-727 B.C.) mentions "Samsi, queen of Arabia," as well as Saba and the Sabeans.[9] Sargon II (721-705 B.C.) writes: "From Pir'u (Pharaoh), king of Egypt, Samsi, queen of Arabia, It'amra, the Sabean, the kings of the seacoast and the desert, I received gold, products of the mountain, precious stones, ivory, seed of the maple, all kinds of herbs, horses, and camels, as their tribute."[10] Sennacherib (704-681 B.C.) mentions "Karibi-ilu, king of Saba'."[11]

The relationship of the Hebrews and the Arabians was relatively close by reason of geography and also of language, Hebrew and Arabic being cognate Semitic tongues. Commercial cooperation evidently existed in the time of King Solomon. The famed Queen of Sheba probably came from the Arabian kingdom of Saba and doubtless visited Solomon for business purposes as well as because of interest in his notable wisdom (I Kings 10:1-10). Likewise the navy of ships which Solomon built in Ezion-geber for trade with Ophir (I Kings 9:26-28) went probably to South Arabia. According to I Kings 10:14f., the trade with Arabia was a not unimportant part of the sources of Solomon's wealth: "The weight of gold that came to Solomon in one year was six hundred and sixty-six talents of gold, besides what came from the traffic of the merchants and from all the kings of the Arabs and from the governors of the land."[12] Intermittent warfare is also recorded. "The Arabians that are beside the Ethiopians" invaded Judah in the time of King Jehoram (II Chronicles 21:16); and Uzziah fought against "the Arabians that dwelt in Gur-baal, and the Meunim" (II Chronicles 26:7).[13] "Geshem the Arabi-

[7] HHA p.34. [8] ARAB I, §611. [9] ARAB I, §778.
[10] ARAB II, §18, cf. 55. [11] ARAB II, §440.
[12] From *The Bible, An American Translation.* cf. II Chronicles 9:13f.
[13] Hezekiah also fought against the Meunim (I Chronicles 4:41).

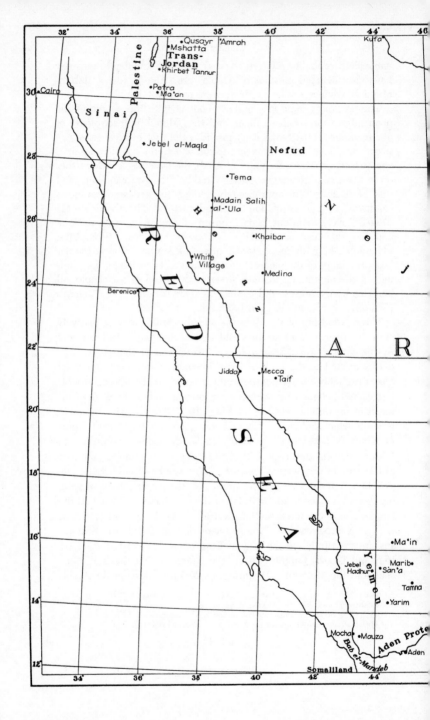

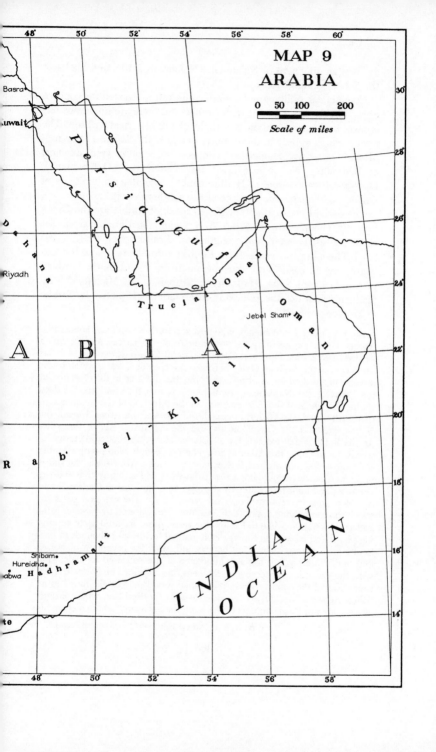

MAP 9
ARABIA

0   50   100   200
Scale of miles

Basra

Kuwait

Persian Gulf

Dehana

Riyadh

Trucial Oman

Oman

Jebel Sham+

A   B   I   A

Rab' al Khali

R   a   b'   a   l

Shibam•
Hureidha•
abwa   Hadhramaut

te

INDIAN

OCEAN

an" was an opponent of Nehemiah (Nehemiah 2:19); and Sheba or the Sabeans raided Job (Job 1:15).

Commercial, military and scientific interests motivated the concern of the Greeks and Romans with Arabia, and there are numerous references to this land in their geographical and historical writings. The names which appear in these sources include the *Sabaei* (Sabeans), *Minaei* (Mineans), *Homeritae* (Himyarites), *Scenitae* (tent-dwellers or Bedouins), *Nabataei* (Nabateans), *Catabanei* (Qatabanians), *Chatramotitae* (people of Hadhramaut), *Omanitae* (inhabitants of Oman), and *Sachalitae* (people of the southern coast line).[14]

The earliest classical authorities to speak of Arabia are the Greek botanist, Theophrastus (c.372-c.287 B.C.), and the Alexandrian mathematician, astronomer and geographer, Eratosthenes (c.276-c.195 B.C.). Theophrastus writes in his *Enquiry into Plants*: "Now frankincense, myrrh, cassia and also cinnamon are found in the Arabian peninsula about Saba, Hadramyta, Kitibaina and Mamali."[15] Eratosthenes provides the following information, as quoted by Strabo in his *Geography*.[16]

But I return to Eratosthenes, who next sets forth his opinions concerning Arabia. He says concerning the northerly, or desert, part of Arabia, which lies between Arabia Felix and Coele-Syria and Judaea, extending as far as the recess of the Arabian Gulf, that from the City of Heroes, which forms a recess of the Arabian Gulf near the Nile, the distance in the direction of the Petra of the Nabataeans to Babylon is five thousand six hundred stadia, the whole of the journey being in the direction of the summer sunrise and through the adjacent countries of the Arabian tribes, I mean the Nabataeans and the Chaulotaeans and the Agraeans. Above these lies Arabia Felix, which extends for a distance of twelve thousand stadia towards the south, to the Atlantic Sea. The first people who occupy Arabia Felix, after the Syrians and Judaeans, are farmers. After these the soil is sandy and barren, producing a few palm-trees and a thorny tree and the tamarisk, and affording water by digging, as is the case in Gedrosia; and it is occupied by tent-dwellers and camel-herds. The extreme parts towards the south, lying opposite to Aethiopia, are watered by summer rains and are sowed twice, like India; and the rivers there are used up in supplying plains and lakes. The country is in general fertile, and abounds in particular with places for making honey; and, with the exception of horses and mules and hogs, it has an abundance of domesticated animals; and, with the exception of geese and chickens, has all kinds of birds. The extreme part of the country above-mentioned is occupied by the four largest tribes; by the Minaeans, on the side towards the Red Sea, whose largest city is Carna or Carnana; next to these, by the Sabaeans, whose metropolis

[14] HHA p.44 n.1.   [15] IX, iv, 2. tr. Arthur Hort, LCL (1916), II, pp.233-235.
[16] XVI, iv, 2.

is Mariaba; third, by Cattabanians, whose territory extends down to the straits and the passage across the Arabian Gulf, and whose royal seat is called Tamna; and, farthest toward the east, the Chatramotitae, whose city is Sabata.

An interesting source of the Roman period which deals with Arabia is *The Periplus of the Erythraean Sea.*[17] The author is unknown but must have been a Greek resident in Egypt and a Roman subject. He was a merchant and made a voyage around Arabia for commercial reasons. The present work, written perhaps about A.D. 60, is a report on that trip and on the various ports, markets and products which the author had observed. *Periplus* means "a sailing round" or "the account of a coasting voyage," and the term Erythraean Sea was at that time applied to the Indian Ocean together with the Arabian Gulf (or Red Sea of modern times) and the Persian Gulf.

Starting from Berenice, Egypt, he crossed the Gulf to White Village, from which as he says "there is a road to Petra, which is subject to Malichas, King of the Nabataeans." "Directly below this place," the author continues, "is the adjoining country of Arabia, in its length bordering a great distance on the Erythraean Sea. Different tribes inhabit the country, differing in their speech, some partially, and some altogether. The land next the sea is similarly dotted here and there with caves of the Fish-Eaters, but the country inland is peopled by rascally men speaking two languages, who live in villages and nomadic camps, by whom those sailing off the middle course are plundered, and those surviving shipwrecks are taken for slaves. And so they too are continually taken prisoners by the chiefs and kings of Arabia; and they are called Carnaites. Navigation is dangerous along this whole coast of Arabia, which is without harbors, with bad anchorages, foul, inaccessible because of breakers and rocks, and terrible in every way. Therefore we hold our course down the middle of the gulf and pass on as fast as possible by the country of Arabia until we come to the Burnt Island; directly below which there are regions of peaceful people, nomadic, pasturers of cattle, sheep and camels.

"Beyond these places, in a bay at the foot of the left side of this gulf, there is a place by the shore called Muza,[18] a market-town es-

---

[17] tr. Wilfred H. Schoff, *The Periplus of the Erythraean Sea, Travel and Trade in the Indian Ocean by a Merchant of the First Century, Translated from the Greek and Annotated.* 1912.

[18] The name seems to include both the modern seaport of Mocha and the inland market-town of Mauza.

tablished by law, distant altogether from Berenice for those sailing southward, about twelve thousand stadia. And the whole place is crowded with Arab shipowners and seafaring men, and is busy with the affairs of commerce; for they carry on a trade with the far-side coast and with Barygaza,[19] sending their own ships there.

"Three days inland from this port there is a city called Saua. . . . And after nine days more there is Saphar,[20] the metropolis, in which lives Charibael, lawful king of two tribes, the Homerites and those living next to them, called the Sabaites; through continual embassies and gifts, he is a friend of the Emperors."

Proceeding on his adventurous voyage, the author of the *Periplus* entered "a narrow strait," the course through which ·was "beset with rushing currents and with strong winds blowing down from the adjacent ridge of mountains." This was the strait now known as Bab el-Mandeb or Gate of Tears.

Having negotiated this passage he arrived at Eudaemon Arabia, or the modern Aden. "After Eudaemon Arabia," he goes on, "there is a continuous length of coast, and a bay extending two thousand stadia or more, along which there are Nomads and Fish-Eaters living in villages; just beyond the cape projecting from this bay there is another market-town by the shore, Cana, of the Kingdom of Eleazus, the Frankincense Country. . . . Inland from this place lies the metropolis Sabbatha,[21] in which the King lives. All the frankincense produced in the country is brought by camels to that place to be stored, and to Cana on rafts held up by inflated skins after the manner of the country, and in boats. And this place has a trade also with the far-side ports, with Barygaza and Scythia and Ommana and the neighboring coast of Persia." Farther than this we will not follow the nameless merchant who has provided such vivid glimpses of first century Arabia.

In the second century A.D. the Greco-Egyptian geographer Ptolemy listed a large number of known places in Arabia. His map of that land is shown in Fig. 208.[22]

[19] The city on the west coast of India now known as Broach.

[20] Saphar is called Zafar by the Arabian geographers and is identified with ruins near modern Yarim.

[21] Probably to be identified with ruins sixty miles west of modern Shibam.

[22] *Geography.* v, 16, 18; vi, 7. Edward L. Stevenson, *Geography of Claudius Ptolemy, Translated into English and Edited, Based upon Greek and Latin Manuscripts and Important Late Fifteenth and Early Sixteenth Century Printed Editions, Including Reproductions of the Maps from the Ebner Manuscript, ca. 1460.* 1932, pp.128f.,130f., 137-140. Sexta Asiae tabula.

1. THE SABEO-HIMYARITE PERIOD, c.1000 B.C.-A.D. c.525[23]

Now we will turn to systematic consideration of a number of the early Arabian kingdoms which have been mentioned in the foregoing accounts. All those to be dealt with have become known to modern archeology through their own monuments and inscriptions as well as through the references of outside peoples such as we have been citing. For the most part the centers of these kingdoms were in South Arabia, an area which has been penetrated by comparatively few scientific explorers. Among those who were pioneers, special prominence attaches to the names of the Dane, Carsten Niebuhr (1763); the Frenchmen, Louis Arnaud (1843) and Joseph Halévy (1869); and the Austrian, E. Glaser (1882-1889).[24] Despite the difficulties, the work of these men and others has resulted in making known many sites and monuments, and in particular in collecting a large body of inscriptions.[25] These are written in an alphabet which is related to the Hebrew and, like it, probably derived from the proto-Sinaitic alphabetic symbols.[26]

References to and descriptions of various ancient monuments are also to be found in the writings of later Arabic authors. In this regard, the most important name is that of al-Hamdani (d. A.D. 945), a native of San'a and a student of astronomy, geography and history. He wrote a geography of Arabia entitled Sifatu Jazirat al-'Arab, and a large treatise on the history and antiquities of Yemen called al-Iklil, The Crown.[27] Book VIII of the latter work deals with the citadels and castles of South Arabia,[28] and will be cited in the following discussion. Where it has been checked by modern explorers it has proved remarkably dependable.

[23] For most of the dates and periods in Arabian history see HHA.

[24] David G. Hogarth, The Penetration of Arabia, A Record of the Development of Western Knowledge Concerning the Arabian Peninsula (The Story of Exploration). 1904, pp.39-62,128-131,200-203,203f.

[25] Corpus Inscriptionum Semiticarum ab Academia Inscriptionum et Litterarum Humaniorum conditum atque digestum. Pars Quarta, Inscriptiones Himyariticas et Sabaeas continens. 1889-.

[26] Martin Sprengling, The Alphabet, Its Rise and Development from the Sinai Inscriptions. OIC 12 (1931), pp.54f.

[27] Reynold A. Nicholson, A Literary History of the Arabs. 2d ed. 1930, pp.11f.

[28] tr. David H. Müller, Die Burgen und Schlösser Südarabiens nach dem Iklîl des Hamdânî. 2 parts. Sitzungsberichte der kaiserlichen Akademie der Wissenschaften, Wien, phil.-hist. Cl. 94 (1879), pp.335-423; 97 (1881), pp.955-1050; Nabih Amin Faris, The Antiquities of South Arabia, Being a Translation from the Arabic with Linguistic, Geographic, and Historic Notes of the Eighth Book of Al-Hamdânî's al-Iklîl, Reconstructed from al-Karmalî's Edition and a MS in the Garrett Collection, Princeton University Library. 1938.

The first kingdoms we will take up are the four which are mentioned by both Theophrastus and Eratosthenes. Theophrastus, it will be remembered, alludes to the lands of Saba, Hadramyta, Kitibaina and Mamali; and Eratosthenes speaks of the Minaeans, Sabaeans, Cattabanians and Chatramotitae. Since Mamali in the text of Theophrastus is probably an error for Minea,[29] the two lists are in agreement. Theophrastus gives the names of the countries; Eratosthenes the names of the peoples inhabiting them. The order of reference in the latter source is evidently geographical, coming down the coast of the Red Sea to the Bab el-Mandeb and then turning eastward to Hadhramaut. We will follow the order in Theophrastus, beginning with Saba, probably the oldest of these kingdoms.

THE SABEANS, c.1000–c.115 B.C.

Since Saba[30] and the Sabeans are mentioned by the Assyrian kings as far back as Tiglath-pileser III, we know that the Sabean kingdom was in existence at least as anciently as the eighth century B.C. If, as the virtual identity of names suggests and as there seems no sufficient reason to doubt, the Biblical Queen of Sheba was from the land of Saba, then that kingdom was also old enough to be contemporaneous with Solomon (c.965–c.926 B.C.). The rule of a queen need not be astonishing, since an Arabian queen is explicitly named by Sargon only two hundred and fifty years later.[31] In the legends of Islam the Queen of Sheba is a prominent figure. She appears in the Qur'an (XXVII, 20–45), and is generally known in the Muslim world by the name of Bilqis.[32]

The oldest known capital of the Sabeans was at Sirwah, a day's journey west of Marib.[33] The ruins at this site include a castle, an elliptical temple, and numerous monolithic pillars. In the center of the temple stands a large block of stone, seventy feet long, thirty-five inches high and eighteen inches thick, covered on both sides with a

---

[29] De Lacy O'Leary, *Arabia Before Muhammad* (Trubner's Oriental Series). 1927, p.107 n.2.

[30] Tkač in Wilhelm Kroll and Kurt Witte, eds., *Paulys Real-Encyclopädie der klassischen Altertumswissenschaft, Neue Bearbeitung begonnen von Georg Wissowa*. Zweite Reihe, I, ii, cols. 1298-1515; and (J. Tkatsch) in EI IV, pp.3-19.

[31] D. S. Margoliouth, *The Relations between Arabs and Israelites Prior to the Rise of Islam* (The British Academy, Schweich Lectures, 1921). 1924, pp.49f.

[32] B. Carra de Vaux in EI I, p.720. Josephus, on the other hand, states that the royal visitor to Solomon was a "queen of Egypt and Ethiopia"; and Ethiopian tradition holds that their first king, named Menelik, was the son of Solomon and Makkeda, the latter being identified with the Queen of Sheba (*Antiquities*. VIII, vi, 5. tr. H. St. J. Thackeray and Ralph Marcus, LCL v [1934], pp.660f. and note e).

[33] HHA p.54.

lengthy Sabean inscription. Many of the pillars also contain inscriptions. The temple was built by a Mukarrib or priest-king named Yada'il Dharih, and was dedicated to Almaqah.[34]

Almaqah (or Ilmuqah) was the moon god, corresponding to Sin in Mesopotamia, and was the chief deity of the Sabeans. Throughout South Arabia this divinity was conceived of as masculine, and was known to the Mineans by the name of Wadd, to the Qatabanians as 'Amm, and to the Hadhramautians as Sin. His consort was the sun, Shams, the same as Shamash in Mesopotamia. Their son, who completed the triad of most important deities, was 'Athtar. He was the planet Venus, and corresponded to the Babylonian Ishtar and Phoenician Astarte. Many other heavenly bodies were considered divine, and were believed to spring from the moon god and sun god.[35]

The later and more famous capital of Saba was Marib.[36] The town is situated 3,900 feet above sea level. The ancient city wall of Marib encloses a parallelogram roughly one thousand yards square. The wall is some three feet thick, and the positions of eight gates are still recognizable in it. According to inscriptions the wall was originally built by a son of the Mukarrib Sumuhu-'alaya Yanaf. Of him it is said that he "built a wall around Marib by command of and with the help of 'Athtar."

Al-Hamdani states that there were three citadels within the city, Salhin, al-Hajar and al-Qashib. Salhin was the royal residence, and al-Hamdani says that it was the citadel of Bilqis. The pillars of the throne were still standing when he wrote, and were so solidly imbedded in the stone, he said, that even many men would not be able to topple them over.[37]

Some distance east of the city are the ruins to which the modern designation of Haram Bilqis attaches. Actually these are the remains of an elliptical temple like the one at Sirwah, and like it, consecrated to the moon god, Almaqah. An inscription of Ilsarah, son of Sumuhu-'alaya, king of Saba, found here, dedicates walls and towers which he had built to Almaqah because this deity had answered his prayer and bestowed benefits upon him. Another dedication to Almaqah was written by Tabi'karib, a priest and a general under three Sabean kings. Yet another stated: "Karib'il Watar Yuhan'im, king of Saba

---

[34] Adolf Grohmann in EI IV, pp.450f.
[35] Ditlef Nielsen in *Handbuch der altarabischen Altertumskunde.* I (1927), pp.177-250.
[36] Adolf Grohmann in EI III, pp.280-294.
[37] Faris, *The Antiquities of South Arabia*, p.36.

and Raidan, son of Dhamar'alayi Bayyin, and Halak'amar, son of Karib'il, restored the wall for Almaqah for the good of the citadel Salhin and the city Marib."[38]

Southwest of the city at a distance of an hour or two was the Marib dam, the most famous structure of all. It was located at the place where the Wadi Dana opens out between the Balaq hills. Although the Wadi is often waterless in the summertime, in the rainy season a stream pours through it of such size and force as often to be uncrossable for some months. In order to protect Marib from floods and to control the waters for irrigation, the Sabeans undertook the construction of an elaborate system of barriers and sluices. The main dam was of earth, over two thousand feet long, and faced on the side which met the water with small stones strongly held together with mortar. On either side were large sluices, in connection with which stone towers and other buildings were erected. From here canals ran out to distribute the waters to the whole Marib plain, enabling it to flourish as a veritable garden-land.

Various inscriptions have been found at the dam. Two of these, on what are probably some of the oldest constructions on the right side nearest the city, name Sumuhu-'alaya Yanuf and his son Yithi'a-mar Bayyin as builders of the sluice-works on that side. These kings probably belong to the earlier part of the Sabean Period.[39] Eventually the great dam weakened, and inscriptions of the fifth and sixth centuries A.D. tell of breaches and of attempts at repair. The last of these records is dated in A.D. 542, and the final disastrous break in the dam must have occurred sometime after that date and before the rise of Islam. This allowed a terrible flood to devastate the valley, which afterward returned to desert.[40]

In the Qur'an this catastrophe is interpreted as a punishment upon the people of Saba for their sins: "For Sheba . . . there was a sign in their dwelling-place—two gardens, on the right and on the left: 'Eat of the provision of your Lord, and show gratitude to him; a good soil and a forgiving Lord.' But they turned away, so We sent upon them the flood of the dam and gave them instead of their two gardens, two which produced bitter fruit, and tamarisks and lote-trees a few."[41]

---

[38] *Corpus Inscriptionum Semiticarum*, Pars Quarta, II, pp.20-28 (Nos. 373-375).

[39] Müller, *Die Burgen und Schlösser Südarabiens nach dem Iklîl des Hamdânî*, II, pp.965-967.

[40] Grohmann in EI III, pp.290f.

[41] XXXIV, 14f. tr. Richard Bell, *The Qur'ān, Translated with a Critical Re-arrangement of the Surahs.* 2 vols. 1937-39, II, p.423.

When al-Hamdani visited Marib the break in the dam had long since taken place, but the aqueducts through which the waters were led to the fields still stood "as though the builders had completed their construction only yesterday." So impressive were the ruins that al-Hamdani was not uninclined to accept the attribution of the original construction of the dam to Luqman ibn-'Ad, a mythical person to whom many institutions of antiquity were ascribed.[42]

Marib is now being excavated by the American Foundation for the Study of Man, under the presidency and leadership of Wendell Phillips.

THE HADHRAMAUTIANS

The Chatramotitae, as Eratosthenes named them, were the people of the land which Theophrastus called Hadramyta and which we know as Hadhramaut.[43] According to Eratosthenes the capital city of Hadhramaut was Sabata, which is identified with the modern town of Shabwa.[44] Pliny (A.D. 23-79) spoke of the city under the name of Sabota and said that it was situated on a lofty mountain, was surrounded by walls and contained sixty temples.[45]

Another ancient town of Hadhramaut was at modern Hureidha, some distance east of Shabwa. Excavations were conducted here in 1937-1938 by Gertrude Caton Thompson.[46] Hureidha is on the Wadi 'Amd. In this Wadi the remains of an extensive ancient irrigation system were traced. As in the case of the larger and more famous system at Marib, there were dams, sluices and channels to control and impound the waters and to lead them to the fields.

In the ruins of the ancient town the most important discovery was that of a temple to the moon god, the first such structure to be excavated in Arabia. As revealed by the digging, this temple stood on a slight eminence in the cultivated valley. It was built upon an oblong platform of paved stone, the corners of which were oriented to the four cardinal points. The main façade faced to the southwest. Three building periods were distinguished, in the course of which the temple was enlarged to its final dimensions. Five stone pillar-

[42] Faris, *The Antiquities of South Arabia*, pp.34f.

[43] Probably to be identified with Hazarmaveth in Genesis 10:26.

[44] HHA p.55; Adolf Grohmann in EI IV, pp.244f.

[45] *Natural History*. VI, xxxii, 155; XII, xxx, 52. tr. H. Rackham, LCL (1938-) II, p.455; IV, p.37.

[46] G. Caton Thompson, *The Tombs and Moon Temple of Hureidha (Hadhramaut)* (Reports of the Research Committee of the Society of Antiquaries of London, XIII). 1944.

bases still stood near the center of the platform. These may have supported wooden pillars upon which the sanctuary roof was carried.

Lying beside one of these pillars was a stone offering table. It was made from a rectangular slab of limestone, and there was a depression in the upper surface evidently intended to receive libations. A projection on one side was roughly shaped into a bull's head, and an inscription (No. 7)[47] gave the name of the one who had dedicated the table.

In one of the shrines later added to the temple there was a large stone altar, and around the base of this were various votive objects. In addition to pottery vessels these included two remarkable pieces of limestone. The first had been roughly hammer-dressed into a conical shape with a flattened base; the second was a rectangular brick with one end crudely shaped into a human head. The place where they were found shows that both stones must have had some sort of religious character. We may call the first a baetyl or sacred stone, and may suppose that it was an aniconic representation of a god. The second stone is clearly a semi-anthropomorphic image, and may be held to represent the worshiper or to be a cult image. In the two, then, we have two stages on the way to the fully sculptured images of which we will present examples in speaking of the Himyarite Period. Crude as they are, the stones are therefore of much significance, and we reproduce them in Figs. 209 and 210.[48]

Some fifty inscriptions were found at Hureidha, written in the Hadhramautic dialect. Twenty-two of these preserve dedications to the moon god, Sin, and there are also explicit references to the temple and the town. Inscription No. 4 refers to the "town of Madabum," thus giving us the ancient name of Hureidha; No. 10 mentions the "anterior façade [of the temple] of Madabum"; and No. 54 names the god of the city, "Sin of Madabum."[49]

Two cave tombs were also excavated and a considerable body of pottery recovered as well as two stone seals and a number of beads. The beads resemble eastern Mediterranean beads of the seventh to fifth centuries b.c.;[50] the seals reveal Achaemenian (sixth to fourth centuries b.c.) influence.[51] A tentative date, therefore, for the Hureidha tombs and temple is in the fifth and fourth centuries b.c.,

---

[47] *ibid.*, pp.160f. ("Epigraphy" by G. Ryckmans).
[48] *ibid.*, Pls. xv,left; xiv,left.
[49] *ibid.*, pp.158-160,162f.,173 (Ryckmans).
[50] *ibid.*, pp.96-101 (H. C. Beck).
[51] *ibid.*, pp.101-103 (Henri Frankfort).

with later phases of the temple building belonging perhaps to the
third century.[52]

THE QATABANIANS

The statement of Eratosthenes concerning the Qatabanians leads
us to locate this people along the strait, Bab el-Mandeb. Their capital, according to the same authority, was Tamna. For some time a
number of inscriptions in the Qatabanian dialect have been known.
These give the names of some of the Qatabanian kings, and tell of
campaigns in which they fought with and also against the Sabeans.
On the basis of these materials it has been judged that the Qatabanian kingdom came into existence around 500 B.C. and endured
until around the beginning of the Christian Era.[53] The site of ancient
Tamna, or Timna,[54] has very recently been identified, forty miles
south of Marib. Explorations and excavations were conducted there
in 1950 and 1951 by the American Foundation for the Study of Man,
under the leadership of Wendell Phillips, with William F. Albright
as chief archeologist. Thick beds of ashes have been revealed, marking the final conflagration in which the capital city was destroyed.
This event, doubtless coinciding with the end of Qataban as an independent kingdom, is now placed about 50 B.C. in round numbers.[55]

THE MINEANS

From the statement of Eratosthenes we gather that the territory
of the Mineans was to the north of that of the Sabeans, and we learn
that their largest city was Carna. Carna is identified with the modern
Ma'in, northeast of San'a. Outposts of Minean power were at Ma'an
near Petra, and at Daydan (Old Testament Dedan) which is represented by modern al-'Ula.[56]

Many inscriptions in the Minean dialect have been found in both
South and North Arabia. The Minean inscriptions which were found

[52] *ibid.*, pp.93,153.

[53] J. Tkatsch in EI II, pp.809-814; and (Tkač) in *Paulys Real-Encyclopädie der
klassischen Altertumswissenschaft.* Zweite Reihe, I, ii, cols. 1457-1459; Nikolaus Rho-
dokanakis, *Der Grundsatz der Öffentlichkeit in den südarabischen Urkunden.* 1915,
pp.33-49; *Katabanische Texte zur Bodenwirtschaft.* 1919 (Sitzungsberichte der [kais.]
Akademie der Wissenschaften in Wien, phil.-hist. Kl., 177, 2 and 194, 2); W. F. Albright in BASOR 119 (Oct. 1950), pp.5-15; cf. A. Jamme in BASOR 120 (Dec. 1950),
pp.26f.

[54] Although Timna is the form now more widely used, Eratosthenes has Τάμνα,
which points to Tamna as more accurately representing the ancient vocalization.

[55] W. F. Albright in BASOR 119 (Oct. 1950), pp.5-15.

[56] HHA pp.52,54. Daydan was the capital of the Lihyanites, whom the Mineans
probably succeeded at that place.

at al-'Ula by the French explorers Pères Jaussen and Savignac contain the names of three kings of Ma'in, Ilyafa' Yashur, Abikarib
Yathi' and Waqah'il Nabat, and refer frequently to the "gods of
Ma'in."[57] One of these inscriptions, naming Abikarib Yathi' and men-
tioning some of the gods of Ma'in, is reproduced in Fig. 211.

It has been thought by some that the Minean kingdom originated
even before the Sabean and went back to 1200 B.C. or earlier. Various
objections have been raised to this view, however, and it now appears probable that the Minean kingdom was later than the Sabean.[58]
Possible dates for its duration are from c.500 B.C. to A.D. c.50.[59]
If, however, the Meunim of the Old Testament are to be identified
with the Mineans, then this people must have been in existence as
early as the eighth century B.C. since both Uzziah (785-747) and
Hezekiah (725-697) are said to have fought against them.[60]

THE HIMYARITES, c.115 B.C.-A.D. c.525

Toward the end of the second century B.C. the dominant power in
South Arabia passed from the Sabeans to the Himyarites.[61] These
were a people related to the Sabeans in race and language, and the
heirs of their culture. The center of the Himyarites was at Raidan,
and about 115 B.C. the title "King of Saba and Raidan" appears in
the inscriptions.[62] Raidan was later known as Saphar (Sephar in
Genesis 10:30) or Zafar, under which name it appears, as we have
seen, in *The Periplus of the Erythraean Sea*. The same source gives
us our first mention by name of the Homerites or Himyarites, and
states that their king (who also ruled over the Sabeans) was Charibael. This ruler is probably the same as the Karib'il Watar Yuhan'im,
king of Saba and Raidan, whom we have already met in a late inscription at the Haram Bilqis at Marib. Pliny[63] also mentions the
Homeritae in connection with the Roman expedition which Aelius
Gallus led to disaster in Arabia in 25 B.C. Gallus, says Pliny, reported
that the Homeritae constituted the most numerous tribe in the land.
Strabo[64] describes the same expedition and states that at the time
Marsiaba (Marib) belonged to the tribe of the Rhammanitae who

---

[57] Jaussen and Savignac, *Mission archéologique en Arabie* (Publications de la Société des Fouilles Archéologiques). II, *El-'Ela, d'Hégra a Teima, Harrah de Tebouk*
(1914), pp.256-263,270-273,301-304 (Nos. 11,12,17,31); Atlas, Pl. LXXIV, No. 17.

[58] Tkatsch in EI IV, pp.12-15.

[59] F. V. Winnett in BASOR 73 (Feb. 1939), pp.3-9.

[60] II Chronicles 26:7; I Chronicles 4:41.

[61] J. H. Mordtmann in EI II, pp.310-312.   [62] HHA p.55.

[63] *Natural History*, VI, xxxii, 161.   [64] *Geography*. XVI, iv, 22-24.

were subject to Ilasarus. Ilasarus is probably the Ilsarah Yahdub, king of Saba and Raidan, who is also known in the inscriptions.

The ruins of the Himyarite capital of Zafar[65] crown the summit of a circular hill near the modern village of Yarim. Al-Hamdani tells of the place at some length and quotes the expressions of various Arabic poets concerning it. He says that the city had nine gates and that from the main gate to the inner city was a mile in distance. The guardhouse at this gate was connected by a golden chain with the place where the king held audience so that the approach of visitors could be signaled. One of the castles at Zafar, reports al-Hamdani, was adorned with silver and white stones on the outside, and paneled with aloe wood, mosaic, onyx and different kinds of precious stones on the inside. So splendid was this castle that legend attributed its erection to the jinn or demons.[66]

Another notable Himyarite castle was the Ghumdan in San'a, which al-Hamdani calls the oldest, most remarkable and most famous of all those with which he deals. According to one view, it was built by none other than Shem, the son of Noah. In the time of al-Hamdani the castle was reduced to a gigantic ruin, opposite the great mosque of San'a, but this authority collected much information on its earlier appearance. It was built in terraces, he says, to a height of twenty stories. Each façade was built of stone of a different color, one front red, one white, one green and one black. The uppermost story was roofed with marble so transparent that, looking up, one could distinguish between a crow and a stork. At the four corners stood lions of copper which roared whenever the wind blew.[67]

The Himyarite Period is divided into two parts, the first from around 115 B.C. to around A.D. 300, the second from that date to about A.D. 525. Early in the first part colonists from South Arabia settled in the "land of Cush" and laid the foundations of the kingdom of Aksum (first century A.D.) which developed into the later Abyssinia. During the second part there were one or two relatively brief times of Abyssinian invasion and rule in Arabia, but mostly the native Himyarite kings maintained their position until the final date indicated.[68]

Both Judaism and Christianity were in South Arabia in the latter part of the Himyarite Period. According to Philostorgius in his

[65] J. Tkatsch in EI IV, pp.1185-1187.
[66] Faris, The Antiquities of South Arabia, pp.20-29.
[67] ibid., pp.8-20.   [68] HHA pp.56f.,60.

Church History (written sometime between A.D. 425 and 433), Christianity was taken to the Himyarites by the Indian Theophilus under the Emperor Constantius (A.D. 337-361). The evangelist succeeded in building churches in several towns, including the metropolis of Tapharon (probably Zafar), Aden, and a place at the mouth of the Persian Gulf. At the same time there were already numerous Jews in the land.[69]

Along with the two monotheistic faiths which had come in from the outside, the indigenous polytheism of Arabia continued to flourish, and worship was still directed to Almaqah, 'Athtar and other deities. Philostorgius says of the Himyarites in the same passage just cited: "They sacrifice to the sun and moon and spirits of the land."

The extant remains by which the popular beliefs are known include many funerary objects. As other peoples throughout the world have done, the ancient Arabians buried with the dead a variety of things which were valuable to them and desired for the life beyond. Among these, for example, are jars and saucers, cosmetic boxes and necklaces of semiprecious stones. Small altars and incense burners attest some kind of religious rites. Most interesting of all are the statuettes and bas-reliefs. These usually provide a representation of the deceased and are presumably animistic in conception, being intended to be a "support" for the soul after the burial of the inanimate body.[70]

The items which will be shown here have all been recovered in various ways from burial places in southwest Arabia. The inscriptions, which are in various South Arabian dialects, provide some clues for dating. For the most part it may be said that the objects belong to the time between 150 B.C. and A.D. 200, that is at the end of the Sabean and in the earlier part of the Himyarite Periods.

Fig. 212 pictures a limestone mask in which the human countenance is represented in a geometrical form. The inscription at the base is in archaic characters, and gives a name which has been read

---

[69] III, 4. ed. Joseph Bidez, *Philostorgius Kirchengeschichte mit dem Leben des Lucian von Antiochien und den Fragmenten eines arianischen Historiographen, herausgegeben im Auftrage der Kirchenväter-Commission der königl. preussischen Akademie der Wissenschaften* (Die griechischen christlichen Schriftsteller der ersten drei Jahrhunderte). 1913, pp.32-34. For the struggles between the Jews and the Christians and the persecution of the Christians by the Jewish king Masruq (dhu-Nuwas in the Muslim tradition), see Axel Moberg, *The Book of the Himyarites, Fragments of a Hitherto Unknown Syriac Work, Edited, with Introduction and Translation* (Skrifter Utgivna Av Kungl. Humanistiska Vetenskapssamfundet I Lund, 7). 1924.

[70] Léon Legrain in AJA 38 (1934), pp.329-337.

as Kaddat or Kadabat.[71] Fig. 213 shows an even more strongly geometrical woman's head executed in alabaster. In Fig. 214 we see a complete statuette in the round, also carved in alabaster. The modeling is done with care, but the lower part of the body is quite out of proportion, due no doubt to considering the head as the most important part. The inscription on the base gives the name of 'Ammyada of Shukaymim.[72]

Of the relief carvings three examples will be shown. The first (Fig. 215) is an alabaster stela with two panels of reliefs. In the upper panel the deceased man is shown at the right, garbed in a long robe and seated upon a low stool. He holds a bowl in one hand, and in front of him is a table with another bowl and a large vase. A servant with cup or bowl stands by the table, while at the left is a woman with a two-stringed musical instrument. This would appear to represent the master at a feast. In the lower panel the same deceased one is shown, evidently returning from an expedition. He rides upon a horse and, with brandished spear, drives a camel before him. At the top an inscription invokes the protection of the god 'Athtar for the monument: "Funeral image and stela of 'Igli, son of Sa'dlati Qurain. And may 'Athtar of the East smite him who effaces it!"[73]

The second relief (Fig. 216) is now but a fragment. At the top is part of an inscription calling the object a tombstone and giving several names; below this is a scene showing a peasant guiding a plow drawn by two oxen; and at the bottom are the heads of three persons.[74]

The third stela (Fig. 217) is identified by the inscription at the top as an "amulet" belonging to Ilza'adi and his brother Hillqahi. The carving shows a front view of the heads of two bulls. Their horns form almost perfect crescents or new moons, and on this ground the heads may probably be interpreted as symbols of Almaqah, the moon god.[75]

THE NABATEANS

In the time with which we have thus far been dealing there were

[71] G. Ryckmans in *Le Muséon, Revue d'études orientales.* 48 (1935), p.175.
[72] *ibid.,* pp.170f.
[73] *Corpus Inscriptionum Semiticarum,* Pars Quarta, ii, pp.143f. (No. 445); J. H. Mordtmann in *Zeitschrift der deutschen morgenländischen Gesellschaft.* 32 (1878), pp.200-203; 35 (1881), pp.432-438,440.
[74] *Corpus Inscriptionum Semiticarum,* Pars Quarta, iii, pp.127f. (No. 706).
[75] *ibid.,* pp.118f. (No. 695); Ditlef Nielsen, *Die altarabische Mondreligion und die mosaische Ueberlieferung,* 1904, pp.110-112.

also various kingdoms in North Arabia, but for the most part they were of less prominence than those in the South. For this reason the important southern kingdoms of the Sabeans and Himyarites have been allowed to give their names to the entire period. Of the northern kingdoms, it will suffice to mention here the earliest and greatest, that of the Nabateans, before passing on to the next main chronological period.

The Nabateans appear first in the inscriptions of Ashurbanipal in the seventh century B.C.,[76] and were mentioned by Eratosthenes, in the passage already quoted, among other North Arabian tribes. They succeeded the Moabites and Edomites in Transjordan, and made their capital at the famous city of Petra which they wrested from the Edomites. Their kingdom flourished from the fourth century B.C. to the second century A.D., reaching its greatest height in the first century A.D.

Petra, the Sela (or Selah) of the Old Testament (Isaiah 16:1; 42: 11; II Kings, 14:7; cf. Jeremiah 49:16; Obadiah 3; II Chronicles 25: 12), was a spectacular city, carved largely out of the solid and colorful rock in a high mountain valley east of the Wadi el-Arabah. Rock-hewn temples like the Khazneh (Fig. 218), houses, tombs, cisterns, aqueducts, and altars remain to attest the splendor which this place enjoyed when caravans brought in and out of it the riches of all the East.[77]

Of the many Nabatean deities the best known was dhu-al-Shara (the lord of Shara) or Dushara. He was worshiped at Petra in the form of an unhewn, rectangular black stone. In an inscription[78] at Petra, dating probably from the first century A.D., a tomb is entrusted to the care of this god in the following words:

This sepulcher, and the large vault within it, and the small vault inside, within which are burying-places fashioned into niches, and the wall in front of them . . . and the rest of all the entire property which is in these places, is the consecrated and inviolable possession of Dushara, the god of our lord, and his sacred throne, and all the gods, [as specified] in deeds relating to consecrated things according to their contents. And it is the order of Dushara and his throne and all the gods that, according to what

[76] ARAB II, §821.

[77] M. Rostovtzeff, *Caravan Cities.* tr. D. and T. Talbot Rice. 1932, pp.37-53; M. A. Murray, *Petra, The Rock City of Edom.* 1939.

[78] Although they spoke Arabic the Nabateans wrote in script derived from the Aramaic, and this developed into the script of North Arabic, particularly the round script called *naskhi* in distinction from the angular writing practiced in the city of Kufa and hence called Kufic (HHA p.70).

is in the said deeds relating to consecrated things, it shall be done and not altered. Nor shall anything of all that is in them be withdrawn; nor shall any man be buried in this sepulcher save him who has in writing a contract to bury, [specified] in the said deeds relating to consecrated things— for ever.[79]

Elsewhere in southern Transjordan the sites of more than five hundred Nabatean towns, fortresses, watch-towers and temples have now been surveyed. For a strikingly located temple we may refer to Khirbet Tannur on the summit of high, isolated Jebel Tannur not far from the Dead Sea. Here, as the sculptured remains show, the Nabateans worshiped Syrian deities like Hadad and his consort Atargatis.[80] Farther south in Arabia another Nabatean center was at Madain Salih or al-Hegr, where the rock-hewn monuments are almost as impressive as at Petra. One of the tombs at this place, dated in the year 1 B.C., is pictured in Fig. 219.[81]

The decisive blow to the Nabatean kingdom was the capture of Petra by the Romans in A.D. 106, after which time the rival city of Palmyra successfully attracted the trade which had previously enriched the merchants of Nabatea. The people of Palmyra, it may be added, were also of Arabian descent, and built in the Syrian desert a caravan city of amazing splendor. Their religion was a distinctive blend of Arabian, Parthian, Babylonian, Syrian and Greek elements, and their gods included a trinity made up of Bel (with Malak-bel as his messenger), Yarhibol and Aglibol, and the other deities Belshamin the rival of Bel, Shamash, Ishtar, Nanaia, Nergal, Hadad, Atargatis, Eshmun, Sama, Allat, Chai al Qaum, Arsu, Azizu and Satrapes.[82]

[79] Corpus Inscriptionum Semiticarum, Pars Secunda, Inscriptiones Aramaicas continens. I (1889), pp.307-311 (No. 350); G. A. Cooke, A Text-Book of North-Semitic Inscriptions, Moabite, Hebrew, Phoenician, Aramaic, Nabataean, Palmyrene, Jewish. 1903, pp.241-244 (No. 94).
[80] Nelson Glueck, The Other Side of the Jordan. 1940, pp.158-200.
[81] Jaussen and Savignac, Mission archéologique en Arabie, I, De Jérusalem au Hedjaz, Médain-Saleh (1909), pp.301-441; II, pp.78-108; Atlas, Pl. XL.
[82] Rostovtzeff, Caravan Cities, pp.91-152; Hoyningen-Huene and David M. Robinson, Baalbek, Palmyra. 1946, pp.59-127.

2. THE JAHILIYAH PERIOD, A.D. c.525-622

FROM the Muslim point of view the entire time prior to the rise of Islam was *jahiliyah*. This word appears several times in the Qur'an and is variously translated "Time of Ignorance" or "Paganism."[83] Finding such a designation not altogether appropriate to the relatively advanced civilizations hitherto discussed, the modern historian is inclined to limit the word to the century just before the establishment of Islam.[84]

The chief feature of Arabian life at this time was the return to nomadism.[85] In the south the breaking of the Marib dam symbolized the downfall of the urban civilization there; in the north the Nabatean state had already disintegrated and its powerful cities lost their greatness. Elsewhere in the north, in Hejaz and Nejd, nomadic life had always been most characteristic of the people.

Only three cities of importance were to be found in Hejaz. These were Taif, Mecca and Medina. Taif[86] enjoyed a picturesque and fertile location in the mountains and Medina[87] (then known as Yathrib) was in a well-watered plain, but Mecca[88] stood in a barren, rocky valley. Despite the sterility and extreme heat of the place, Mecca enjoyed the possession of a famous well called Zamzam and an ancient sanctuary known as the Ka'bah, and was also where important commercial routes intersected.

The Bedouins of the desert, who comprised the majority of North Arabia's population, were basically animistic in their religion. Springs and wells, stones and trees were the dwelling-places of spirits, and wild animals and fearsome places of the wilderness were inhabited by jinn or demons. Higher gods also were worshiped, and among these the most important, for our account, were Allah, Allat, al-'Uzza and Manat.[89]

While Allah is best known as the principal god of Mecca, he was also worshiped in other places throughout Arabia as is shown by the occurrence of the name in Sabean, Minean and particularly Lihya-

---

[83] III, 148; v, 55; XXXIII, 33; XLVIII, 26. tr. Bell, I, pp.60,101; II, pp.414,523.
[84] HHA p.87.
[85] Giorgio Levi della Vida in FAH pp.43f.,55.
[86] H. Lammens in EI IV, pp.621f.   [87] Fr. Buhl in EI III, pp.83-92.
[88] H. Lammens in EI III, pp.437-442.
[89] J. Wellhausen, *Reste arabischen Heidentums gesammelt und erläutert.* 2d ed. 1897; Theodor Nöldeke in HERE I, pp.659-673; cf. Samuel M. Zwemer, *The Influence of Animism on Islam, An Account of Popular Superstitions.* 1920.

nite inscriptions.[90] The Qur'an (xxix, 61) refers to the belief of the pagans in Allah as the creator of the heavens and the earth; and Muhammad's own father bore the name of 'Abd Allah or 'Abdullah, meaning the slave or worshiper of this god. In Mecca, Allah was worshiped in the Ka'bah and possibly represented by the famous Black Stone in that place.

Allat, according to recent study of the complicated inscriptional evidence,[91] is believed to have been introduced into Arabia from Syria, and to have been the moon goddess of North Arabia. If this is the correct interpretation of her character, she corresponded to the moon deity of South Arabia, Almaqah, Wadd, 'Amm or Sin as he was called, the difference being only the oppositeness of gender. Mount *Sinai* (the name being an Arabic feminine form of *Sin*) would then have been one of the centers of the worship of this northern moon goddess.

Similarly, al-'Uzza is supposed to have come from Sinai, and to have been the goddess of the planet Venus. As the moon and the evening star are associated in the heavens, so too were Allat and al-'Uzza together in religious belief, and so too are the crescent and star conjoined on the flags of Arab countries today.

As for Manat, her original home seems to have been in Hejaz. The etymology of the name is judged to be connected with the root *mana*, meaning "to determine" or "to mete out," and it is thus suggested that she was a goddess of fortune or fate. The same root is at the basis of the name of the god Meni or Destiny mentioned in Isaiah 65:11.

Prior to the rise of Islam, these three goddesses were associated with Allah as his daughters,[92] and all were worshiped at Mecca and other places in the vicinity. Articles about all three of them were written by the scholar Ibn al-Kalbi (d. A.D. c.820) in his Kitab al-Asnam or Book of Idols, extensive portions of which are preserved in the *Geographical Dictionary* of Yaqut (d. A.D. 1229).[93] According to Ibn al-Kalbi the sanctuary of Allat was in Taif where the goddess was represented by a rectangular block of stone, over which a build-

[90] HHA p.100.

[91] F. V. Winnett in *The Moslem World*. 30 (1940), pp.113-130.

[92] In the tablets found at ancient Ugarit (Ras Shamra), three daughters are ascribed to Baal, which strengthens the theory of North Syrian influence in the formation of the Meccan pantheon. Cyrus H. Gordon, *The Loves and Wars of Baal and Anat and Other Poems from Ugarit*. 1943, p.23.

[93] The extracts in Yaqut are collected and translated by Wellhausen, *Reste arabischen Heidentums*, pp.10-64. See now N. A. Faris, *The Book of Idols*. 1952.

ing was erected.[94] Al-'Uzza "stood," says the same authority, in the valley of Nakhla to the right of the road from Mecca to Iraq. This manner of speech leads us to suppose that al-'Uzza also was worshiped in the form of a stone pillar, and Ibn al-Kalbi speaks expressly of the house which was built over her. Manat was the oldest of the three deities, according to the same authority, and was a large stone in the valley of Qudaid between Mecca and Medina. The Aus and Khazraj tribes of Medina were the most prominent worshipers of Manat, while the Quraish of Mecca paid much reverence to Allat and al-'Uzza, most of all to the latter. The Quraish were the tribe to which Muhammad belonged, and Ibn al-Kalbi states that before the prophet began to preach his own message he himself once offered a white sheep to al-'Uzza. Such was the "paganism" in which Muhammad was reared and which he later came to believe it was his mission to dispel.

The milieu of the prophet was not one, however, of polytheistic paganism untouched by any other influences. As in South Arabia, so too in North the monotheistic faiths of Judaism and Christianity had long since become known. When the first Jewish communities were established in North Arabia we do not know, but a plausible hypothesis supposes that the enhanced commercial opportunities consequent upon the residence at Tema (Taima) of the Babylonian king Nabonidus (Nabunaid) attracted colonists as early as the latter half of the sixth century B.C. From there they followed on down the main caravan route to establish other colonies in Khaibar, Medina and Mecca.[95] The influence of Christianity was brought to bear upon Arabia both from Syria in the northwest and from Mesopotamia in the northeast. In the sixth century A.D. the Arabic kingdoms of the Ghassanids in Syria and the Lakhmids in Mesopotamia were allied respectively with the Byzantine and the Persian empires and were strong centers respectively of Monophysite and of Nestorian Christianity. From these regions and in this time if not also earlier, Christian ideas spread on into the farther reaches of Arabia.[96]

[94] The idol-stone of Allat which Charles M. Doughty was shown at Taif in the last century was an "unshapely crag" of gray granite nearly twenty feet in length (*Travels in Arabia Deserta.* 1921, II, p.516).

[95] Charles C. Torrey, *The Jewish Foundation of Islam* (The Hilda Stich Stroock Lectures [Established 1927] at the Jewish Institute of Religion). 1933, pp.10-15; cf. Ilse Lichtenstädter in *Proceedings of the American Academy for Jewish Research.* 10 (1940), pp.185-194.

[96] Richard Bell, *The Origin of Islam in Its Christian Environment* (The Gunning Lectures, Edinburgh University, 1925). 1926, pp.18-28.

A careful study of the relevant data particularly in the Qur'an shows that Muhammad had a very considerable store of knowledge of Judaism and Christianity, and that it was of the sort which he would have been most likely to obtain through oral channels and personal observation over a long period of time. He was specially impressed, it seems, with the fact that both the Jews and the Christians were People of a Book, and it was his desire likewise to provide his own people with a Book which would be to them what the Torah was to the Jews and the Bible to the Christians.[97]

[97] Julian Obermann in FAH pp.58-119; cf. Heinrich Speyer in EI IV, pp.1146-1148; W. F. Albright in JAOS 60 (1940), p.301; W. St. Clair-Tisdall, *The Sources of Islam, A Persian Treatise.* tr. William Muir. 1901.

3. THE AUTHORITATIVE WRITINGS OF ISLAM

THE QUR'AN

THE book which Muhammad gave to his people was the Qur'an (Koran).[98] The name of this book is the noun from the verb *qara'a* which is used in the work itself with the meaning "to read," "to discourse," or "to recite"; hence it must signify something like "lecture," "discourse," or "what is uttered."[99] More than fifty other names are applied to the Qur'an, of which one of the most frequent is Kitab, simply meaning "book" or "scripture." The individual chapters of the book, of which there are one hundred and fourteen, are called Surahs, a word the derivation of which has not been satisfactorily explained.[100] Smaller sections are known as *aya* (plural *ayat*), probably meaning "token," or "token of belief."

The contents of the Qur'an are extremely miscellaneous in character, as might indeed be expected from its own statement that it is "a clear setting forth of everything" (xii, 111). Not only the variety of subject matter but also the abruptness of transitions and the great number of repetitions conduce to the impression of confusion given by the materials of the Qur'an.

Critical study of these materials attempts to bring them into some sort of chronological order. According to present investigation,[101] three periods may be distinguished. In the first, Muhammad was still

---

[98] tr. George Sale, *The Koran, Commonly Called the Alcoran of Mohammed, Translated into English Immediately from the Original Arabic; with Explanatory Notes, Taken from the Most Approved Commentators. To Which is Prefixed a Preliminary Discourse.* 1734. 6th ed. 1876; E. M. Wherry, *A Comprehensive Commentary on the Qurán: Comprising Sale's Translation and Preliminary Discourse, with Additional Notes and Emendations, Together with a Complete Index to the Text, Preliminary Discourse, and Notes* (Trübner's Oriental Series). 4 vols. 1896; J. M. Rodwell, *El Kor'ân; or, the Korân: Translated from the Arabic, The Suras Arranged in Chronological Order; with Notes and Index.* 1861. 2d ed. 1876; E. H. Palmer in SBE VI, IX. 1880; Maulvi Muhammad Ali, *The Holy Qur-án, Containing the Arabic Text with English Translation and Commentary.* 2d ed. 1920; Richard Bell, *The Qur'ān, Translated, with a Critical Re-arrangement of the Surahs.* 2 vols. 1937-39; cf. Allama Sir Abdullah al-Mamun al-Suhrawardy, *The Sayings of Muhammad* (Wisdom of the East). 1941. For other translations and the literature related to the Qur'an see Gustav Pfannmüller, *Handbuch der Islam-Literatur.* 1923, pp.206-229. The translation employed in this chapter is that by Bell.

[99] D. S. Margoliouth in HERE X, pp.538f.; F. Buhl in EI II, pp.1063f.; and in A. J. Wensinck and J. H. Kramers, eds., *Handwörterbuch des Islam.* 1941, pp.347f.

[100] F. Buhl in EI IV, pp.560f.

[101] Bell, *The Qur'ān, Translated, with a Critical Re-arrangement of the Surahs,* I, pp.v-vii; II, pp.689f.; John E. Merrill in *The Moslem World.* 37 (1947), pp.134-148; cf. Theodor Nöldeke, *Geschichte des Qorāns.* 2d ed. by Friedrich Schwally. 1909-19, I, pp.58-234.

in Mecca, and his preaching was a summons to the worship of Allah alone, based specially upon "signs" which Allah had set forth in nature. A sample passage from this period runs as follows (XIII, 2): "Allah it is who hath raised up the heavens without pillars that ye can see; then sat firm upon the throne managing the affair; and hath subjected the sun and the moon to service, each running its course to a fixed term; he maketh the signs distinct, mayhap of the meeting with your Lord ye will be convinced."

The second period covers the latter part of Muhammad's time in Mecca and the first year or two of his residence in Medina. In this period Muhammad recited many stories with which he had become familiar in the traditions of the Jews and the Christians, and evidently felt that he was preaching to his own people the same revelation which had already come to the peoples of the Law and the Gospel. Passages originating in this period may be found in Surah XXVI, for example, where stories of Moses, Abraham, Noah and others are related.

The third period is that of the prophet's later time in Medina. He had now become opposed to Judaism and Christianity and had determined upon the establishment of a religious community independent of both. For that community he consciously undertook to prepare a Book which would have the same place as was occupied by the Old Testament and the New Testament among the Jews and the Christians.

The transition to this period and to the type of material characteristic of it may be seen in Surah II, which is believed to have been composed for the most part during Muhammad's second and third years at Medina. Some portions of the Surah contain appeals to the Jews, but in verses 105-107 the prophet speaks against Jews, Christians, and pagan Arabs alike:

They say: "No one but those who are Jews or Christians will enter the Garden"; that is what they take on trust; say (thou): "Produce your proof, if ye speak the truth."

Nay, whoever surrenders himself to Allah, being a well-doer, has his reward with his Lord, fear rests not upon him nor does he grieve.

The Jews say: "The Christians have no ground to stand on," and the Christians say: "The Jews have no ground to stand on"; (this) though they both recite the Book. So also those who have no knowledge[102] say much the same. Allah will judge between them on the Day of Resurrection in regard to that in which they have been differing.

[102] These are the pagan Arabs who have no knowledge of revealed religion.

While the Jews and the Christians both want him to accept their teachings, he feels that he will be under the divine displeasure unless he adheres to the revelation of which he has been made the recipient, and to that alone. These are the words which come to him (v.114): "Neither the Jews nor the Christians will be satisfied with thee until thou followest their creed; say: 'The guidance of Allah is the guidance': if thou followest their desires after the knowledge which has come to thee, there will be for thee from Allah neither protector nor helper."

After all, the religion which he is proclaiming is older, he believes, than either the Law of Moses or the Gospel of Jesus. It is, indeed, nothing other than the original religion of Abraham (v.129): "They say: 'Be ye Jews or Christians and ye will be guided'; Say (thou): 'Nay, the creed of Abraham, who was a Hanif, but was not one of the idolaters.'" The word Hanif, applied here to Abraham, occurs frequently in the Koran as the name of those who have the true religion.[103] In other verses (125f.) Muhammad calls Abraham a Muslim even more explicitly: "Who is averse to the creed of Abraham but him who is essentially stupid? We surely have chosen him in this world, and in the Hereafter he is among the upright. When his Lord said to him: 'Surrender thyself,'[104] he said: 'I have surrendered myself to the Lord of the worlds.' Abraham charged his sons therewith, and Jacob also: 'O my sons, Allah hath chosen the religion for you, so die not without becoming submissive.'"[105]

As an outward sign of the new independence of his movement, Muhammad changed the Qibla[106] or direction of prayer for his followers. Hitherto they had practiced the Jewish custom of praying in the direction of Jerusalem. In preparation, possibly, for the change, Muhammad declared (v.109): "To Allah belong the East and the West; whichever way ye turn, the face of Allah is there; verily Allah is unrestricted, knowing." Then he brought the following message, abrogating for his adherents the observance of the Jewish Qibla and instituting the custom of praying toward the Ka'bah in Mecca (vv. 136-139): "The stupids among the people will say: 'What has turned them from the qibla which they have been observing?'; say (thou): 'To Allah belongs the East and the West; he guideth whom he willeth to a straight path.' Thus have We made you a community in the middle, that ye may be witnesses in regard to the people, and

103 Fr. Buhl in EI II, pp.258-260.   104 That is, "become Muslim."
105 That is, "becoming Muslims."   106 C. Schoy in EI II, pp.985-989.

the messenger be in regard to you a witness. We appointed the qibla which thou hast been observing only that We might know those who would follow the messenger from those who would turn on their heels, though it was a big thing except to those whom Allah guided. But Allah was not one to let your faith go lost; verily Allah is with the people gentle and compassionate. We see thee turning thy face about in the heaven. So We shall put thee in possession of a qibla that will satisfy thee; turn thy face in the direction of the Sacred Mosque, and wherever ye are, turn your faces in its direction. Those to whom the Book has been given know that it is the truth from their Lord, and Allah is not neglectful of what they do."

Such are some of the main points in Surah II, a chapter which Muhammad very probably intended to serve as the first in the new and definitive Book which he was to give to his people. In line with this, we find in the first sentence of the Surah (v.1) the statement: "That is the Book, in which there is no doubt, guidance for those who act piously."

Are we to suppose that Muhammad was personally responsible for the recording of his revelations and pronouncements? It is not impossible that he was, either by dictation to others or by actually doing the writing himself. Dr. Bell, whose hypothesis as to the chronological periods in which the various Surahs originated has here been followed, is of the opinion that Muhammad wrote personally. He pictures the prophet as setting down his messages on small pieces of writing material as occasion permitted, and from time to time revising, correcting, and making additions between the lines, on the margins and on the backs of the sheets. Thus it is possible to explain the abundant confusion in the materials.[107]

Whether or not the theory just mentioned is correct, there can be little doubt that written collections of the prophet's sayings were in existence shortly after his death. The orthodox belief is that the scattered portions of the Qur'an were brought together in the year after the prophet's death by his secretary, Zayd ibn-Thabit, and again revised by the same person under the Caliph 'Uthman (A.D. 644-656). Modern critical study of the text of the Koran leads to the conclusion, rather, that there were various codices with varying readings in different Muslim centers until 'Uthman designated as authoritative the text used at Medina and ordered the others destroyed.[108]

[107] Bell, *The Qur'ān, Translated, with a Critical Re-arrangement of the Surahs,* I, p.vi.
[108] Arthur Jeffery, ed., *Materials for the History of the Text of the Qur'ān, The Old*

The arrangement of the Surahs in the completed Qur'an was in accordance with their length, running from the longest (Surah II) to the shortest (Surah CXIV). The following short prayer was placed as a preface to the entire collection (Surah I):

In the Name of Allah, the Merciful, the Compassionate.
Praise belongs to Allah, the Lord of the worlds,
The Merciful, the Compassionate.
Wielder of the Day of Judgment.
Thee do we serve, and on Thee do we call for help;
Guide us (in) the straight path,
The path of those upon whom thou hast bestowed good,
Not (that) of those upon whom anger falls, or those who go astray.

The making of copies of the Qur'an was always an important expression of Islamic faith, and as time went on much attention was devoted to executing these in the most beautiful manner possible. The art of calligraphy, practiced largely on such works, was most highly regarded throughout the Muslim world. Thus a fourteenth century author, Muhammad ibn-Mahmud al-Amuli, in an encyclopedic work on Muslim arts and sciences entitled *Nafa'is al-Funun*, says: "The art of writing is an honorable one and a soul-nourishing accomplishment; as a manual attainment it is always elegant, and enjoys general approval; it is respected in every land. . . . The Prophet (peace be upon him!) said: 'Beauty of handwriting is incumbent upon you, for it is one of the keys of man's daily bread.' "[109]

As we have already noted,[110] there were two kinds of North Arabic script, a round form called *naskhi* and an angular variety known as Kufic. The latter name is derived from Kufa, a city which was founded by the Muslims in A.D. 638 near the site of Babylon, and which became a very important center of Qur'anic studies.[111] The Kufic script was evidently regarded as possessing a sort of hieratic character, and for the first four centuries or so almost all the copies of the Qur'an seem to have been written in it.[112] Later the round

Codices, The Kitāb al-Maṣāḥif of Ibn Abī Dāwūd Together with a Collection of the Variant Readings from the Codices of Ibn Ma'sūd, Ubai, 'Alī, Ibn 'Abbas, Anas, Abū Mūsā and Other Early Qur'ānic Authorities Which Present a Type of Text Anterior to That of the Canonical Text of 'Uthmān. 1937, pp.7f.

109 tr. Thomas W. Arnold, *Painting in Islam, A Study of the Place of Pictorial Art in Muslim Culture.* 1928, p.2.

110 cf. above p.480 n.78; and see B. Moritz in EI I, pp.381f.,387f.

111 K. V. Zettersteen in EI II, pp.1105-1107.

112 See Section I in B. Moritz, ed., *Arabic Palaeography, A Collection of Arabic Texts from the First Century of the Hidjra till the Year 1000* (Publications of the Khedivial Library, Cairo, No. 16). 1905.

script was used too, of course with certain variations in the different countries into which the Muslims went.

One of the oldest known copies of the sacred book of Islam is the famous Samarkand Kufic Qur'an. This is a parchment codex which was long in the Mosque of Khodzah-Akhrar in Samarkand, was sent to the St. Petersburg Public Library in 1869, and was returned in the early days of the Soviet Government to Samarkand. Although it is said not to have been heard of since its return, the manuscript was photographed in Russia by Dr. S. Pissareff in 1905. It is believed to have been written not later than the beginning of the second century of the Muslim era, perhaps in Iraq.[113] A photograph of a page of this manuscript is reproduced in Fig. 220.[114]

A handsome and relatively early example of a Qur'an in the Naskhi writing is the manuscript numbered N.E.-P. 27 in the University Museum of the University of Pennsylvania. This is a Persian Qur'an of the Seljuq Period, richly illuminated and definitely dated. The date appears in a colophon at the end, where we are also given the name of the master calligrapher and illuminator who did the work, as well as the place of its execution. This colophon reads: "Mahmud ibn al-Husayn, the scribe from Kirman[115] wrote it and illuminated it in the city of Hamadhan,[116] may Allah who is exalted guard it, in the last days of Jumada I of the year 559 [April, 1164]. Praise to Allah, the Lord of the Worlds, and blessing on Muhammad and his family and his relatives." The first (fol. 212-b) of the two pages containing the colophon is shown in Fig. 221. The text, with the name of the scribe and the city, appears in the narrow rectangles at the top and bottom of the page; the center is filled with a diamond-shaped figure featuring a rosette of intersecting circles together with half-circles and arabesques. The page (fol. 2-a) containing the beginning of Surah II of the Qur'an is reproduced in Fig. 222. The border of the page is composed of interlacing designs of geometrical character. As is the case throughout the work, between the lines of the text an Arabic commentary is written, on the slant, in a smaller Naskhi script.[117]

[113] Isaac Mendelsohn in *The Moslem World.* 30 (1940), pp.375-378; citing A. Shebunin in *Zapiski Vostochnago Otdieleniia Imperatorskago Russkago Arkheologicheskago Obshchestva.* 6 (1891), pp.69-133.

[114] S. Pissareff, *Curan coufique de Samarcand écrit d'après la tradition de la propre main du troisième calife Osman qui se trouve dans la bibliothèque impériale publique de St. Pétersbourg.* 1905.

[115] The same as Kerman.

[116] A rare but still standard spelling of Hamadan.

[117] Richard Ettinghausen in *Bulletin of the American Institute for Persian Art and Archaeology.* 4 (1935-36), pp.92-102.

For another example of the exquisite and detailed work lavished upon copies of the Qur'an, we show in Fig. 223 a page from a Qur'an of the Mamluk Sultan, Sha'ban (A.D. 1363-1376). It is dated in A.H. 770 = A.D. 1369.[118]

THE HADITH

Next to the Qur'an in authority for the Muslim world stands the great body of tradition known as Hadith.[119] This word means "news" and can relate to a communication or narrative of any kind. Here it is used for the whole mass of inherited information about the doings and sayings of Muhammad and his companions. At first this information was handed down orally, and then later was committed to writing in various collections.

The first of the written collections was made, according to Muslim belief, about one hundred years after the time of Muhammad, and other compilations were certainly prepared in the next two centuries or so. Any given tradition to be complete should contain two parts: first, the *isnad* or "support" which is a list of the persons who have handed down the information from one to another; second, the *matn* or text itself. In the earlier compilations the materials were arranged according to their transmitters, and such a collection was called a *musnad* or body of "supported" traditions. In the later arrangements the traditions were put together according to their content, and a collection so ordered was known as *musannaf* or "arranged."

Of the first type of collection the most important example was doubtless the Musnad of Ahmed ibn-Hanbal[120] who lived in Baghdad in the second century of the Muslim era (A.D. 780-855). As edited by his son 'Abd Allah, this voluminous work contained nearly thirty thousand traditions grouped under the names of seven hundred companions of the prophet.

Of the second type, some six collections, all of which arose during the third Muslim century, attained the highest recognition. These were made by the following authorities: (1) al-Bukhari (d. A.D. 870); (2) Muslim (d. A.D. 875); (3) Abu Dawud (d. A.D. 888); (4) al-Tirmidhi (d. A.D. 892); (5) al-Nasa'i (d. A.D. 915); (6) ibn-Madja

[118] B. Moritz, ed., *Arabic Palaeography, A Collection of Arabic Texts from the First Century of the Hidjra till the Year 1000* (Publications of the Khedivial Library, Cairo, No. 16). 1905, Pl. 57.

[119] Th. W. Juynboll in EI II, pp.189-194; Alfred Guillaume, *The Traditions of Islam, An Introduction to the Study of the Hadith Literature.* 1924; cf. A. J. Wensinck, *A Handbook of Early Muhammadan Tradition.* 1927.

[120] Goldziher in EI I, pp.188-190.

(d. A.D. 886). Together these works are known as "the six books" (al-Kutub al-Sitta), while the first two are singled out for designation as *sahih* or "sound," meaning that their tradition is utterly faultless. The first, by al-Bukhari, is the most highly regarded. Its remarkable author is said to have been acquainted with six hundred thousand traditions, to have himself memorized more than two hundred thousand, and to have put more than seven thousand in his book. His labors were performed with the utmost piety. His inspiration came, he said, from a dream in which he was driving flies away from Muhammad. An interpreter explained the flies as falsehoods which had gathered around the tradition of the prophet, and it was these which he made it his task to dispel. He never put a tradition in his collection without first making an ablution and offering a prayer.

So vast was the total literature of the Hadith that it became desirable also to make synopses and anthologies. Of these we may mention, for a single example, the Mishkatu-l-Masabih or The Niche of the Lamps by Waliu-l-Din Abu 'Abd Allah, who flourished in the fourteenth century A.D.

4. THE LIFE AND TEACHINGS OF MUHAMMAD

THE three most important sources for the life of Muhammad are the Qur'an, the Hadith, and the Arabic biographies of the prophet.[121] The nature of the first two has been dealt with in the preceding section; here we may also cite an important example of the last. This is the large biographical work of ibn-Sa'd, who died in Baghdad in A.D. 845. It is entitled Kitab al-Tabaqat or Book of the Classes, and narrates the lives of Muhammad and of his companions and successors down to the author's own time.[122]

HIS CAREER

The first definitely fixed date in the life of Muhammad is that of his migration from Mecca to Medina which took place in A.D. 622. The year of this event, known as the Hijra (Hegira), was taken as the first year of the Muslim era (A.H.).[123] Since tradition regularly places the call of Muhammad thirteen years before the Hijra, and makes the prophet forty years of age at the time of his call, we may suppose that he was born around A.D. 570. The date of his death was ten years after the removal to Medina, or A.D. 632.[124]

Many legends cluster around the birth of Muhammad, and the Qur'an itself contains a passage (LXI, 6) in which Jesus is stated to have predicted his coming: "Jesus, son of Mary, said: 'O Children of Israel, I am Allah's messenger to you, confirming the Torah which was before me, and announcing the good tidings of a messenger who will come after me, bearing the name Ahmed.'" The possible basis for this is John 16:7 where in Greek the word for Comforter(παράκλητος) is very similar to the word for "renowned" (περι-

121 Pfannmüller, Handbuch der Islam-Literatur, pp.128-132.

122 E. Mittwoch in EI II, pp.413f.

123 The Hijra occurred on September 25 but the era was reckoned from the beginning of the year which was on July 16, A.D. 622. B. Carra de Vaux in EI II, pp.302f.; Leone Caetani, Chronographia islamica ossia riassunto della storia di tutti i popoli musulmani dall'anno 1 all'anno 922 della Higrah (622-1517 dell'Era Volgare), corredato della bibliografia di tutte le principali fonti stampate e manoscritte. 1912-, I, p.3. Since the Muslim year has only 354 days, it shifts all the while in relation to the Christian year. Thus the New Year of A.H. 1367 began on November 15, 1947.

124 For the life of Muhammad see Tor Andrae, Mohammed, The Man and His Faith. tr. Theophil Menzel. 1936; D. S. Margoliouth, Mohammed and the Rise of Islam (Heroes of the Nations). 3d ed. 1905; William Muir, The Life of Mohammad from Original Sources. rev. ed. by T. H. Weir. 1912; M. M. Ali, Mohammad, the Prophet. 1924; G. I. Kheirallah, Islam and the Arabian Prophet. 1938; A. Sprenger, Das Leben und die Lehre des Mohammad nach bisher grösstentheils unbenutzten Quellen. 3 vols. 1861-65.

[494]

κλυτός), the latter being the meaning of the names Ahmed and Muhammad.

It is fact that Muhammad was a member of the Quraish tribe in Mecca. His father was 'Abdullah and his mother Aminah. The father died before the son was born, and the mother when he was only six. He was raised then in the home of his grandfather, 'Abd al-Muttalib, who was in charge of giving water from the well Zamzam to pilgrims to Mecca. This well, incidentally, was believed to have sprung up at the command of Allah to provide water for Ishmael, son of Hagar and ancestor of the Arabs. After the grandfather's death two years later, Muhammad was kept by his uncle, Abu Talib. Although he never became a Muslim, Abu Talib always defended his nephew strongly. At the age of twenty-five Muhammad married Khadijah, a wealthy widow of forty years of age. She likewise was always a great source of strength to him. As he later thought upon Allah's kindness to him in all these regards, as well as in showing him the true religion, Muhammad wrote (Surah xcIII):

> By the morning brightness,
> By the night when it is still,
> Thy Lord hath not taken leave of thee, nor despised thee.
> The last is for thee better than the first;
> Assuredly in the end thy Lord will give thee to thy satisfaction.
> Did he not find thee an orphan and give (thee) shelter?
> Did he not find thee erring, and guide (thee)?
> Did he not find thee poor, and enrich (thee)?
> So as for the orphan, be not (thou) overbearing;
> And as for the beggar, scold not;
> And as for the goodness of thy Lord, discourse (of it).

The vision which came to Muhammad in the fortieth year of his life and which marked his call to be a prophet is described as follows in the Qur'an (LIII, 1-12): "By the star when it falls, your comrade has not gone astray, nor has he erred; nor does he speak of (his own) inclination. It is nothing but a suggestion suggested, taught (him) by One strong in power, forceful; he stood straight, upon the high horizon, then he drew near, and let himself down, till he was two bow-lengths off or nearer, and suggested to his servant what he suggested. The heart did not falsify what it saw. Do ye debate with it as to what it sees?" The "One strong in power" who thus appeared to him may have been thought of by Muhammad as Allah himself, since this deity is described by the similar epithet of "Possessor of Strength" in LI, 58. On the other hand he may have

[495]

been regarded as an angel, since in another account (LXXXI, 19f.) of the same vision the divine visitant is called "a noble messenger, powerful, beside him of the throne established."

For thirteen years Muhammad is said to have preached in Mecca. His proclamation of the message of Allah seems not always to have involved a complete repudiation of the old "paganism." According to a tradition which is hardly likely to have been invented, Muhammad at one time taught that the three goddesses worshiped at Mecca as daughters of Allah were in fact angels to whom requests for intercession with the one god might properly be addressed. "Have ye considered Allat, and al-'Uzza, and the third, Manat, the other (goddess)?" Muhammad said, "These are the swans exalted; whose intercession is to be hoped for."[125] Later this compromise with polytheism was repudiated, the uttering of the teaching attributed to the inspiration of Satan, and the offending words removed from the Qur'an.[126]

When Muhammad boldly attacked the ancient Meccan faith and called for worship of Allah alone, he aroused the strong opposition of the Quraish. They called him an "insolent liar" (Surah LIV, 25f.) and subjected him to some persecution. Certain followers were won, however, among whom were the prophet's own wife Khadijah, his cousin 'Ali, son of Abu Talib, his more distant relative Abu Bakr, and 'Umar, destined to play an important part in the political establishment of Islam. Muhammad was also encouraged by the reception of further revelations, and by the experience called the "night-journey." As reported in Muslim tradition, the latter was a miraculous trip in which the prophet was taken by night from the Ka'bah at Mecca to the Temple at Jerusalem and from there up into the Seventh Heaven. The celestial part of the journey was variously supposed to have begun at the Wailing Wall or the Sacred Rock in Jerusalem, and transportation was provided by Buraq, a winged horse with a woman's head and a peacock's tail. The Qur'an makes the following reference to this event (XVII, 1): "Glory be to him who journeyed by night with his servant from the Sacred Mosque to the Furthest Mosque around which We have bestowed blessing, that We might show him some of our signs; verily he is the one who hears and sees."

In A.D. 620 the two persons who had done most to strengthen and

[125] Surah LIII, 19f. Bell, *The Qur'ān, Translated, with a Critical Re-arrangement of the Surahs*, II, p.540 n.8.
[126] cf. Surah XXII, 51. SBE IX, p.62 n.1.

protect the prophet, Khadijah and Abu Talib, died. In danger of his life in Mecca and perceiving opportunity in Medina, Muhammad made the fateful "flight" to that city in A.D. 622. Whereas the single tribe of the Quraish, now his avowed enemies, dominated Mecca, in Medina the Aus and Khazraj tribes were in strife with one another and the time seemed ripe for the arrival of a strong leader.

Taking full advantage of his opportunities, and drawing upon his continuing revelations for authorization, the prophet now embarked upon a remarkable political and military career. He speedily gained the loyalty of the people of Medina save for the three tribes of Jews resident there, and all of these, when it became evident that they could not be converted, he either drove out or slaughtered. The caravans of his old enemies, the Quraish, were raided even in the month of truce, and several pitched battles were fought with the same foes. Remarkable as it may seem, eight years after he had fled from Mecca in danger of his life, Muhammad returned to the same city as conqueror, and ere he died two years later he was actually the master of most of Arabia. Of these campaigns it is not necessary to tell more here. A detailed account may be read in the Kitab al-Maghazi or Book of the Wars by al-Waqidi, an Arab historian who lived in Medina in the second century of the Muslim era (d. A.D. 822).[127]

The home of Muhammad in Medina was a natural center for his followers. The story is that when the prophet first rode into Medina on his camel, he took the place where the beast stopped as the site for his residence. This dwelling place was built of sun-dried mud bricks, and had a large open courtyard. After the death of Khadijah, Muhammad had married two more wives, the widow Sawdah and the child 'A'ishah, and apartments were constructed for them against the outer wall of the courtyard at the south end of the east side. As the prophet took yet other wives additional places were built for them until finally there were nine huts in all. Each house was known as a *hujrah*, and had a curtained door opening into the court.

The simplicity of these structures is evident from references to them in the writings of Ibn Sa'd. This historian quotes the reports of men who saw the place within the first century of the Muslim era, as follows: " 'Abd Allah ibn-Yazid relates that he saw the houses in which the wives of the Prophet dwelt, at the time when 'Umar ibn-

---

[127] tr. J. Wellhausen, *Muhammed in Medina, Das ist Vakidi's Kitab alMaghazi in verkürtzter deutscher Wiedergabe.* 1882.

'Abd al-'Aziz, governor of Medina [A.H. c.100], demolished them. They were built of unburnt bricks, and had separate apartments with partitions of palm-branches, daubed with mud; he counted nine houses, each having separate rooms, in the space extending from the house of 'A'ishah to the house of Asma' daughter of al-Husain. . . . A citizen . . . was present . . . when the dispatch of the Caliph 'Abd al-Malik (A.H. 86-88) was read aloud, commanding that these houses should be taken down and the site brought within the area of the Mosque, and he never witnessed sorer weeping than there was amongst the people that day. One exclaimed: 'I wish, by the Lord! that they would leave these houses alone just as they are; then would those that spring up hereafter in Medina, and strangers from the ends of the earth, come and see what kind of building sufficed for the Prophet's own abode, and the sight thereof would deter men from extravagance and pride.' "[128]

Although it was a private residence, the courtyard of Muhammad's home was used as a place for prayers and for the conversations of the prophet with those who came to see him. There were three doors, the principal one, through which visitors came, on the south, and one on the west and one on the east, the last being regularly used by Muhammad himself. The direction of prayer was at first toward the north, that is toward Jerusalem, and the north wall was left unbroken. When the Qibla was changed, the south door was walled up and the main entrance placed in the north wall. It is said that the companions who joined Muhammad in prayers complained of the heat of the sun in the open courtyard, and so a portico was built with palm trunks as columns supporting a roof of palm branches covered with mud. From the flat roof Muhammad later had the stentorian-voiced Abyssinian, Bilal, utter the summons to prayer. The use of the formal call to prayer (*adhan*) was decided upon by the prophet a year or two after coming to Medina as a mark of distinction from the Christians who summoned their faithful to church with a wooden gong, and from the Jews who employed horns. The discourses of Muhammad were delivered at first as he leaned casually against a palm trunk in the place of prayer. As his prominence increased and more people came to listen, he had a sort of pulpit constructed of tamarisk wood. This was known as a *minbar*, and consisted of three steps on the top one of which the prophet would sit to speak.

[128] tr. Muir, *The Life of Mohammad from Original Sources*, pp.534f.

The home of Muhammad was also his place of death and burial. The prophet died in the arms of his beloved wife 'A'ishah, and when the question of the burial place was raised, Abu Bakr recalled that Muhammad had once said that a prophet is buried where he passes away. He was laid to rest, therefore, in the apartment of 'A'ishah, where in their turn both Abu Bakr and 'Umar also at last were placed. 'A'ishah herself, however, by her own wish was interred in the cemetery of Baqi outside the eastern city wall of Medina.[129]

HIS RELIGION

The religion instituted by Muhammad is outlined in terms of five duties to be performed and five doctrines to be believed. Since Muhammad was not a systematic theologian, we may take it that this schematization was the work of later theologians. Nevertheless the elements of the outline are already present in the Qur'an.

The five practical duties are known as the "pillars of Islam."[130] These are the following: (1) Recital of the Profession of Faith. The profession of faith (*shahada*) comprises two conjoined affirmations: "I witness that there is no god but Allah and I witness that Muhammad is the apostle of Allah." This is virtually a combination of Surah xxvii, 26: "Allah, there is no god but he";[131] and vii, 157: "I am the messenger of Allah to you all."

(2) Recital of Prayers (*salat*). Traditionally, there are five times of prayer every day: dawn, midday, afternoon, sunset, and nightfall. The Qur'an simply says (Surah ii, 239): "Remember the prayers, the middle prayer included, and stand (in worship) to Allah reverently." The call to prayer (*adhan*), uttered from the minaret (*ma'-dhana*) of a mosque by the muezzin (*mu'adhdhin*), consists of repetition of the phrases: "Allah is most great (*Allahu akbar*). I witness that there is no god but Allah. I witness that Muhammad is the apostle of Allah. Come to prayer! Come to salvation! Allah is most great. There is no god but Allah." At the morning call the words, "Prayer is better than sleep," are added, usually between the fifth and sixth of the foregoing formulas.[132] Before prayers, ablutions must be performed in accordance with Surah v, 8: "When ye stand up for the prayer, wash your faces and your hands up to the elbows, and

[129] Nabia Abbott, *Aishah, The Beloved of Mohammed.* 1942, pp.69,86,100,215,218.
[130] A. J. Wensinck, *The Muslim Creed, Its Genesis and Historical Development.* 1932, p.19 n.5; H. Lammens, *Islām, Beliefs and Institutions.* tr. E. Denison Ross. 1929, pp.56-62.
[131] cf. Surah xxviii, 88.
[132] Th. W. Juynboll in EI I, p.133.

[499]

wipe your heads and your feet up to the ankles." The verse following provides that sand may be used for this if water is not available. Certain postures and prostrations are also prescribed in tradition to accompany the prayers. A complete set of prostrations together with the recital of the first Surah and at least two more verses of the Qur'an is called a *rak'a*.

(3) Almsgiving (*zakat*). This is inculcated in the Qur'an in passages like the following: "They will ask thee (for) what they should contribute; say: 'The good ye have contributed is for parents, relatives, orphans, the poor, and the follower of the way; whatever good ye do Allah knoweth" (Surah ii, 211); "What ye give for usury that it may increase amongst the wealth of the people will gain no increase with Allah, but what ye give as Zakat desiring the favor of Allah—these are the ones who gain the double" (Surah xxx, 38).

(4) Fasting (*sawm*). "O ye who have believed, fasting is prescribed for you as it was for those before you; mayhap ye will show piety," declares the Qur'an (ii, 179). As the passage immediately following specifies, the required fast is that of "the month of Ramadan, in which the Qur'an was sent down as guidance for the people." The fast must be kept during every day of this month, but eating and drinking are permitted throughout the night "until so much of the dawn appears that a white thread may be distinguished from a black." Other fasts are voluntary.[133]

(5) Pilgrimage to Mecca (*hajj*). "Pilgrimage to the house is due to Allah from the people, whoever is able to make his way thither," states the Qur'an (iii, 91), and more details concerning the observance are specified by tradition.[134] The practice of pilgrimage was in fact very important: necessitating long journeys and meetings with pilgrims from other nations, many of whom had at least a smattering knowledge of Arabic, it furthered the diffusion of ideas and helps to explain the rather uniform appearance of Muslim art in spite of tremendous distances, differences in ethnic stock and national heritage.

The five basic doctrines are listed in a negative statement in Surah iv, 135: "Whoever disbelieves in Allah and his angels and his books and his messengers and the last day, has strayed into error far." Teachings of Muhammad on each of these five points are scattered throughout the Qur'an.

[133] C. C. Berg in EI iv, pp.192-199.
[134] A. J. Wensinck in EI ii, pp.196-201.

(1) Allah. A concise definition of the nature of Allah appears in Surah CXII, a verse which Muhammad himself is traditionally reported to have declared equal in value to two-thirds of the Qur'an:[135]

> Say: "He is Allah, One,
> Allah, the Eternal;
> He brought not forth, nor hath he been brought forth;
> Co-equal with him there hath never been any one."

Slightly longer is the "verse of the throne" (Surah II, 256), often inscribed in mosques:[136] "Allah—there is no god but he, the Living, the Eternal; slumber affects him not nor sleep; to him belongs whatever is in the heavens and whatever is in the earth; who is there that will intercede before him except by his permission? He knoweth what is before them and what is behind them, and they comprehend not anything of his knowledge but what he willeth; his throne extendeth over the heavens and the earth, to guard them wearieth him not; he is the Exalted, the Mighty."

All together, it is reckoned that ninety-nine appellations are applied to Allah in the Qur'an, and the repetition of these names is regarded as a matter of merit in accordance with the injunction of Surah VII, 179: "To Allah belong the most beautiful names; so call upon him by them."[137]

Many-sided as this multiplicity of names would indicate the character of Allah to be, his chief attribute is undoubtedly his unlimited power. In line with this, predestination is a dominant doctrine in the Qur'an.[138] Surah LXXIV, 34 states: "Thus Allah doth send astray whom he willeth and guideth whom he willeth"; and Surah III, 139 declares: "It is not given to anyone to die except by permission of Allah written and dated." Hence it is appropriate that Islam, literally meaning "submission (to the will of Allah)," is the name of the Muhammadan faith, and Muslim, meaning "one who has submitted," is the designation of an individual believer.

(2) Angels. While Muhammad repudiated polytheism, he accepted, presumably from pagan, Jewish and Christian influences, belief in demons and angels. He taught that the demons (*jinn*) were created by Allah out of fire (Surah XV, 27), and it is stated (Surah XLVI, 28; cf. LXXII, 1) that he once preached to a band of these spirits.

[135] Grace H. Turnbull, *Tongues of Fire, A Bible of Sacred Scriptures of the Pagan World.* 1929, p.403 n.5.
[136] *ibid.*, p.395 n.2.
[137] Wherry, *A Comprehensive Commentary on the Qurán*, II, p.242 n.181.
[138] D. S. Margoliouth, *Mohammed* (What Did They Teach?). 1939, pp.35f.

The angels were regarded as heavenly beings who sing hymns to Allah and intercede on behalf of men. "The heavens almost split asunder from above while the angels give glory with praise of their Lord, and ask pardon for those upon the earth" (Surah xlii, 3).

Of the angels the foremost was Gabriel, through whom the revelations of the Qur'an were brought to Muhammad. "Whoever is an enemy to Gabriel—verily he hath brought it down upon thy heart with the permission of Allah confirming what was before it, and as guidance and good tidings to the believers" (Surah ii, 91). The chief spirit of evil was called Iblis, the name probably being a corruption of the Greek word for Devil (διάβολος).[139] According to Surah ii, 32, the evil character of Iblis dates from his refusal to do homage to Adam as commanded by Allah: "We said to the angels: 'Prostrate yourselves to Adam'; they prostrated themselves, with the exception of Iblis; he refused in his pride and became one of the unbelievers." While from this passage Iblis would seem to have once been one of the angels, in another reference (Surah xviii, 48) to the same act of rebellion it is explicitly stated that he was one of the jinn.

(3) Books. In addition to the book of his own revelations, Muhammad makes mention of the Torah (*Tawrat*) of Moses,[140] the Psalms (*Zabur*) of David,[141] and the Gospel (*Injil*, from εὐαγγέλιον) of Jesus.[142] All these books were sent down by Allah, the Qur'an of course being the last and containing the climactic revelation. "Verily We have sent down the Torah containing guidance and light; by it the prophets who surrendered themselves[143] gave judgment. . . . In their footsteps We caused Jesus, son of Mary, to follow, . . . and We gave him the Evangel, containing guidance and light. . . . To thee also have We sent down the Book with the truth" (Surah v, 48-52).[144]

(4) Messengers. Muhammad recognized a series of apostles who were divinely sent to particular nations or communities, and also numerous prophets who bore witness to the divine message. Of the prophets perhaps two dozen are named in the Qur'an, and of the apostles the following eight: Noah, Lot, Ishmael, Moses, Shu'aib, Hud, Salih, and Jesus. Shu'aib is to be identified with Jethro the Midianite, while Hud and Salih were messengers to Arab tribes.[145]

139 A. J. Wensinck in EI ii, pp.351f.
140 J. Horovitz in EI iv, pp.706f.
141 J. Horovitz in EI iv, pp.1184f.
142 Carra de Vaux in EI ii, pp.501-504.   143 That is, were Muslims.
144 For the Psalms see Surah xvii, 57: "To David We gave Psalms."
145 C. R. North, *An Outline of Islâm*. 1934, pp.76f.

Jesus ('Isa)[146] is called the Messiah (Surah III, 40; IV, 169) and "pure" (Surah XIX, 19), and it is stated that "Allah raised him to himself" (Surah IV, 156).

(5) The Last Day. Here is how Muhammad described the day of judgment (Surah LXIX, 13-32):

> So when on the trumpet shall be blown a single blast,
> And the earth and the mountains shall be moved, and shattered at a single blow,
> Then will happen the thing that is to happen,
> The heaven shall be rent asunder, for then it will be weak,
> The angels (will be) on its borders, and above them eight shall then bear the throne of thy Lord.
> That day ye shall be mustered, not one of you concealed;
> As for him who is given his book[147] in his right hand, he will say: "Here, read my book,
> Verily I thought that I should meet my account."
> He shall be in pleasing life,
> In a Garden lofty,
> With clusters near:
> "Eat and drink with relish, for what ye paid in advance in the days gone-by."
> But as for him who is given his book in his left hand, he will say: "Oh, would that I had not been given my book,
> And had not known my account.
> Oh, would that it had been the finish-off![148]
> My wealth has not profited me,
> My authority has gone from me."
> "Take him and bind him,
> Then in the Hot Place roast him,
> Then in a chain of seventy cubits' reach insert him."

Other passages fill in the details concerning the realms of future blessedness and punishment. This is the prospect which awaits faithful Muslims: "Lo, the pious are in Gardens and delight, enjoying what their Lord hath bestowed upon them, and their Lord hath protected them from the punishment of the Hot Place. 'Eat and drink with relish, for what ye have been doing' " (Surah LII, 17-19). "Upon couches set with jewels, on which they recline facing each other, while round them circle boys of perpetual youth, with goblets and jugs, and a cup of flowing (wine), from which they suffer neither headache nor intoxication, and with fruit of their own choice, and

[146] D. B. Macdonald in EI II, pp.524-526.
[147] This is the book which contains the record of the man's deeds (cf. Surah XVII, 14f.).
[148] The man wishes that death had been the end.

bird's flesh, of what they desire; and (maidens [*houris*]) with dark, wide eyes, like pearls treasured—a recompense for what they have been doing" (Surah LVI, 15-23). But this is what confronts unbelievers: "Verily We have prepared for the wrong-doers a Fire, the awnings of which have encompassed them, and if they call for aid they will be sprinkled with water like molten metal which will broil their faces; a bad drink, and a bad place to lie in!" (Surah XVIII, 28).

As the discussion and clarification of these doctrines proceeded through the centuries, detailed and lengthy creeds were formulated. Reference to one of these will show how the implications of the Muslim faith were set forth. The creed here selected is the so-called Fiqh Akbar II, which probably originated in the first half of the tenth century A.D. It consists of twenty-nine Articles, the nature of which will be indicated by the following much abbreviated quotations:

1. The heart of the confession of the unity of Allah and the true foundation of faith consist in this obligatory creed: I believe in Allah, his angels, his books, his apostles, the resurrection after death, the decree of Allah the good and the evil thereof, computation of sins, the balance, Paradise and Hell; and that all these are real.

2. Allah the exalted is one, not in the sense of number, but in the sense that he has no partner.

3. The Koran is the speech of Allah.

4. Allah is thing, not as other things but in the sense of positive existence.

5. Allah has not created things from a pre-existent thing.

6. Allah created the creatures free from unbelief and from belief. Allah did not compel any of his creatures to be infidels or faithful. He created them as individuals, and faith and unbelief are the acts of men.

7. All acts of obedience are obligatory on account of Allah's command. All acts of disobedience happen through his knowledge, decision, decree and will; not according to his wish, good pleasure, or command.

8. All the prophets are exempt from sins, yet stumbling and mistakes may happen on their part.

9. Muhammad is his beloved. He did not serve idols, nor was he at any time a polytheist, even for a single moment. And he never committed a light or a grave sin.

10. The most excellent of men after the apostle of Allah is abu Bakr; after him, 'Umar; after him, 'Uthman; after him, 'Ali.

11. We declare no Muslim an infidel on account of any sin.

12. The moistening of the shoes is commendable.[149]

13. Prayer behind every faithful man, be he of good or of bad behavior, is valid.

14. We do not say that sins will do no harm to the faithful.

[149] This refers to sectarian arguments about foot washing.

15. If any work be mixed with ostentation, its reward is forfeited.

16. The signs of the prophets and the miracles of the saints are a reality.

17. Allah will be seen in the world to come.

18. Faith consists in confessing and believing.

19. We know Allah with adequate knowledge.

20. The intercession of the prophets is a reality.

21. The weighing of works in the balance on the day of resurrection is a reality.

22. Allah guideth whomsoever he pleaseth, by grace, and he leadeth astray whomsoever he pleaseth, by justice.

23. The interrogation of the dead in the tomb by Munkar and Nakir[150] is a reality.

24. It is allowable to follow scholars in expressing the qualities of Allah in Persian, in all instances except in the case of Allah's hand.

25. Allah's being near or far is not to be understood in the sense of a shorter or longer distance. The obedient is near to him, without how, and the disobedient is far from him, without how.

26. The Koran is revealed to the apostle of Allah. The verses are all equal in excellence and greatness.

27. Kasim, Tahir and Ibrahim were the sons of the apostle of Allah. Fatimah, Rukaiya, Zainab and Umm Kulthum were all of them daughters of the apostle of Allah.

28. When a man is uncertain concerning any of the subtleties of theology, it is his duty to cling for the time being to the orthodox faith.

29. The report of the ascension is a reality. The descent of 'Isa from heaven, as well as the other eschatological signs according to the description thereof in authentic tradition, are a reality that will take place. Allah guideth to the straight way whomsoever he willeth.[151]

MECCA AND MEDINA

The two cities which were the chief foci of the life and work of Muhammad have remained virtually inaccessible to the outside world. The prophet himself forbade the visit of unbelievers to Mecca, declaring after his taking of that city: "O ye who have believed, the polytheists are simply filth, so after this present year they shall not approach the Sacred Mosque" (Surah ix, 28); and the interdict has generally been held to apply also to Medina, the sacred burial place of the founder of Islam. Known as al-Haramain, the restricted region has been penetrated by a few western visitors from whose reports it is possible to gain some conception of Islam's two most holy sites.[152]

As seen by Eldon Rutter in 1925-1926, Mecca was "a little old ugly

150 These are two angels.
151 tr. Wensinck, *The Muslim Creed*, pp.188-197.
152 Samuel M. Zwemer in *The Moslem World*. 37 (1947), pp.7-15.

Arab town, bare of ornament, but full of fascination."[153] The pilgrim road from Jidda leads in toward the heart of the city and connects through the narrow Zugag es-Suwag with the Suq es-Saghir. The latter is a wadi not infrequently filled with flood water, and at the same time a market street and the main thoroughfare leading to the Sacred Mosque.

The Masjid al-Haram, as the Sacred Mosque is called, is surrounded by a wall with nineteen gates and six minarets. Within the wall are colonnades running around the sides of a large open area. In the center stands the Ka'bah, a roughly cubical structure, approximately thirty-eight feet long, thirty-one feet wide, and thirty-four feet high. The famous Black Stone is embedded in the southeast corner of the Ka'bah, about five feet from the ground. Having inspected it carefully, Richard F. Burton was persuaded that it was originally an aerolite.[154] Other structures in the Haram are the building over the well Zamzam, the great pulpit, and two small mosques. A general view of the city and the Sacred Mosque is shown in Fig. 224; a closer view of the Ka'bah itself in Fig. 225.

As in Mecca, so too in Medina the most sacred shrine stands in the heart of the city. This is the Masjid al-Nebi or Prophet's Mosque, which is the home of Muhammad transformed by successive rebuildings into an actual mosque. This development was natural enough in view of the prophet's use of his courtyard as a place of prayer and of address, and a strong impetus in the same direction came from the fact of his burial there in the apartment (hujrah) of 'A'ishah. Today the mosque is in the form of a large courtyard, marked out with tall minarets at the corners, and surrounded by domed colonnades. In the southeast corner of the mosque there is a rectangular enclosure, within which is a five-sided chamber some twenty feet in height. Surmounting the chamber is a large green dome. This is still called the Hujrah, and is supposed to have once been the apartment of 'A'ishah. Within the sanctified darkness of this place are said to be the three tombs of Muhammad, Abu Bakr and 'Umar, while one empty place is traditionally reserved for 'Isa on his second coming. Adjacent to the Hujrah is a smaller enclosure containing the reputed sepulcher of Fatimah, daughter of Muhammad and Khadi-

[153] Eldon Rutter, *The Holy Cities of Arabia.* 1928, I, p.124; cf. C. Snouck Hurgronje, *Bilder aus Mekka, mit kurzem erläuterndem Texte.* 1889.
[154] Richard F. Burton, *Personal Narrative of a Pilgrimage to al-Madinah and Meccah.* 1907, II, p.169.

jah, and wife of 'Ali. The Mosque of the Prophet is illustrated in Fig. 226. The large dome in line with the minaret is that above the grave of the prophet and his successors.[155]

[155] Rutter, *The Holy Cities of Arabia*, II, p.234; John F. Keane, *My Journey to Medinah: Describing a Pilgrimage to Medinah, Performed by the Author Disguised as a Mohammedan.* 1881, pp.108f.; Traugott Mann, *Der Islam einst und jetzt* (Monographien zur Weltgeschichte). 1914. Fig. 25.

5. THE ORTHODOX CALIPHS, A.D. 632-661

As STATED in Article 27 of the creed quoted in the preceding section, Muhammad had several sons, but none of these survived him. Upon his own death, therefore, the leadership of his movement passed in turn to a series of four of his closest associates. These were the "most excellent of men" named in Article 10 of the same creed, and the dates of their rule were as follows: Abu Bakr, A.D. 632-634; 'Umar, 634-644; 'Uthman, 644-656; 'Ali, 656-661. They bore the title of Caliph (khalifah)[156] meaning Successor (of Muhammad), and each was chosen to office by a sort of informal election upon the death of his predecessor. Upon the four, Arab historians bestow the designation of "orthodox." The first three ruled at Medina, while 'Ali made his capital at Kufa. Within the period of their rule, Syria, Palestine, Iraq, Persia and Egypt were all subjugated to Islam.

Wherever they went the Muslims fiercely maintained their loyalty to the teachings of Muhammad, and as he had instructed them continued to turn their faces to Mecca in prayer. When they had a formal place of prayer it was known as a mosque, the Arabic word being *masjid*, meaning a place of prostration.[157] The fundamental elements of a mosque were those which we have already seen in Muhammad's home in Medina: a court, a shelter over the worshipers, and a pulpit. There too, it will be remembered, the call to prayer was uttered from the roof. In the fully developed Arab mosque, a tall tower or minaret (*ma'dhana*) provided a vantage point from which to give the call to prayer (*adhan*), while the courtyard not only served as a kind of neutral zone shielding the inner sanctuary from the busy outer world, but also had in its center the fountain where ablutions were performed before prayer. The place of prayer proper was usually an arcaded or colonnaded rectangle, much wider than it was deep; thus it was well qualified to house a congregation which during prayer was like a body of soldiers, arranged in long rows of worshipers and performing certain movements of the body. The direction of prayer (*qibla*) was marked by a *mihrab* or niche in the wall toward which the worshipers faced, and not far away was the *minbar* or pulpit. Genetically connected with the apse in a Christian basilica, the *mihrab* was much different in character.[158] Whereas the

---

[156] Thomas W. Arnold, *The Caliphate.* 1924, pp.19-54; Pringle Kennedy, *Arabian Society at the Time of Muhammad.* 1926, pp.31-100.
[157] J. Pedersen, R. A. Kern and E. Diez in EI III, pp.315-389
[158] E. Diez in EI III, pp.485-490.

basilican apse housed the altar and provided a place for religious pictures in the form of mosaics or paintings, the *mihrab* was left empty and usually only decorated with floral, geometric or epigraphic designs. The ornamentation of the whole mosque was also carried out only in decorative script, usually texts from the Qur'an, and in the intricate patterns known as arabesques.[159] Here too the abstract character of strictly monotheistic Islam is clearly revealed.

In the course of time and in the various lands into which Islam went, Muslim architecture naturally underwent variation. Some mosques were built as tombs, others for the purpose of housing the *madrasa* or religious academy which became so important in Islam. In Persia, the *madrasa*-mosque assumed a distinctive form in that there was a large hall or *iwan* running out from each side of the courtyard, which served as a lecture room for one of the four faculties in Muslim theology and jurisprudence. Characteristic, too, was a lofty dome erected above the *mihrab* or the founder's tomb. In Turkey, Byzantine influence accentuated the importance of the dome, and the Turkish mosque was usually an immense centralized domed building.

At the outset, Islamic expansion involved in many cases the conquest of a town in the Christian world. Here the Muslims might simply arrange to share in the use of one of the churches which was already there, employing some agreed-upon part of it as their own place of devotion; or they might take it over outright and convert it into a mosque. The marks of this process may still be seen at Hama in Syria, for example, where the front of a Christian church of the fifth or sixth century is preserved in the west wall of the Great Mosque.[160]

In the event of the foundation of a new city it was of course necessary to arrange a place of worship from the beginning. The first town so founded was Basra in Mesopotamia, which was settled to some extent in A.D. 635 and permanently occupied from 638 on. At the outset the place of prayer here was simply a marked out area, possibly enclosed by a fence of reeds. Later it was walled with sun-dried bricks and roofed on the Qibla side with brushwood. Similarly at Kufa, founded in A.D. 637, the place of prayer was a square area surrounded by a ditch, perhaps with a roofed colonnade at the south or Qibla side. In Egypt the new Muslim capital was called al-Fustat

[159] E. Diez, *Glaube und Welt des Islam.* 1941, pp.176-179.
[160] CEMA I, p.14.

(from Latin *fossatum* = camp) since it was the place where the conqueror, 'Amr ibn-al-'Asi, made his camp.[161] A mosque was built by 'Amr at the same time that the town was started (A.D. 641/42). It was probably built of mud bricks and covered with a roof of palm branches and mud supported on palm trunk pillars.[162]

Along with Mecca the most holy places of the Muslim world were Medina, sanctified by the later life, death and burial of the prophet, and Jerusalem, rendered more sacred by the traditional visit of Muhammad on his "night-journey." The early Caliphs probably interested themselves in at least limited building works in all three places. In A.D. 638 'Umar went on pilgrimage to Mecca, and finding that the Ka'bah had been washed away by a great flood, rebuilt this sanctuary, enlarging and walling in the surrounding space. At about the same time 'Umar also made enlargements in the former residence of Muhammad at Medina, which was increasingly in use for the purposes of a mosque. The same year (A.D. 638) was the date of the surrender of Jerusalem to the Muslim forces. There the Temple Area had evidently remained in ruins since the time of Titus (A.D. 70). It is probable that 'Umar caused this area to be cleared, and in it constructed a relatively simple, timber-roofed mosque. If this is correct this is the origin of the Aqsa Mosque at Jerusalem, a structure often rebuilt in later centuries.[163] 'Uthman, successor of 'Umar, is known to have carried out further enlargements in the sanctuaries at Medina and Mecca.[164]

[161] This was in the vicinity of modern Cairo.
[162] CEMA I, pp.15-18,28.
[163] It is not to be confused with the Dome of the Rock which will be described later.
[164] CEMA I, pp.19,25,31.

6. THE UMAYYADS OF DAMASCUS, A.D. 661-750

AFTER the four "orthodox" Caliphs there were several great dynasties which held sway in the Islamic world.[165] The first of these was established by Mu'awiyah, who had been governor of Syria and a rival of 'Ali. With his victory, finally accomplished by the murder of 'Ali, Damascus became the capital of the Muslim empire. He was able to hand down his authority to his son, and the hereditary principle thus introduced into the succession was influential from then on. Himself the son of Umayyah, the line which he established was known as that of the Umayyad Caliphs,[166] and it endured from A.D. 661 to 750. In this period the Muslim conquests were extended in the east to the Indus Valley and beyond the Oxus River to the borders of China, and in the west all the way across North Africa and into Spain.

Of the Umayyad Caliphs the two of most interest for our account are 'Abd al-Malik (A.D. 685-705) and his son al-Walid (A.D. 705-715). The former was the builder of the Dome of the Rock at Jerusalem, and the latter of the Great Mosque at Damascus.

THE DOME OF THE ROCK AT JERUSALEM

The authority of 'Abd al-Malik was contested during the early part of his reign by a rival Caliph, Ibn al-Zubayr of Mecca. According to the Arabic historian Ya'qubi (A.D. 874), the latter made a practice of seizing and exploiting Syrian pilgrims to Mecca. Hence 'Abd al-Malik resolved to make the Sacred Rock (as-Sakhra) at Jerusalem, rather than Mecca, the place of pilgrimage for his subjects. This was the ancient rock which formed the highest point in the Temple Area and on which David's altar probably once stood.[167] It was also easily possible to suppose that this was the precise point from which Muhammad had made his miraculous ascent to heaven. So 'Abd al-Malik proceeded as follows, as Ya'qubi relates:

Then 'Abd al-Malik forbade the people of Syria to make the pilgrimage [to Mecca]; and this by reason that 'Abd Allah ibn al-Zubayr was wont to seize on them during the time of the pilgrimage, and force them to pay him allegiance—which, 'Abd al-Malik having knowledge of, forbade the people to journey forth to Mecca. But the people murmured thereat, say-

165 Philip K. Hitti, *The Arabs, A Short History.* 1946, p.64.
166 For the genealogical interrelationships of the Umayyads, 'Abbasids and Fatimids, see the table in HHA p.184 n.2.
167 FLP p.151.

[511]

ing, "How dost thou forbid us to make the pilgrimage to Allah's house, seeing that the same is a commandment of Allah upon us?" But the Caliph answered them, "Hath not ibn-Shihab al-Zuhri [a famous student of tradition, d. A.D. 742] told you how the Apostle of Allah did say: *Men shall journey to but three Masjids, al-Masjid Haram [at Mecca], my Masjid [at Medina], and the Masjid of the Holy City [Jerusalem]*? So this last is now appointed for you in lieu of the Masjid al-Haram [of Mecca]. And this Rock, of which it is reported that upon it the Apostle of Allah set his foot when he ascended into heaven, shall be unto you in the place of the Ka'bah." Then 'Abd al-Malik built above the Sakhra a Dome, and hung it around with curtains of brocade, and he instituted door-keepers for the same, and the people took the custom of circumambulating the Rock, even as they had paced round the Ka'bah, and the usage continued thus all the days of the dynasty of the Umayyads.[168]

The structure which 'Abd al-Malik thus erected in Jerusalem was not a mosque (*masjid*) but a shrine (*mashhad*) or "place of witness," that is a sanctuary built over a sacred object, in this case the ancient Rock. Its proper name is the Dome of the Rock (Kubbet as-Sakhra). In its essential structure, a circle of four masonry piers and twelve marble columns encloses the great rock and upholds a drum and lofty timber dome; surrounding this inner circle is an octagonal colonnade and an outer octagonal wall in each face of which are five windows; and in the drum above the roof of the octagon are sixteen windows. The entire impression is one of extraordinary symmetry.[169]

The Dome of the Rock is the oldest existing monument of Muslim architecture, and one of the oldest known Islamic inscriptions is preserved in the mosaics which run around the octagon. This inscription is written in Kufic script and contains verses from the Qur'an. At the east end of the south face the inscription contains a dedication which begins, "Hath built this dome the servant of Allah," and ends, "In the year two and seventy—Allah accept of him!" The year A.H. 72 is equivalent to A.D. 691 and falls within the reign of 'Abd al-Malik, whose name without doubt stood originally in the middle of the inscription. The name that is there now, however, is that of the 'Abbasid Caliph al-Ma'mun (A.D. 813-833), who undertook restorations on the Dome of the Rock over a century after its erection. At that

[168] Quoted in CEMA I, p.43. Shelomo Dov Goitein questions this account by Ya'qubi and thinks that the building of the Dome of the Rock was motivated primarily by the desire to erect a structure which would rival the splendid Christian churches of the time. See JAOS 70 (1950), pp.104-108.
[169] Ernest T. Richmond, *The Dome of the Rock in Jerusalem, A Description of Its Structure and Decoration.* 1924, pp.7-10.

time he removed the name of 'Abd al-Malik and inserted his own, not, however, remembering to change the date too![170]

The photograph reproduced in Fig. 227 shows a portion of the interior of this structure, particularly revealing the arrangement of the columns and piers which support the drum and dome.[171]

THE GREAT MOSQUE AT DAMASCUS

Al-Walid's most notable architectural work was the Great Mosque at Damascus, a structure which takes rank as perhaps the most famous mosque in Islam and the sanctuary of greatest holiness after Mecca, Medina and Jerusalem. In part at least the motive back of its erection was the desire to provide for the Muslims a place of worship which would rival the churches of the Christians in Syria. This fact is stated by the Arabic geographer al-Muqaddasi (A.D. 985) in the following words: "Now one day I said, speaking to my father's brother, 'O my uncle, verily it was not well of the Caliph al-Walid to expend so much of the wealth of the Muslims on the Mosque at Damascus. Had he expended the same on making roads, or for caravanserais, or in the restoration of the Frontier Fortresses, it would have been more fitting and more excellent of him.' But my uncle said to me in answer, 'O my little son, thou hast not understanding! Verily al-Walid was right, and he was prompted to a worthy work. For he beheld Syria to be a country that had long been occupied by the Christians, and he noted herein the beautiful churches still belonging to them, so enchantingly fair, and so renowned for their splendor, even as are the Qumama [the Church of the Holy Sepulcher at Jerusalem], and the churches of Lydda and Edessa. So he sought to build for the Muslims a mosque that should prevent their regarding these, and that should be unique and a wonder to the world.' "[172]

As made known both by actual remains and by notices of ancient authors, the Great Mosque had an extremely interesting history which is probably to be reconstructed somewhat as follows. The area which the mosque occupies was originally the precinct of a Roman temple, dedicated to Jupiter Damascenus and inscriptionally dated in the third century A.D. At the end of the fourth century under the Emperor Theodosius the Great (A.D. 379-395) the pagan temple became a place of Christian worship. Probably a Christian church

[170] CEMA I, pp.46f.
[171] Richmond, *The Dome of the Rock in Jerusalem*, Fig. 3; see also FLP Figs. 63,64.
[172] Quoted in CEMA I, p.101.

of limited size was built within the western part of the entire temple enclosure. Because the "head" of John the Baptist was transferred here at a later date the church received the name of that personage. When the Muslims first took Damascus (A.D. 635) they shared the large temple enclosure with the Christians and had their place of prayer at one end while the church was at the other. This situation is referred to by the Arab historian Ibn Shakir (d. A.D. 1362) when he says that the Christians and Muslims "entered by the same doorway, which was that of the original temple, placed on the south side where is now the great mihrab. Then the Christians turned to the west towards their church, and the Muslims to the right to reach their mosque."[173] Finally when al-Walid became Caliph, both because of the reason already cited from al-Muqaddasi and because of the large increase in the number of Muslims, the entire area was taken over, the church torn down, and the whole turned into a mosque. Four Roman towers stood at the four corners of the ancient temple enclosure, and these were used for minarets or places from which the call to prayer (*adhan*) was given.[174] Notable mosaics provided the decorations.[175]

As described by the Arab travelers, Ibn Jubayr (last quarter of the twelfth century) and Ibn Batuta (second quarter of the fourteenth century), the Great Mosque at Damascus was a place of much splendor. "I entered Damascus on Thursday 9th Ramadan 726 [August 9, A.D. 1326]," writes Ibn Batuta, "and lodged at the Malikite college called ash-Sharabishiya. Damascus surpasses all other cities in beauty, and no description, however full, can do justice to its charms. Nothing, however, can better the words of Ibn Jubayr in describing it. The Cathedral Mosque, known as the Umayyad Mosque, is the most magnificent mosque in the world, the finest in construction and noblest in beauty, grace and perfection; it is matchless and unequalled."[176]

Several times destroyed and reconstructed in following centuries, a view of this famous mosque is given in Fig. 228.[177]

While the Umayyad capital was at Damascus, these rulers never forgot their Bedouin heritage and lived by preference at camps in

[173] Quoted in CEMA I, p.135.
[174] CEMA I, pp.38f.
[175] Marguerite van Berchem in CEMA I, pp.229-252; AJA 51 (1947), p.194.
[176] tr. H. A. R. Gibb, *Ibn Battúta, Travels in Asia and Africa, 1325-1354, Translated and Selected* (The Argonaut Series). 1929, p.65.
[177] CEMA I, Pl. 38,c.

the desert. There they constructed various residences and forts, the ruins of which still stand. It will suffice to mention two examples of these secular sites.

QUSAYR 'AMRAH

Qusayr 'Amrah, meaning the "little castle of 'Amrah," stands on the edge of a wadi in the desert east of the northern end of the Dead Sea. The site and structure are shown in an air view in Fig. 229. The building, which is made of limestone blocks, comprises a rectangular audience hall with vaulted roof and apsidal rooms at the end, and a bath with two rooms vaulted and one covered by a dome.

The most remarkable feature of Qusayr 'Amrah are the frescoes with which its walls and vaults are painted. In an alcove which was directly opposite the main entrance and which probably served as a throne recess there is a painting of a monarch seated upon a throne and resting his feet upon a footstool. At the south end of the west wall of the main room is a painting showing six royal figures. Accompanying superscriptions in Arabic and Greek lead to the identification of these persons with sovereigns of states overcome by the Umayyads, and make probable a date for the building and its paintings in the reign of al-Walid. Other subjects among the frescoes include figures which symbolize Poesy, History and Philosophy; scenes of the bath, gymnasium, dance and hunt; and a painting, in the dome of the bath, of the signs of the Zodiac.[178]

MSHATTA

Mshatta, located between Qusayr 'Amrah and the Dead Sea, belongs almost certainly to the Umayyad Period and may have been built by al-Walid II who reigned but briefly A.D. 743-744. His death would account for the unfinished state in which the work was left. The ruins consist of a large walled enclosure strengthened with numerous half-round towers, inside which are various courts, halls and rooms. The entrance is in the center of the south side of the enclosure, and here the walls and two half-octagonal towers are decorated with extremely rich carvings.

The nature of this decoration may be seen in Fig. 230 where a portion of the tower flanking the west side of the entrance is shown. The leading motifs are triangles, rosettes and tendrils. Beneath the

---

[178] CEMA I, p.264, Pl. 47,b; Jaussen and Savignac, *Mission archéologique en Arabie,* III, *Les châteaux arabes de Qeseir 'Amra, Harâneh et Tûba.* 1922, pp.97f.,111; Ernst Diez, *Die Kunst der islamischen Völker* (Handbuch der Kunstwissenschaft). 1917, p.27.

central rosette is a chalice out of which a lion, on the left, and a griffin, on the right, are drinking. Another lion sits in the lower right corner, and some other animal in the lower left corner. Amidst the tendrils around the rosette are a number of birds, and in the rosette are leaves and perhaps a sunflower. The upper parts of the carving are not completely finished.[179]

[179] CEMA I, pp.397f.,403, Pl. 71.

7. THE 'ABBASIDS, A.D. 750-1258

IN THE middle of the eighth century, the 'Abbasids, descendants of an uncle of Muhammad named al-'Abbas, wrested power from the Umayyads. At first they ruled over the whole caliphate, with the exception of Spain; after some time, however, they progressively lost parts of the western regions and eventually ruled only over the eastern part of the Muslim world. The period of their dominion was the golden age of Islamic civilization, and Baghdad, their capital, became a city of fabulous wealth and splendor. Their most famous ruler was the Caliph Harun al-Rashid (A.D. 786-809).

While Baghdad was completely destroyed by the Mongols in A.D. 1258, we learn from descriptions that it was built in circular form, with a surrounding moat and three concentric walls. Four gates placed at equal distances in the walls gave access from the southwest, southeast, northeast and northwest. The distance from one outer gate to the next was said to be seventy-five hundred feet, so that the total circumference of the city was over five and one-half miles. From each of the gates a main thoroughfare led directly to the central circle within the city where were the palace of the Caliph, called the Golden Gate or the Green Dome, and beside it the Great Mosque.[180]

A tremendous intellectual activity unfolded at this time. It was manifest during the first century of the 'Abbasid Period by the translation into Arabic of Persian, Sanskrit, Syriac and Greek writings, and after that by the development of original and notable work in the sciences of medicine, astronomy, geography, mathematics and alchemy leading to chemistry, and in philosophy, history, ethics and literature.[181]

THE SECTS OF ISLAM

Major sectarian divisions also were now fully evident within Islam. According to a tradition cited by the theologian al-Baghdadi (d. A.D. 1037) in the beginning of his work on Muslim schisms and sects, Muhammad himself had prophesied that his followers would form no less than seventy-three groups, surpassing the sectarian separations of both Jews and Christians: "The tradition has come down to us through the following chain of authorities: Abu Sahl

---

[180] Joseph Hell, *The Arab Civilization*. tr. S. Khuda Bukhsh. 1926, pp.67f.
[181] Hitti, *The Arabs, A Short History*, p.118.

Bishr ibn-Ahmad ibn-Bashshar al-Isfara'ini, 'Abd Allah ibn-Najiyah, Wahb ibn-Bakiyyah, Khalid ibn-'Abdallah, Muhammad ibn-'Amr, Abu Salmah, Abu Hurairah that the last said, the prophet of Allah —peace be unto him—said: 'The Jews are divided into 71 sects, and the Christians are divided into 72 sects, and my people will be divided into 73 sects."[182]

The two chief groups are those of the Sunnites and the Shi'ites. The Sunnites constitute the orthodox party in Islam, and numerically speaking are greatly in the majority. They are devoted to the *sunnah* or "usage" of Muhammad as embodied in the tradition (*hadith*).[183] The Shi'ites comprise the "following" of 'Ali. This man, it will be remembered, was the cousin of Muhammad and husband of the prophet's daughter Fatimah, and was murdered in the midst of the struggles by which the Umayyad dynasty was established. 'Ali was rightfully succeeded, the Shi'ites believe, by his son al-Hasan, then by his other son al-Husayn, and then by nine descendants of the latter, one after another. These twelve personages are called Imams by the Shi'ites, and regarded as having a divine right of rule.[184] The last of the twelve, a young man named Muhammad, disappeared, they say, in A.D. 878 in the cave of the mosque at Samarra. He is thought to be still alive, but "hidden," and it is believed that he will eventually reappear as the Mahdi or "divinely guided one" to restore the true religion, conquer the world for Islam and reign in a splendid millennium.[185] The chief center of the Shi'ites is in Persia,[186] although. this has not at all times been the case; in the tenth to twelfth centuries, for example, Egypt under the Fatimids was the foremost Shi'ite state.

Of the other sects, most interest attaches to the Sufis. These are

---

[182] tr. Kate C. Seelye, *Moslem Schisms and Sects (Al-Farḳ Bain al-Firaḳ), Being the History of the Various Philosophic Systems Developed in Islam, by abū-Manṣūr 'abd-al-Ḳāhir ibn-Ṭāhir al-Baghdādi* (d. 1037), Part I, Translated from the Arabic (Columbia University Oriental Studies, 15). 1919, p.21. Part II of this work is translated by Abraham S. Halkin, 1935.

[183] W. M. Patton in HERE XII, pp.114-119.

[184] HHA pp.440f.; W. M. Patton in HERE XI, pp.453-458; Dwight M. Donaldson, *The Shi'ite Religion, A History of Islam in Persia and Iraḳ.* 1933.

[185] D. B. Macdonald in EI III, pp.111-115; D. S. Margoliouth in HERE VIII, pp.336-340.

[186] It was in Persia in A.D. 1844 that 'Ali Muhammad claimed to be the Bab or "gate" through whom communication could be had with the Hidden Imam. The Bab was put to death only six years after his "manifestation," but in 1863 a new "manifestation" was found in Baha'u'llah or "the Splendor of God" (d. 1892). Known at first as Babism, the religion thus founded is now called Bahaism. Edward G. Browne in HERE II, pp.299-308; Mann, *Der Islam einst und jetzt*, pp.147-150; Mirza Ahmad Sohrab in Vergilius Ferm, ed., *Religion in the Twentieth Century.* 1948, pp.307-314.

the mystics of Islam. Deriving their name from the *suf* or wool of which their white cloaks were made, they have commonly organized themselves in brotherhoods and sought by practices of devotion and contemplation to achieve union with the divine love. Members of the orders are often called Dervishes, this word signifying mendicants and being applicable to ascetic devotees. Philosophically, the Sufis attribute reality to God alone, but teach that through the beatific vision the finite soul of man may attain knowledge of the divine Unity and be absorbed in it. In the words of Von Grunebaum, "Love is the mood of the Sûfî, gnosis his aim, ecstasy his supreme experience."[187]

Orthodoxy and mysticism were combined in the teachings of the man who was probably the greatest theologian ever to arise in Islam and who lived in the period of which we are now speaking. This was al-Ghazzali,[188] who was born at Tus in A.D. 1058, lived as a recluse at Damascus and Jerusalem, taught at Baghdad and Nishapur, and died in Tus in 1111. A single quotation must suffice to suggest the nature of his thought and writing: "Know, therefore, that your companion who never deserts you at home or abroad, when you are asleep or when you are awake, whether you are dead or alive, is your Lord and Master, your Creator and Preserver, and whensoever you remember him he is sitting beside you. For God himself hath said, 'I am the close companion of those who remember me.' And whenever your heart is contrite with sorrow because of your neglect of religion he is your companion who keeps close to you, for God hath said, 'I am with those who are broken-hearted on my account.' And if you only knew him as you ought to know him you would take him as a companion and forsake all men for his sake. But as you are unable to do this at all times, I warn you that you set aside a certain time by night and by day for communion with your Creator that you may delight yourself in him and that he may deliver you from evil."[189]

[187] Gustave E. von Grunebaum, *Medieval Islam, A Study in Cultural Orientation* (An Oriental Institute Essay). 1946, p.133. For the Sufis see pp.133-141 in this work, and also Louis Massignon in EI IV, pp.681-685; Reynold A. Nicholson, *The Mystics of Islam.* 1914; and in HERE XII, pp.10-17; Arthur J. Arberry, *An Introduction to the History of Ṣūfism* (The Sir Abdullah Suhrawardy Lectures for 1942); D. S. Margoliouth in HERE IV, pp.641-643; John P. Brown, *The Darvishes or Oriental Spiritualism.* ed. H. A. Rose. 1927.
[188] Margaret Smith, *Al-Ghazālī the Mystic, A Study of the Life and Personality of Abū Ḥāmid Muḥammad al-Ṭūsī al-Ghazālī, Together with an Account of His Mystical Teaching and an Estimate of His Place in the History of Islamic Mysticism.* 1944; Samuel M. Zwemer, *A Moslem Seeker after God: Showing Islam at Its Best in the Life and Teaching of Al-Ghazali, Mystic and Theologian of the Eleventh Century.* 1920.
[189] tr. Zwemer, *A Moslem Seeker after God,* pp.248f.

SAMARRA

The most impressive extant monuments of the 'Abbasid Period are the ruins of Samarra. This was a city sixty miles up the Tigris River from Baghdad to which the eighth 'Abbasid Caliph, al-Mu'tasim (A.D. 833-842), transferred the seat of government (836) and which remained the capital until 892. The reason for the removal was the unrest created in Baghdad by al-Mu'tasim's introduction of Turkish troops for his bodyguard. This action indeed foreshadowed future events, inasmuch as other Turks eventually assumed the rule, the Seljuqs from A.D. 1037 and the Ottoman Turks from 1299 on.[190]

At Samarra al-Mu'tasim built an enormous palace known as the Jausaq al-Khaqani. Of this, the best preserved portion is the Bab al-'Amma or Hall of Public Audience, the façade of which, consisting of three great arches, still stands to a height of nearly forty feet. Other identified parts of the palace include the throne room, harem, great esplanade, little and great serdabs,[191] treasury, barracks and polo ground. As at Qusayr 'Amrah the walls were adorned with paintings, and these include pictures of dancers, hunting scenes, animals and birds.[192]

The second successor of al-Mu'tasim, al-Mutawakkil (A.D. 847-861), built the Great Mosque of Samarra, as is stated in the following words by the geographer al-Ya'qubi (A.D. 891): "He [al-Mutawakkil] built the Great Mosque at the beginning of al-Hair in a broad space beyond the houses and not in contact with the allotments and markets. He made it good and spacious and strong. He placed a fountain in it, which played without ceasing. He provided access to it by means of three great, wide rows coming from the street which leads from the Wadi Ibrahim ibn-Riyah. In each row there were shops containing all sorts of merchandise and [products of] art and trade. The breadth of each row was one hundred black cubits, in order that the approach to the mosque should not be too narrow for the Caliph, when he visited the mosque on Fridays with his troops and followers, cavalry and infantry. From each row there were alleys and passages to the neighboring one, in which were the allotments of a number of common people. The dwellings and houses of the

[190] Among other and lesser Turkish dynasties which also found establishment in this period was the one we have already met (p.179) at Ghazni in Afghanistan.

[191] Serdabs, still a feature of houses in southern Mesopotamia, are underground rooms used as retreats from the heat. CEMA II, p.64 n.5.

[192] *Die Ausgrabungen von Samarra* (Forschungen zur islamischen Kunst), III, Ernst Herzfeld, *Die Malereien von Samarra*. 1927.

people had plenty of space, and the people of the markets and crafts-men and artificers had room in their shops and markets, which lay in the rows of the Great Mosque."[193]

The ruins of the Great Mosque are shown in an aerial view in Fig. 231, with the modern walled city of Samarra in the back-ground.[194] As may be clearly seen, the mosque is in the form of an immense rectangle with a spiral minaret outside the walls at one end. The rectangle is walled with kiln-dried bricks, and measures about 787 by 512 feet, which makes it the largest mosque in the world. The main axis runs from northeast to southwest, almost ex-actly in the direction of Mecca. The minaret stands precisely on this line outside the northeast wall, and on the same line in the center of the southwest wall is a rectangular recess (*mihrab*) marking the direction of prayer. The foundations of the twenty-four rows of col-umns which divided the mosque into twenty-five aisles and carried its roof may still be seen, while in the middle of the open court (*sahn*) are the remains of the famous fountain which al-Ya'qubi said played continuously.

The most striking feature of all is the minaret, known as the Mal-wiya or "spiral." It is a helicoidal tower, about one hundred and nine-ty-five feet high, with a ramp running up around it for five complete turns in a counterclockwise direction. This ramp is about seven and one-half feet wide and ascends at a constantly increasing angle, since otherwise the amount of rise would be reduced as the diameter of each turn became smaller. It is almost certainly correct to recog-nize the influence of the ancient Babylonian ziggurat in the construc-tion of this remarkable tower.

According to Yaqut the cost of the Great Mosque at Samarra was a sum equal to nearly two million dollars.[195]

[193] tr. in CEMA II, p.254.   [194] CEMA II, Pl. 63,b.
[195] CEMA II, p.261.

8. THE AGHLABIDS (A.D. 800-909), TULUNIDS (A.D. 868-905) AND FATIMIDS (A.D. 909-1171)

EGYPT and North Africa were conquered by the Muṣlims, it will be remembered, in the days of the Orthodox Caliphs and the Umayyads. In A.D. 800 Harun al-Rashid appointed Ibrahim ibn al-Aghlab governor of what is now Tunisia, and he established a dynasty which ruled in relative independence for a little over a century and dominated most of North Africa and the Middle Mediterranean.

THE GREAT MOSQUE OF QAYRAWAN

The capital of the Aghlabids was at al-Qayrawan (Kairouan). This town is said to have been built originally, with its mosque, in A.D. 674/75 by 'Uqbah ibn-Nafi', a governor sent out by Mu'awiyah. In A.D. 836 the third Aghlabid ruler, Ziyadat-Allah I (817-838), rebuilt the mosque of al-Qayrawan completely. The geographer al-Bakri (A.D. 1068) states that Ziyadat-Allah "had all the mosque demolished, and even ordered the mihrab to be destroyed. People pointed out to him that all his predecessors had abstained from touching this part of the edifice, because 'Uqbah ibn-Nafi' had constructed it; he persisted in his resolution, not wishing that the new building should exhibit the least trace of work that was not his. In order to turn him from his intention, one of the builders proposed that the old mihrab should be enclosed between two walls, in such a way that no part of it was visible from the interior of the mosque. This plan was adopted, and down to our time the mosque of Qayrawan has remained just as Ziyadat-Allah left it. The present mihrab, as well as all that surrounds it, from top to bottom, is constructed of white marble openwork covered with carving. Part of this decoration consists of inscriptions, the rest forms arabesques of various patterns. Round the mihrab are extremely beautiful columns of marble. The two red columns of which we have spoken[196] are placed in front of the mihrab, and serve to support the [semi-]dome of which they form a part. The mosque contains 414 columns, forming seventeen naves. Its length is 220 cubits, and its width 150. The maqsurah was formerly in the interior of the mosque, but as a result of the alterations which Ziyadat-Allah continued to make in this building, it is now only a house on the south side of the mosque which has

196 Al-Bakri had already told how the mosque of 'Uqbah was rebuilt earlier (A.D. 703) by Hassan, and how the latter brought to it from an ancient church "the two red columns spotted with yellow, of which the beauty is unsurpassed."

its entrance in the Fruit Bazaar. It has a second doorway which opens at the side of the pulpit and it is by this one that the Imam enters the mosque, after having stopped in the house to await the hour of prayer. Ziyadat-Allah spent 86,000 *mithqal* for the construction of the mosque."[197]

While Ziyadat-Allah gave to the Great Mosque of Qayrawan the size and shape which it has today, additional work was done on the building by later rulers. Abu Ibrahim Ahmad in A.D. 862/63 decorated the mihrab with marble panels and faïence tiles, made a dome in front of it, and built a magnificent pulpit; Ibrahim II ibn-Ahmad (A.D. 874-902) constructed a beautifully decorated dome at the end of the nave which leads to the mihrab; and al-Mu'izz ibn-Badis, who governed the region in the first half of the eleventh century for the Fatimid Caliph of Egypt, gave the splendid wooden *maqsurah*, or enclosure for the use of the ruler at prayers.[198]

The photograph in Fig. 232 shows the Great Mosque from the northwest, with the massive square minaret in the foreground and the domes above the sanctuary in the background. The central aisle of the sanctuary is pictured in Fig. 233. The mihrab of Ahmad may be seen in the wall straight ahead. It is a recess over six feet wide, flanked by two orange-red marble columns, and lined with carved marble panels, many in openwork. The face of the arch and the rectangular surface surrounding it are adorned with luster tiles, some in monochrome and some in polychrome, featuring varied floral motifs.[199]

To the right of the mihrab is the minbar or pulpit, a side view of which is shown in Fig. 234. Likewise probably erected by Ahmad, it is the oldest and most famous minbar in Islam.[200] Constructed of plane tree wood, it has the usual staircase form with seventeen steps leading up to the speaker's platform. The sides are adorned with openwork panels of remarkable intricacy and beauty. There are geometrical patterns and arabesques employing trees, pine cones, palmettes, acanthus whorls, vine leaves and bunches of grapes. Yet farther to the right of the minbar and partially visible in both of our photographs is the handsome maqsurah of wood with which the mosque was endowed by al-Mu'izz ibn-Badis.

While the Aghlabids were ruling in North Africa, the Tulunid dynasty made itself independent in Egypt. This dynasty was founded

[197] tr. in CEMA II, pp.209,213.
[198] CEMA II, pp.213f.,224.
[199] CEMA II, Pls. 46,b; 83,a.
[200] CEMA II, p.317, Pl. 89,a.

by Ahmad ibn-Tulun (A.D. 868-884), who was sent to Egypt as governor and soon made himself independent, and it endured until A.D. 905. Al-Fustat was still the capital, and here the Mosque of 'Amr, although several times reconstructed, had become too small for the increased numbers of Muslims. Ibn-Tulun consequently built a new mosque which was completed in A.D. 879.

THE MOSQUE OF IBN-TULUN

The Mosque of ibn-Tulun is shown in a general view in Fig. 235. The entire area occupied is a square about five hundred and thirty feet on the side. Within this area there is first an outer court known as a *ziyada* or extension, which once contained places of ablution and subsidiary buildings and which served to separate the mosque proper from its secular surroundings. The wall of the mosque proper is pierced with doors and pointed-arched windows and crested with openwork adornment. In the interior (Fig. 236) the arcades were constructed with brick piers rather than columns, and with pointed arches. Bands of stucco ornamentation adorn the arches, and openwork grilles fill the windows with delicate lacework. Under the ceiling remains a part of a famous Kufic inscription, carved in solid wood, and containing originally about one-fifteenth of the entire Qur'an. The original minaret of the mosque is believed to have resembled that of the Great Mosque of Samarra, which is where ibn-Tulun spent his youth, but the present minaret was probably built by the Mamluk Sultan Lajin (A.D. 1296-1298).[201]

The Fatimids concern us next. They were a Shi'ite dynasty claiming descent from Fatimah and 'Ali through al-Husayn. In A.D. 909 a leader of theirs named 'Abdullah al-Husayn al-Shi'i destroyed the Aghlabid dynasty and began to rule at al-Qayrawan as the Imam 'Ubaydullah al-Mahdi (A.D. 909-934). In A.D. 969 a famous general, Jawhar, took Egypt from the Ikhshidids who had held it briefly, and completed the establishment of the Fatimid empire along the entire southern coast of the Mediterranean. At al-Fustat, Jawhar laid out a new quarter which he named al-Qahirah (the triumphant) after the planet Qahir al-Falak (the triumphant of heaven, Mars) which was then in the ascendant, and in 973 this place, now called Cairo, became the Fatimid capital.[202]

[201] CEMA II, pp.337,354, Pls. 96,99.
[202] HHA p.619.

THE MOSQUE OF AL-AZHAR

The first and most famous mosque constructed by the Fatimids was that of al-Azhar, built in al-Qahirah by Jawhar in A.D. 972. Under the Caliph al-'Aziz (A.D. 975-976) this mosque became a place of teaching as well as prayer, and is today the principal university of the Muslim world. The central part of the structure preserves its original form, but otherwise much rebuilding has been done. The photograph in Fig. 237 shows the façade of the mosque from the court. The various minarets are relatively late, dating from the fifteenth to the eighteenth century.[203]

Interestingly enough we possess the very name of al-'Aziz, just mentioned as the inaugurator of the teaching program in the Mosque of al-Azhar, inscribed on the beautiful rock-crystal ewer shown in Fig. 238. Aside from its historical importance in this regard, the object illustrates a high degree of skill in the productions of Muslim artists of the time.[204]

Another striking object of the Fatimid Period, probably of the eleventh century, is the great bronze griffin (Fig. 239) which probably once stood in some royal palace and is now in the Campo Santo at Pisa.[205] The making of such an image as this was in general frowned upon in the Islamic world because it savored of idolatry and might carry an implication of disrespect to the sole creative power of Allah. It will be noted, however, that the body of the griffin is covered with engraved patterns, and that there is a Kufic inscription running around the chest and sides. This decoration has nothing in common with the nature of the animal and serves rather to negate the form of the object. Thus it was shown that the image need not be taken for a living being nor an affront in any wise to the Creator.[206]

---

[203] Louis Hautecoeur and Gaston Wiet. *Les mosquées du Caire.* 1932, I, pp.218-220; II, Pl. 10; E. T. Richmond, *Moslem Architecture, 623 to 1516, Some Causes and Consequences.* 1926, pp.79-83; Mrs. R. L. Devonshire, *Eighty Mosques and Other Monuments in Cairo.* 1930, pp.97f.

[204] A. H. Christie in Thomas Arnold and Alfred Guillaume, eds., *The Legacy of Islam.* 1931, p.144, Fig. 65.

[205] Gaston Migeon, *Les arts musulmans* (Bibliothèque d'histoire de l'art). 1926, p.32.

[206] Richard Ettinghausen in FAH pp.259f.

9. THE UMAYYADS OF CORDOVA, A.D. 756-1031

WHEN the 'Abbasids overthrew the Umayyads of Damascus (A.D. 750) they destroyed all the members of the house they were able to seize. One youth named 'Abd al-Rahman escaped, however, and ultimately made his way to Spain. There he was able to establish an independent western branch of the Umayyad dynasty which maintained power for two and three-quarters centuries (A.D. 765-1031) and was the chief agency through which the influence of Arab culture was brought to bear upon the western world. 'Abd al-Rahman I and his first successors took only the title of amir, but with the eminent 'Abd al-Rahman III (A.D. 912-961) the title of caliph was assumed.

The capital of the dynasty was at Cordova. Just outside the city 'Abd al-Rahman I built his palace which he named al-Rusafah after the residence of his grandfather Hisham, tenth caliph of Damascus. To a solitary palm tree in the garden, said to be the first imported from Syria, he addressed these verses: "In the midst of Rusafah has appeared to us a palm tree in a Western land far from the home of palm trees. So I said, this resembles me, for I also live in distant exile and separated by a great distance from my children and my family. Thou hast grown up in a foreign land and we are both exiled and far from home."[207]

THE GREAT MOSQUE OF CORDOVA

In A.D. 788, two years before his death, 'Abd al-Rahman I founded the great and famous mosque of Cordova. In its original form, portions of which can still be detected in the present structure, it seems to have consisted of a large court and a sanctuary divided into eleven aisles by ten arcades, each containing twelve arches. Antique columns were used, and in order to gain additional height two tiers of arches were employed to support the ceiling.

At first there was no minaret, but one was added by 'Abd al-Rahman's son and successor, Hisham I (A.D. 788-796); and later an entirely new minaret was erected by 'Abd al-Rahman III. This has been found to still exist inside the present Campanile. Extensive enlargements were also carried out by 'Abd al-Rahman II (A.D. 822-852), al-Hakam II (961-976) and Hisham II (976-1009).[208]

[207] tr. in CEMA II, p.139.
[208] CEMA II, pp.140-145,155; Ernst Kühnel, *Maurische Kunst* (Die Kunst des Ostens,

The building was made into a Christian cathedral in A.D. 1236, and survives today, still being popularly known as La Mezquita or "the mosque." It is an enormous rectangle, measuring about 585 by 410 feet, and comprises an open court and a sanctuary or hall of nineteen aisles. The wonderful vistas through the veritable forest of columns in the interior are suggested by the photograph in Fig. 240.

---

9). 1924, pp.16f.,64; Heinrich Glück and Ernst Diez, *Arte del Islam* (Historia del arte labor, v). 1932, pp.65f.

10. THE MAMLUKS, A.D. 1250-1517

THE high point of Arab expansion was reached in the periods with which we have now dealt. If not in exhaustive recital, at least in selected episodes we have told how the followers of the Arabian prophet carried his religion throughout the Middle East and into northern Africa and western Europe. The halting of Arab expansion and the reducing of Arab power were accomplished by such events as the Christian reconquest of Spain in the west, largely carried out by the middle of the thirteenth century (Cordova fell in 1236); the Crusades in the Near East, launched by the famous speech of Pope Urban II in 1095; and the conquest and destruction of Baghdad (1258) in the Middle East by Hulagu, grandson of Jenghiz Khan.

It was the Mamluks who stopped the Mongols from further progress westward, drove out of Syria and Egypt the last of the Crusaders, and established in the Near East the last and in some respects most remarkable of the medieval Arab dynasties. The name Mamluk means "possessed" and was the common designation for a slave. These rulers were erstwhile slaves who by energetic and ruthless endeavor fought their way to leadership. This domination they maintained from the middle of the thirteenth century until 1517 when the new non-Arab caliphate of the Ottoman Turks was established.[209]

The capitals of the Mamluks were Cairo and Damascus. The title borne by the rulers was Sultan, a designation literally meaning "he with authority" (al-sultan) and first borne officially by the Seljuq monarchs.[210] The most famous of the earlier Mamluk Sultans included Baybars (A.D. 1260-1277), distinguished for his campaigns against the Mongols and the Crusaders, Qalawun (1279-1290), specially remembered for the great hospital he built in Cairo, and al-Nasir (1293-1294, 1298-1308, 1309-1340), also a builder of important public works; and of the later Mamluks Qa'it-bay may be singled out, whose reign was relatively long (1468-1495) and successful.

Warlike as the times were, the Mamluk Period was notable for its architectural and artistic activity, and Egypt in particular was adorned with the finest monuments erected there since the times of the Ptolemies and the Pharaohs. Characteristic of the style which prevailed in this climactic period of Arab architecture were a cruciform plan and the use of striped masonry as well as of arabesque decoration and Kufic lettering.

[209] HHA p.671.   [210] HHA pp.464,474.

THE MOSQUE OF QA'IT-BAY

The single structure we select for illustration is the Mosque of Qa'it-bay in Cairo. This remarkable building, a general view of which is shown in Fig. 241, was completed in A.D. 1474 and comprises not only a mosque proper but also a tomb, a school and a fountain. Notable are the fine proportions, the red and white striped masonry, the lofty minaret, and the dome decorated with a lacework of conventionalized foliage and rosettes. Within there is a corresponding richness of exquisite ornamentation as may be seen in Fig. 242, showing the prayer niche and the pulpit.[211]

Of the superb calligraphic art which was lavished upon copies of the Qur'an under the Mamluks we have already given an example (Fig. 223).

[211] GCE I, p.231; Heinrich Glück and Ernst Diez, *Die Kunst des Islam* (Propyläen-Kunstgeschichte, v). 3d ed. 1925, p.186, Pl. III.

11. THE IL-KHANS (A.D. 1256-1335) AND THE TIMURIDS
(A.D. 1369-1506)

IN THE east, meanwhile, the world had been overrun by the Mongols. Of the fall of 'Abbasid Baghdad to Hulagu, grandson of Jenghiz Khan, in A.D. 1258 we have already spoken. This conqueror took the title Il-Khan, meaning "lord of the tribe," and founded a dynasty which ruled all Iran until about 1335. Then, after a brief feudal period, came Timur Lang, better known as Tamerlane (A.D. 1336-1405). Having become king in Samarkand in A.D. 1369, he went forth on his campaigns, conducted with boundless cruelty, in Iran, Mesopotamia, Russia, India, Syria and Asia Minor. The dynasty which he established ruled Transoxiana and Persia until shortly after A.D. 1500, the approximate date up to which we are carrying this chapter.

The first of the Il-Khans, including Hulagu (A.D. 1256-1265), Abagha (1265-1281) and Arghun (1284-1291), may have shown interest in Buddhism and also in Nestorianism, but the later ones such as Ghazan (1295-1304) and Oljaitu (1304-1316), were converted to Islam. Related as they were to the Yüan dynasty rulers of China (p.376), a strong Chinese influence was felt in their realm. As for Tamerlane, he was a Muslim from the outset.[212]

The architectural monuments of the time and region are massive, mighty structures, expressive of tremendous force, built of brick and surfaced with a ceramic decoration of shimmering color.[213] Two examples are shown here. The first (Fig. 243) is the Masjid-i-Jami' or cathedral mosque built at Varamin, south of Teheran, in A.D. 1325-1326 by Abu Sa'id (A.D. 1316-1335), the last of the Il-Khans. In ruins as it is, the impressive unity of the great building is still manifest, and, on the façade, portions of the original blue faïence remain to give an intimation of its original beauty.[214] The second monument (Fig. 244) is the Gur-i-Mir or Tomb of Timur at Samarkand. This is a cross-formed hall, contained within an octagon and surmounted by a high drum and lofty, swelling dome. Both dome and drum are adorned with blue enameled brickwork, the drum also carrying an inscription in large Kufic characters. Within, the body of the famous conqueror lies beneath a great block of green nephrite.[215]

[212] GCE I, pp.296f.,308f.
[213] Ernst Cohn-Wiener, *Asia, Einführung in die Kunstwelt des Ostens.* 1929, pp.137,139.
[214] PSPA IV, Pl. 405,B.
[215] Ernst Cohn-Wiener, *Turan, islamische Baukunst in Mittelasien.* 1930. pp.30f., 45; PSPA IV, Pl. 419.

PERSIAN PAINTING

Of Muslim architecture, particularly as manifested in imposing mosques, and of calligraphy, as devoted to the production of ornamental inscriptions for the mosques and the making of beautiful copies of the Qur'an, we have had frequent occasion to speak. Alongside these two prime arts of Islam the art of painting also played at least a limited role.

Theologically, this art had long been the object of disapproval, for it was held that the painter who depicted the figure of an animal or a human being was arrogating to himself something of the creative power which belonged alone to Allah. This attitude took form in the traditions in such sayings as the following.[216]

Those who will be most severely punished on the Day of Judgment are the murderer of a prophet, one who has been put to death by a prophet, one who leads men astray without knowledge, and a maker of images or pictures.

A head will thrust itself out of the fire and will ask, Where are those who invented lies against God, or have been the enemies of God, or have made light of God? Then men will ask, Who are these three classes of persons? It will answer, The sorcerer is he who has invented lies against God; the maker of images or pictures is the enemy of God; and he who acts in order to be seen of men, is he that has made light of God.

While this disapprobation served quite universally to keep painted pictures out of the mosques, it did not prevent the art of painting from being practiced and enjoyed in a secular way. At certain times and in certain countries, particularly among the ruling classes, the art asserted itself. Of this we have already encountered examples in the frescoes of Qusayr 'Amrah and Samarra. In the realm and era of the Il-Khans and the Timurids, with which we are now dealing, a notable activity unfolded in the production of miniature illustrations for books. Here, too, in the larger number of cases the books illustrated were of a secular nature, being scientific works on plants, animals, or medicine; collections of poems, or fables; or treatises on history. In the historical works it of course happened not infrequently that persons of religious significance were treated; also manuscripts on religious subjects were sometimes illustrated. In these cases, however, the representations which might be made of Muhammad or other religious leaders remained purely of historical significance; they were not intended as objects of devotion. Thus the

[216] Arnold, *Painting in Islam*, p.6; cf. Hans Much, *Islamik*, 1921, p.8.

miniatures, interesting as they are to us, were only of ephemeral importance in Islamic civilization as a whole.

Turning to this art because of its interest from our historical point of view, we find that the painting may best be described as truly Persian, but influenced by 'Abbasid art on the one side and eventually even more strongly by Chinese on the other.

In A.H. 707 = A.D. 1307/08 a fine illustrated copy was made of The Chronology of Ancient Nations (al-Athar al-Baqiya), a work which was written, it will be remembered, in A.D. 1000 by the scholar al-Biruni. From this manuscript we show in Fig. 245 the painting of Muhammad preaching his farewell sermon on the occasion of his last visit to Mecca. The prophet speaks from upon a minbar, and behind the heads of both himself and his listeners are round halos. The style of the painting is still that of the Arab tradition.[217]

Another historical work of great importance by a Muslim author was the Jami' at-Tawarikh or Universal History of Rashid-al-Din (A.D. c.1247-1318). This historian lived in the city of Tabriz and served as prime minister under the Il-Khans, Ghazan and Oljaitu.[218] An illustrated manuscript of this book made in A.H. 714 = A.D. 1314 contains miniatures showing episodes from the Bible and from Buddhist, Muslim and Chinese history. The picture reproduced in Fig. 246 shows Muhammad replacing the Black Stone in the Ka'bah at Mecca. The story is that the Ka'bah was damaged by a flood and had to be rebuilt. When it came to putting the Black Stone back in its place a dispute arose as to who should have the honor. Muhammad, then about thirty-five years of age, appeared on the scene and was chosen for the purpose. In the painting, Muhammad stands in front of the Ka'bah and takes up the Black Stone which four prominent citizens of Mecca are presenting to him on a long strip of carpet. In other miniatures in the same manuscript, particularly where landscapes are depicted, a definite Chinese influence is to be seen.[219]

Under the favorite son and successor of Timur, Shah Rukh (A.D. 1404-1447), the Timurid capital was established at Herat in Khorasan. Like his father, Shah Rukh was a patron of the arts, and so too was his son, Baysunqur Mirza (A.D. 1397-1433). The last named is said to have employed forty calligraphers and painters in his library, and presumably the staff in his father's establishment was

217 Arnold, *Painting in Islam*, pp.95f.; GCE I, p.302.

218 E. Berthels in EI III, pp.1124f.

219 M. S. Dimand, *A Handbook of Mohammedan Decorative Arts* (The Metropolitan Museum of Art). 1930, p.22.

even larger. With such royal encouragement the school of Herat became the foremost center of Persian painting, and with the experience gained from earlier developments this art now attained its classical form.

A work devoted entirely to religious subject matter provides some of the finest examples of the art. This is a manuscript of an Apocalypse of Muhammad called the Mi'raj Namah, which is wholly occupied with a detailed account of the famous "night-journey" of the prophet through the realms of heaven and hell. The book was copied in Uighur (Eastern Turki) script at Herat by a certain Malik Bakhshi in A.H. 840 = A.D. 1436, that is under Shah Rukh. From the very beautiful miniature paintings with which the manuscript is adorned we reproduce in Fig. 247 the picture of Muhammad's visit to paradise. In accordance with tradition the prophet rides upon the wonderful steed Buraq, and is guided by the archangel Gabriel. Both Muhammad and Gabriel have halos of flame. Paradise is shown as a wonderful garden, and since the day is Friday, the Islamic holiday, the houris are out traveling, visiting and exchanging gifts of flowers.[220]

Continuing to the end of the Timurid Period, the last of the Timurids was Sultan Husayn Bayqara who came to the throne in Herat in A.D. 1468 and died in 1506. His minister was Mir 'Ali Shir Nawa'i (A.D. 1440-1501), himself a talented writer and a patron of men of letters and art.[221] From an illustrated manuscript, dated A.H. 890 = A.D. 1485, containing a work by Nawa'i entitled Nazm al-Jawahir, we reproduce the miniature in Fig. 248. In this we see Muhammad, distinguished by a flame-halo, seated in front of the mihrab of a mosque. The mihrab and surrounding wall are shown decorated with tiles colored in green and blue, above is a green dome, and at one side an ornate minbar. Thus appeared, no doubt, some mosque in Herat or Samarkand with which the painter was familiar, although in the scene the prophet was of course supposed to be in Medina. In front of Muhammad is a brazier from which flames arise vigorously. Gathered around are a number of the companions of the prophet. Seated by the brazier writing at Muhammad's dictation is a secretary, possibly Zayd ibn-Thabit. The man standing at the left is identified by his black face as Bilal, the Abyssinian whom Muhammad chose on account of his stentorian voice to be the first

[220] Basil Gray in *Persian Painting, From Miniatures of the XIII.-XVI. Centuries.* 1940, p.12; Arnold, *Painting in Islam,* p.109 (for Buraq see pp.117-122).
[221] Edward G. Browne, *A History of Persian Literature under Tartar Dominion* (*A.D. 1265-1502*). 1920, pp.390f.,505f.

muezzin.[222] The standing figure at the right is 'Ali, with his famous two-pointed sword.[223]

Among those who enjoyed the patronage of Husayn Bayqara and Mir 'Ali Shir Nawa'i was Kamal al-Din Bihzad, considered the greatest of all Persian painters.[224] Born at Herat about A.D. 1440, he studied under a certain Pir Saiyid Ahmad of Tabriz, worked at Herat throughout the entire reign of Husayn Bayqara, and continued afterward to labor at Tabriz. A contemporary historian, Khwandamir, wrote in his *Habib as-Siyar* (A.D. c.1523) concerning Bihzad: "He sets before us marvelous forms and rarities of art; his draftsmanship which is like the brush of Mani[225] has caused the memorials of all the painters of the world to be obliterated, and his fingers endowed with miraculous qualities have wiped out the pictures of all the artists among the sons of Adam. A hair of his brush, by its mastery, has given life to the lifeless form. My revered master attained to his present eminence through the blessing of the patronage and of the kind favor of the Amir Nizam al-Din 'Ali Shir, and His Majesty the Khan showed him much favor and kindness; and at the present time too this marvel of the age, whose belief is pure, is regarded with benevolence by the kings of the world and is encompassed by the boundless consideration of the rulers of Islam. Without doubt thus will it be for ever."[226]

Famous as he was, Bihzad had many admirers and imitators and the identification of his own originals is not always positive. The picture we choose for illustration (Fig. 249) is certainly in his style, however, and may safely be attributed to either Bihzad or his school and dated around A.D. 1500. It shows a band of dancing dervishes, surrounded by musicians and spectators. Outstanding features are

[222] HHA pp.106,259; Fr. Buhl in EI I, pp.718f.
[223] Arnold, *Painting in Islam*, p.97.
[224] Basil Gray, *Persian Painting*. 1930, pp.57-66.
[225] The founder of Manicheism (cf. above p.115) was himself a famous painter, and his followers practiced the art vigorously, producing many illuminated manuscripts. In A.D. 923 fourteen sacks of Manichean books were burned in Baghdad and trickles of gold and silver ran out of the fire; and in 1092 Mani's own picture-book called *Arzhang* was still in existence in Ghazni. Manichean painting was doubtless one of the influences contributing to the development of the later Persian painting which we are discussing. Arnold, *Painting in Islam*, pp.61f. In modern times portions of actual Manichean manuscripts with pictures dating from around A.D. 750-850, have been recovered at the Oasis of Turfan. A. von Le Coq, *Die buddhistische Spätantike in Mittelasien* (Ergebnisse der kgl. preussischen Turfan-Expeditionen). II, *Die manichaeischen Miniaturen*. 1923.
[226] tr. Thomas W. Arnold and Adolf Grohmann, *The Islamic Book, A Contribution to Its Art and History from the VII-XVIII Century*. 1929, p.75.

the delicacy of execution, gracefulness of the figures, liveliness of the motion, beauty of the landscape, and, in the original, effectiveness of the combination of the colors, pink, vermilion, dark red, brick red, and various shades of yellow, green and blue.[227]

With the adding of painting to calligraphy and mosque architecture the most typical expressions of Islamic art have now come before our view, and this chapter must be closed. Concerning Islam in India, further information will be given in the beginning of the following chapter.[228]

[227] Dimand, *A Handbook of Mohammedan Decorative Arts*, p.36.
[228] For China see Marshall Broomhall, *Islam in China, A Neglected Problem*. 1910.

CHAPTER X

Sikhism

SIKHISM is a religion which arose in India around A.D. 1500 and which has today over five million followers. Since it is of comparatively recent origin and since it has neither mythology nor idols, it presents fewer archeological materials than the faiths previously considered. It is properly included in our study, however, both because of its magnitude and because of its significant origin as an effort toward the reconciliation of Hinduism and Islam in India. Even though Sikhism did not accomplish that goal, the story of its early work toward such an end may testify to the growing desire to find a common understanding among the great religions of the modern world.

1. INDIA IN THE MUSLIM PERIOD, A.D. 1206-1857

THE TURKS AND AFGHANS, A.D. 1206-1526

THE period of Sikhism's rise and distinctive development fell within the Muslim Period in Indian history.[1] It will be remembered (p.179) that the Turk Mahmud (A.D. 999-1030), son of Sabuktigin, of Ghazni played an important part in the establishment of Islam in India.[2] This ruler's triumphal tower still stands at Ghazni and is shown in Fig. 250. Later, Qutb-ud-din Aibak, slave and viceroy of the Ghaznavid Muhammad Ghori, occupied Delhi (A.D. 1191) and, upon the death of his master, became sultan (A.D. 1206-1210) and founder of the so-called Slave dynasty. It was in commemoration of the capture of Delhi that Aibak founded in that city the mosque known as Quwwat-ul-Islam or "the might of Islam." An outstanding feature of this mosque was the Qutb Minar (Fig. 251) or "axis-pillar," an imposing tower begun by Aibak and completed by Shams-ud-din Iltutmish (A.D. 1211-1236), probably intended as a minaret for the muezzin but soon regarded as a tower of victory.[3]

[1] For the chronology in the time of the Turks and Afghans see CHI III, p.690; and of the Mughals see CHI IV, p.614.
[2] Murray T. Titus, *Indian Islam, A Religious History of Islam in India* (The Religious Quest of India). 1930, p.6.
[3] John Marshall in CHI III, pp.575-579.

The dynasty of Qutb-ud-din and his successors held sway in Delhi for some sixty years and then gave way to the house of Balban (A.D. 1266-1290). After that came the dynasty of the Khaljis (A.D. 1290-1320), whose king 'Ala-ud-din (A.D. 1296-1316) subjected Gujarat and the Deccan to Islam. Then the Tughluqs reigned (A.D. 1320-1414), and their king Firuz (A.D. 1351-1388) founded Firuzabad or New Delhi just south of Old Delhi, built four other towns and, it is said, constructed or restored four mosques, thirty palaces, two hundred caravanserais, five reservoirs, five hospitals, one hundred tombs, ten baths, ten monumental pillars and one hundred bridges.[4]

In A.D. 1398 Timur (p.530) invaded India and sacked Delhi, and when Khizr Khan (A.D. 1414-1421), reputed descendant of the prophet Muhammad, established the new Sayyid dynasty (A.D. 1414-1451) at Delhi it was in a position as viceroy to Shah Rukh (p.532), Timur's successor. The Sayyids in turn were displaced by the Lodi dynasty (A.D. 1451-1526), which was founded by Buhlul, an Afghan of the tribe of Lodi. Buhlul ruled from A.D. 1451 to 1489, and fought numerous battles, not always successful, on behalf of the supremacy of Delhi. He was succeeded by his son Sikandar (A.D. 1489-1517), who was the most powerful of the three kings of this house. Sikandar campaigned victoriously and administered his enlarged realms vigorously. In connection with a movement against the district of Gwalior he transferred his capital from Delhi to Agra, a city which attained much importance under the later Mughal (= Mogul) emperors. He was under the strong influence of the theologians of Islam, and displayed his intolerance by the wholesale destruction of Indian temples. Another example of this attitude appeared during a four-year stay in Sambhal, beginning in A.D. 1499. It was reported that a Brahman of Bengal had publicly maintained that the Muslim and Hindu faiths were both true and were but different paths to God. Sikandar had the Brahman brought to his court, and likewise summoned thither Islamic theologians from various parts of his kingdom. Consideration was given to the question of whether it was permissible to preach religious peace as the Brahman had been doing, and the Muslim doctors proposed the following decision. Since the Brahman had admitted the truth of Islam, let him accept it or be put to death. Sikandar agreed with this conclusion, and when the Brahman refused to change his faith the king caused him to be executed.[5]

[4] Wolseley Haig in CHI III, p.175.   [5] Haig in CHI III, p.240.

THE MUGHAL EMPIRE, A.D. 1526-1857

The last of the Lodi kings was Ibrahim who, after a reign of nine years (A.D. 1517-1526), was slain on the battlefield of Panipat by an invader from Kabul named Babur. Babur was the last of the Timurids, being the fifth in descent from the founder of that dynasty, and he attained his own greatest ambition when after the defeat of Ibrahim he entered Delhi and on April 27, 1526, was acclaimed in the Grand Mosque as Emperor of Hindustan. Thus was founded the mighty Mughal (from Mongol) Empire of Delhi which endured until A.D. 1857.

Babur (d. A.D. 1530) was a strong Muslim, and in the year of his victory erected at least two mosques which still survive, the Kabuli Bagh at Panipat and the Jami' Masjid at Sambhal.[6] Neither is of special architectural significance, and indeed Babur did not have any very high opinion of the abilities or achievements of his new subjects in general. He wrote in his *Memoirs*: "Hindustan is a country that has few pleasures to recommend it. The people are not handsome. They have no idea of the charms of friendly society, of frankly mixing together, or of familiar intercourse. They have no genius, no comprehension of mind, no politeness of manner, no kindness or fellow-feeling, no ingenuity or mechanical invention in planning or executing their handicraft works, no skill or knowledge in design or architecture; they have no horses, no good flesh, no grapes or muskmelons, no good fruits, no ice or cold water, no good food or bread in their bazaars, no baths or colleges, no candles, no torches, not a candlestick."[7]

The eldest son and successor of Babur was Humayun, who came to the throne in A.D. 1530 and died by accident in 1556. His reign was not distinguished and he was even driven into exile for a time while Shir Shah, a rebel Afghan of Bengal, ruled Hindustan (A.D. 1538-1545). Shir Shah was a man of culture and a great builder, however, and his splendid island mausoleum at Sasaram is still in existence.[8] Humayun's own tomb, a beautiful structure yet standing at Delhi, was erected by his widow some eight years after his death, when Akbar had fully reestablished Mughal authority throughout the country.

[6] Marshall in CHI III, p.524.
[7] tr. John Leyden and William Erskine, *Memoirs of Zehīr-ed-Dīn Muhammed Bābur, Emperor of Hindustan, Written by Himself, in the Chaghatāi Tûrki.* rev. by Lucas King, 1921. II, p.241.
[8] Percy Brown in CHI IV, pp.526-528; Fergusson, *History of Indian and Eastern Architecture*, II, pp.217-219.

Akbar[9] was the son of Humayun, born while the latter was in exile, but himself destined to become the greatest of all the Mughal emperors. During his reign of nearly fifty years (A.D. 1556-1605), Akbar brought under his own sway more of India than had ever before been ruled by one man, and in the administration of this vast realm displayed much wisdom and inaugurated important financial and military reforms. In religion he was a mystic, and while originally a strict and orthodox Muslim he gradually departed from this belief and proclaimed a doctrine of universal tolerance (*sulh-i-kull*). In his new city of Fatehpur Sikri, Akbar erected a Hall of Worship (*'Ibadat-Khana*) in which not only Muslims but also Hindus, Jains, Zoroastrians and Christians were invited to participate in religious discussions. From his studies in the various religions the emperor at last evolved a composite creed and code of rites on the basis of which he believed all of his subjects could be united in a common faith. The teaching was monotheistic with a tinge of pantheism, and the practice of the cult included the public worship of the sun and the veneration of fire and lights. Known as the Din-i-Ilahi or Divine Faith, the new religion was seriously promulgated with Akbar as its head, but it never attracted more than a few thousand adherents and it ceased to exist after the death of the emperor.[10] The rather beautiful mausoleum of this remarkable ruler was completed by his son, Jahangir, and still stands at Sikandra about five miles from Agra. The entrance gateway of the tomb, with its fine inlaid stonework, is shown in Fig. 252.[11]

Jahangir, son of Akbar, became the next of the Mughal rulers (A.D. 1605-1627). Soon after his accession, he faced a revolt by his own son, Khusrau, but crushed this successfully. After his own death, another son, Shah Jahan, succeeded him upon the throne, although not without a struggle against other contenders. Under the rule of Shah Jahan (A.D. 1628-1658) the Mughal empire attained its greatest magnificence and Mughal architecture achieved its golden age. Buildings of surpassing beauty were erected by the Shah throughout the land. Of these we may recall the imposing Jami' Masjid at Delhi, India's largest and most eminent mosque; and the peerless white marble Taj Mahal at Agra (Fig. 253), the mausoleum of Mumtaz-i-Mahal, the emperor's favorite wife, and at last his own burial place

---

[9] Vincent A. Smith, *Akbar, The Great Mogul, 1542-1605*. 2d ed. 1919.

[10] Haig in CHI IV, pp.119-132.

[11] Brown in CHI IV, pp.549-551; Fergusson, *History of Indian and Eastern Architecture*, II, pp.298-302; Glück and Diez, *Die Kunst des Islam*, p.338.

as well. Religiously, both Jahangir and Shah Jahan were Muslims, but the former manifested a certain tolerance while the latter was intolerant and in particular caused the demolition of many Hindu temples.

The throne of Shah Jahan was seized in A.D. 1658 by his son Aurangzib, and the great emperor spent the rest of his life in imprisonment in the fort of Agra. The son did not even complete the father's own mausoleum, which had been planned as a black marble replica of the Taj Mahal, to stand across the river from the same and be connected with it by a bridge, "an architectural composition which for romance, imagination and magnificence would have had no equal."[12] As for Aurangzib himself, he enjoyed a long reign (A.D. 1658-1707) and made some additional conquests, but was not an outstanding ruler. Actually the decay of the Mughal power had already set in, and art and culture were showing signs of decadence. After his death the decline of the Mughal empire continued, and a series of weak kings held the throne for brief reigns until the last of them was banished in A.D. 1857.

Such in brief outline was the history of India during the time in which the religion of the Sikhs arose.

[12] Brown in CHI IV, p.566.

2. THE SIKH SCRIPTURES

As WE proceed now to speak of Sikhism itself, it will be helpful to describe at the outset the scriptures recognized in this religion.

THE ADI GRANTH

The literary collection which has the place of chief authority is called the Granth, the Granth Sahib, or the Adi Granth.[13] The Sanskrit word *grantha* means "book," "treatise" or "written code," and thus the title of this collection is simply the Book, the Lordly Book, or the First Book. For the most part its contents are composed in Hindi or Hindustani and written in the Gurmukhi script of the Punjab. All together it is a very extensive compilation, comprising not less than 3,384 hymns with 15,575 verses, and it serves the Sikhs as a hymnbook, a prayer book and a book of doctrinal theology. A custodian, reader or expounder of the Granth is known as a *granthi*.

The collecting of the materials of the Adi Granth was done largely by Arjun, the fifth Guru or Teacher of the Sikh religion who was head of the faith from A.D. 1581 to 1606. He is said to have felt the need of recording the exact words of his predecessors and specially of Guru Nanak, the founder of the religion, in order to have a source of authoritative guidance for his disciples. For the purpose of doing this work he took up his abode in a secluded and pleasant place at Amritsar. There, with the assistance of numerous followers and helpers, he gathered materials for the compilation and also composed hymns of his own. When all the texts suitable for inclusion had been determined, Guru Arjun sat in his tent and dictated them to a scribe named Bhai Gur Das who wrote them out in Gurmukhi. After much labor the volume was completed in A.D. 1604, and Arjun wrote these words in conclusion:

Three things have been put into the vessel [the Granth]—truth, patience, and meditation.
The ambrosial name of God the support of all hath also been put therein.
He who eateth and enjoyeth it shall be saved.
This provision should never be abandoned; ever clasp it to your hearts.

[13] Ernest Trumpp, *The Ādi Granth, or the Holy Scriptures of the Sikhs, Translated from the Original Gurmukhī, with Introductory Essays.* 1877; Winternitz, *Geschichte der indischen Litteratur,* III, p.587; Von Glasenapp, *Die Literaturen Indiens von ihren Anfängen bis zur Gegenwart,* p.204.

By embracing God's feet we cross the ocean of darkness; Nanak, everything is an extension of God.[14]

While the Granth compiled by Guru Arjun contained the bulk of the materials now found in that work, certain additions were made after his time. It was a third edition which was produced by the last of the Gurus, Gobind Singh (A.D. 1675-1708). In this, some verses of Gobind Singh and some of his father, Teg Bahadur, were added.

In its final form, then, the Adi Granth contained materials from three chief sources. First, there were hymns of the Gurus from Nanak to Arjun, and those of Teg Bahadur and Gobind Singh as well.

Second, there were verses which were composed by various Bhagats or Devotees, many even earlier than Nanak. The names of these Bhagats follow, with identifications when particulars are known: (1) Beni; (2) Bhikan; (3) Dhanna, said to have been a Jat or cultivator by caste and a disciple of Ramananda; (4) Shaikh Farid, a famous Muslim saint who died A.D. 1266; (5) Jaidev, a Sanskrit poet who lived at the court of King Lakshmanasena (twelfth century A.D.) of Bengal and wrote the Gitagovinda; (6) Kabir, a later disciple of Ramananda, who probably lived A.D. 1440-1518; (7) Namdev, a saint who lived A.D. 1270-1350 and emancipated himself from Hindu idolatry; (8) Parmananda; (9) Pipa, raja in a state called Gagaraungarh, and a disciple of Ramananda; (10) Ramananda, a religious leader of around A.D. 1400 and an adherent of the teachings of Ramanuja who had lived in the eleventh century A.D.; (11) Ravidas, a leatherworker who lived at Benares at a date not long after Kabir whom he mentions, and who was a disciple of Ramananda; (12) Sadhna, a butcher by trade and a contemporary of Namdev; (13) Sainu, a court barber and disciple of Ramananda; (14) Sur Das, a Brahman born in A.D. 1528 and governor of a province under the Emperor Akbar; (15) Trilochan, a saint of the Vaisya caste and a contemporary of Namdev.

Third, the Granth contained eulogies of the Gurus written by Bhatts or professional bards. These Bhatts presumably lived in the times of the Gurus they praised, and their names were: (1) Bhalhau; (2) Bhika; (3) Dasu; (4) Ganga; (5) Haribans; (6) Jalan; (7) Jalap; (8) Kalu; (9) Kalasu; (10) Kalasahar; (11) Kiratu; (12) Mathura; (13) Nal; (14) Rad; (15) Sal.[15]

[14] Max A. Macauliffe, *The Sikh Religion, Its Gurus, Sacred Writings and Authors.* 1909, III, p.64.

[15] Trumpp, *The Ādi Granth*, pp.cxix-cxx; Macauliffe, *The Sikh Religion,* VI.

As far as its order of arrangement is concerned, the Granth is divided into three parts. The first part is composed of four portions all intended for devotional purposes. These are: (1) the Japji, an introductory book of praise, composed by Nanak, and used in morning worship; (2) the So-daru; (3) the So-purkhu; (4) the So-hila; the last three comprising hymns for use as evening prayers, extracted chiefly from the Rags which will be mentioned next.

The second part of the Granth is the main body of the work, and is made up of a large number of hymns arranged in thirty-one Rags according to the musical measures in which they are sung. The names of these Rags are: (1) Siri; (2) Majh; (3) Gauri; (4) Asa; (5) Gujri; (6) Devgandhari; (7) Bihagra; (8) Vadhansu; (9) Sorathi; (10) Dhanasari; (11) Jaitsiri; (12) Todi; (13) Bairari; (14) Tilang; (15) Suhi; (16) Bilavalu; (17) Gaud; (18) Ramkali; (19) Natnarain; (20) Maligaura; (21) Maru; (22) Tukhari; (23) Kedara; (24) Bhairau; (25) Basantu; (26) Sarang; (27) Malar; (28) Kanara; (29) Kalian; (30) Prabhata; (31) Jaijavanti. Of them all, the first four are the most extensive and contain the most important materials.

The third part of the work serves as conclusion of the whole and is called the Bhog. Here there are many verses or Sloks by various ones of the Gurus, Bhagats and Bhatts. Throughout the entire work there is much repetition and the leading ideas appear again and again in almost endless variations.[16]

THE GRANTH OF THE TENTH GURU

The tenth recognized great teacher of the Sikh religion was Guru Gobind Singh who exercised authority as head of the church from A.D. 1675 to 1708. As we have already noted, at least a small amount of his writing was incorporated in the Adi Granth. All together his literary work was very extensive, however, and in the year 1734 his compositions and translations, as well as those of bards associated with him, were brought together in a large compilation. This was done in Amritsar by Bhai Mani Singh, and the work became known as the Daswan Padshah ka Granth or Granth of the Tenth King, referring to the Guru. It has considerable authority among the Sikhs but certainly much less than that of the Adi Granth.

Its contents include the Japji or psalms of praise; the Akal Ustat or praise of the creator; the Vachitar Natak or wonderful drama,

[16] Trumpp, *The Ādi Granth*, pp.cxx-cxxi.

with an account of Guru Gobind Singh's life and battles, and with hymns in praise of Durga, the goddess of war; the Gyan Parbodh or awakening of knowledge, giving tales of twenty-four Hindu incarnations of deity; the Hazare shabd, quatrains praising God and condemning idolatry; the Shastar Nam Mala, listing weapons used at that time, with special reference to divine attributes; the Tria Charitar, stories illustrating the qualities of women; the Zafarnama, a letter of the Guru to Aurangzib; and some additional metrical narratives.[17]

THE JANAMSAKHIS

In addition to the Adi Granth and the Granth of the Tenth Guru the Sikhs also have a third body of writings to which they attach importance and which are known as the Janamsakhis or Birth Stories. These are for the most part narratives of the life of Guru Nanak, written at various times after his death. In general, these are highly legendary in character, and the later they are the more of the miraculous they contain.[18] We will return to the Janamsakhis when we deal with the life of Nanak.

[17] Macauliffe, *The Sikh Religion*, v, pp.260-331; H. A. Rose in HERE VI, p.390.
[18] Von Glasenapp, *Die Literaturen Indiens von ihren Anfängen bis zur Gegenwart*, p.230.

3. THE FORERUNNERS OF NANAK

IT IS clear from the inclusion of writings of so many different authors in the Adi Granth that the Sikh religion originated out of the work of more than a single teacher. While Guru Nanak ranks properly as the founder of the faith, he was preceded by other leaders whose teachings were enough in harmony with his own to be adjudged worthy of a place in the Sikh Bible. Of these forerunners two were of outstanding importance, Ramananda and Kabir.

RAMANANDA

Ramananda probably lived in the end of the fourteenth and the first half of the fifteenth century. He was originally a follower of the teachings of Ramanuja, an eleventh century Hindu who was devoted to the worship of Vishnu under the form of Narayan, and of Lakshmi, and who inculcated extreme strictness in culinary matters. Ramananda wandered widely throughout India and visited Benares where he came in contact with Muslims. He gradually changed his theological views and founded a sect which worshiped Rama and Sita, and relaxed the strict culinary rules of Ramanuja. He admitted disciples of all castes to this group, and taught that all its members might eat and drink together regardless of birth.

In the hymn of Ramananda found in the Adi Granth, he declines an invitation to attend a religious service of Vishnu and tells how he has learned to recognize the universal God who may be found everywhere.

> Whither shall I go, Sir? I am happy at home.
> My heart will not go with me; it hath become a cripple.
> One day I did have an inclination to go;
> I ground sandal, took distilled aloe wood and many perfumes,
> And was proceeding to worship God in a temple,
> When my spiritual guide showed me God in my heart.
> Wherever I go I *find only* water or stones.[19]
> But Thou, O God, art equally contained in everything.
> The Vedas and the Puranas all have I seen and searched.
> Go thou thither, if *God* be not here.
> O true guru, I am a sacrifice unto thee
> Who hast cut away all my perplexities and doubts.
> Ramanand's Lord is the all-pervading God;
> The guru's word cutteth away millions of sins.[20]

[19] i.e., rivers of pilgrimage or idols.
[20] Macauliffe, *The Sikh Religion*, VI, pp.105f.

Among the disciples of Ramananda were Dhanna the cultivator, Pipa the raja, Ravidas the leatherworker, and Sainu the barber, all of whom are represented by hymns in the Adi Granth. The wide variety of their callings attests the broadness of the appeal of Ramananda.

KABIR

Kabir, who probably lived A.D. 1440-1518, was also a disciple of Ramananda. According to a very legendary account of his life,[21] he was born of a widowed mother and left on a blossoming water lily on a lake called Lahar Talao near Benares. A Muslim weaver named Niru found the child there, and took him to his home. In order to find a name for their charge the new foster parents summoned a Kazi or Muslim judge, and a lot was cast with the Qur'an. The Arabic word *kabir*, meaning "great" and employed in the Qur'an as one of the names of Allah, presented itself, and this name was accordingly bestowed upon the child.

Although Kabir grew up in a Muslim home he was still subject to the strong Hindu influences of Benares, and is said to have conversed not only with Muslim but also with Hindu teachers. Then after a time he became a follower of Ramananda. While he continued to work as a weaver, he also did many unusual deeds of kindness to men and even wrought miracles such as curing the Emperor Sikandar Lodi when the latter contracted a fever upon a visit to Benares. Thus Kabir became a great saint, and upon his death the Muslims and Hindus are supposed to have contended for possession of his remains.

In his teachings Kabir transcended caste and separate religions, and called upon all men to worship the one God whom he called Rama, or the True Name, or the True Guru. He was opposed to all formalism in religion, and he declared that idolatry was false and pilgrimages futile. Theistic and mystical in his beliefs, he retained the Hindu conceptions of Karma and transmigration.

So influential was the work of Kabir that he still has some 650,000 followers, known as the Kabirpanthis. They cherish a book containing his teachings, called the Bijak; and, as we have already seen, other of his hymns are preserved in the Adi Granth of the Sikhs. From the texts ascribed to Kabir, Professor John Clark Archer has selected among others the following as giving the gist of his teachings:

[21] Macauliffe, *The Sikh Religion*, vi, pp.122-141; for his hymns, see *ibid.*, pp.142-316.

God is one; there is no second. The One is everywhere.
Search in thy heart; there is His abode.
O men and women, seek the sanctuary of the One.
He pervadeth thy body and the universe as well. . . .

Sacrifice, the rosary, pilgrimage, fasting and alms are cloaks of false-
hood.
Why perform so many ceremonies! Of what avail to Hindus to bathe,
and to Moslems to pray at the mosque?
Some pride themselves on the practice of yoga.
Put away suspension of the breath and all the attitudinal in devotion. . . .

Worship God, thou fool!
Renounce family, caste and lineage, lest thou think the Maker thus
distinguished men. . . .

Birth is in accordance with penalties for deeds;
Through wanderings and error man keeps coming to his house
[i.e., the body].
If attention be fixed on God, the dread of and the fact of rebirth are
at an end. . . .

I have met God who dwells within the heart. . . .

Renounce honors, renounce boasting.
They who crave for liquor and incline to drunkenness nowhere find
content. . . .

When thy stewardship is ended, thou must render an account. . . .
Repeat the name of Ram, thou madman!
The ocean of existence is difficult to cross;
The name of God savest him who has tasted of its savour. . . .

I take no thought of sin or virtue; neither go I to a heaven or a hell;
I shall not die as the rest of the world of men.
The soul that is joined with Him is indestructible. . . .[22]

[22] Archer, *The Sikhs in Relation to Hindus, Moslems, Christians, and Ahmadiyyas,
A Study in Comparative Religion.* 1946, pp.53f.

4. THE LIFE AND TEACHINGS OF GURU NANAK

IN TELLING of the life of Nanak it may be of interest to follow one of the Janamsakhis or Birth Records. As has already been stated, this type of literature is in general far from trustworthy, being composed without due historical sense and embellished with a great deal of the miraculous. The Janamsakhi here to be cited is relatively early, however, as such literature goes. It is preserved in a manuscript with characters the style of which suggests the time of Guru Arjun or his immediate successor. As compared with yet later accounts, it is at least free of many fantastic details, and even contains points unfavorable to Nanak which are carefully eliminated in versions of a later date. The title of the manuscript is "A Book of Nanak, Referring to His Birth (or Life)."[23]

This manuscript is now in the Commonwealth Relations Office Library, London; its first page is reproduced in Fig. 254. We also show in Fig. 255 a page in a later illuminated Janamsakhi manuscript, likewise in the Commonwealth Relations Office Library.

The account begins: "In Sambat 1526, Baba[24] Nanak was born in the month of Vaisakh; in a moonlight night at an early hour, while yet about a watch of the night was remaining, he was born. Unbeaten sounds were produced at the gate of the Lord. The 33 krores of gods paid homage. The 64 Yoginis, the 52 heroes, the 6 ascetics, the 84 Siddhas, the 9 Naths, paid homage, 'because a great devotee has come to save the world; to him homage should be paid!' "

The date, Sambat 1526, or Year 1526, is reckoned according to the Vikrama Era which began in 58/57 B.C. (p.220); Nanak was born, therefore, in A.D. 1469. The month of Vaisakh is equivalent to the period from the middle of April to the middle of May; other Janamsakhis, however, place Nanak's birth in the month of Katak which falls in October-November.

The record states that the place of Nanak's birth was Talwandi, which was a village, later called Rayapur and now Nankana Sahib, on the Ravi River near Lahore. The name of his father is given as Kalu, and it is said that he was a Khatri, i.e. a Kshatriya by caste; and a Vedi by clan, this being a group which claimed descent from a famous student of the Hindu Vedas, hence the name Vedis.

---

[23] Trumpp, *The Ādi Granth*, pp.ii-xlv.
[24] A title of respect.

While Nanak was thus of Hindu background, he lived in the time of Muslim supremacy in India, and his home was under the rule of Rai Bular, a convert to Islam and a retainer of the Muslim king of Delhi. It has been estimated that the proportion of Muslims in upper India at this time was ten or fifteen per cent of the total population.[25]

Of Nanak's youth the Janamsakhi says: "When he became big, he began to play with the boys, but the views of the boys and his were different. In his spirit he was occupied with the Lord."

Later he was married and had children, but still spent much time in seclusion and meditation. "Then came the order of the Lord, that in the house of Guru Nanak two sons should be born, Lakhmi Das and Sri Chand. But Nanak's retirement from the world was not given up; Guru Nanak going to trees remained [there] retired from the world."

Then a wonderful event took place. Nanak fell asleep one day in a garden in the shade of a tree. By chance the ruler Rai Bular came by and noticed that while the shadows of all the other trees had moved on around, that of the tree under which Nanak was sleeping had remained stationary. Rai Bular thereupon summoned Kalu, who was known to be displeased by his son's religious preoccupations, and declared to him, "Kalu, thou hast become exalted and I also am exalted, in whose town this one has been born"; but Kalu only made a derogatory remark and went away.

It is further explained that the entire family of Nanak regarded him with displeasure because of his exclusive association with religious mendicants and his neglect of daily work. "Guru Nanak kept company with faqirs, with anyone [else] he did not converse. The whole family was grieved thereby, and said: 'He has become mad.' Then came the mother of Guru Nanak and said to him: 'Son, it does not behoove thee, to sit with faqirs, thou hast a house and family, daughters and sons, do some work! leave off making continually good words! the people laugh at us, that the son of Kalu has become mad.' Such words his mother spoke, but they made no impression whatever on the heart of Nanak. He went away again and fell down. As he had fallen, so he passed four days. When she had ceased rubbing him,[26] the wife of the Baba came to her mother-in-law and said: 'O mother-in-law, how canst thou sit down, whose son has fallen? It is now the fourth day, he does neither eat nor drink.' Then his

[25] Archer, *The Sikhs*, p.65.
[26] i.e., in an attempt to revive him from the swoon.

[549]

mother came and said: 'Son, it does not become thee to fall down; eat and drink something and look after thy fields and crops! be a little attentive to thy work! thy whole family is grieved.' "

At last Nanak received his decisive vision and commission. This occurred when he was bathing one day in the river. "As he was doing so, according to the order of the Lord, servants [i.e., angels] took him away to the threshold of the Lord. The servants said: 'Sir, Nanak is present.' Then he obtained a sight of the true court [of God]; the Lord was kind [to him]. . . . Then a cup of nectar was filled and given him by the order [of the Lord]. The command was given: 'Nanak, this nectar is a cup of my name, drink it!' Then Guru Nanak made salutation and drank it. The Lord was kind and said: 'Nanak, I am with thee, I have made thee exalted and who will take thy name, they will all be made exalted by me. Having gone, mutter my name and make also other people mutter it! Remain uncontaminated from the world! Remain in the name, [in giving] alms, in performing ablutions, in worship and remembering [me]! I have given thee my own name, do this work!' "

A servant was with Nanak when he went to bathe, and became greatly alarmed when his master went into the river and did not come out again. The Khan was called and fishermen were set to searching for the presumably lost man, but to no avail. Three days later, however, Nanak returned to his home unharmed. Straightway he gave away his worldly belongings and went forth to his religious work.

Nanak's first public proclamation at this time was the bold and simple affirmation: "There is no Hindu and no Muslim." This attracted much attention, and both Hindus and Muslims began to pay heed to the teachings of this new Guru. As he continued to preach, it was the custom of Nanak to compose and utter verses, and in this he was accompanied by a minstrel named Mardana who played for him upon the rebec. Although not mentioned in this Janamsakhi, other accounts also tell of a certain Bhai Bala who was a prominent disciple and companion of Nanak.

From this time on, Nanak is described as leading a "retired" life, no doubt referring to separation from all worldly concerns and complete devotion to religious work. Five periods follow, according to the Janamsakhi, in each of which Nanak concentrated his efforts in a different geographical area. "First," we read that Nanak "passed his retired life in the East." In this period he visited many places including the great city of Benares, and underwent manifold experiences.

At one time during this period he halted at a village but could find no one who would allow him to stay there. "There was one faqir there, to his hovel he went. That faqir was leprous. The Baba having gone there stood and said: 'O faqir, allow me to remain here during the night!' The faqir said: 'Animals are destroyed, who come near me, but it is the favor of God that a human shape has come again into my sight.' He remained there. The faqir began to lament. . . . The Guru became compassionate and said: 'Mardana, play the rebec!' [Here follow certain verses which Nanak recited to Mardana's accompaniment.] Then in consequence of the interview [with the Guru] the leprosy was removed and his [the faqir's] body was healed. He came and fell down at [Nanak's] feet and became a votary of the name; he began to mutter: 'Guru, Guru!' "

Not long after this, Nanak and Mardana were taken prisoner by an officer of Babur who was then making his conquest of the Lodi kingdom of Delhi. The two were treated as slaves, but when certain wonderful happenings transpired and were reported to the king, he said: "A town in which there are such faqirs should not have been struck." Later Babur visited Nanak in person, and declared: "In the face of this faqir God is coming into sight."

The second period of Nanak's "retired" life was spent in the south, where he visited various places in the Deccan and also went to Ceylon. The third period was passed in the north; the fourth in the west, where he is said to have gone as far as Mecca.

In the fifth and last period of his life, Nanak returned to the banks of the Ravi River to end his days. There he selected a very devoted disciple, Guru Angad, to be his successor, passing over his own two sons who had hoped for the preferment. As the time of his death drew near, "the Hindus and Muslims, who were votaries of the Name, began to say, the Muslims: 'We shall bury him,' and the Hindus: 'We shall burn him.' Then the Baba said: 'Put ye flowers on both sides, on the right side put those of the Hindus and on the left those of the Muslims. If the flowers of the Hindus will remain green tomorrow, then they shall burn me; and if the flowers of Muslims will remain green, then they shall bury me.' Then the Baba ordered the society that they should recite the praises [of God]. [Here follow certain verses, and then there are broken places in the leaf of the manuscript.] . . . he fell asleep. . . . When they lifted up the

sheet, there was nothing at all. The flowers of both parties had remained green. The Hindus took theirs and went and the Muslims
took theirs and went. The whole society fell on their knees. Say:
Wahiguru [Hail, Guru]! In Sambat 1595 [A.D. 1538] . . . Baba Nanak was absorbed [i.e., died] in Kartarpur."[27]

HIS TEACHINGS

It is already evident that the teaching of Nanak was in general
agreement with that of his predecessor, Kabir, on such points as its
transcendence of religious divisions, its opposition to formalism, and
its inculcation of devotion to one God.

For his own formulation of his doctrines we may turn to the Japji
or book of praise which is found as the introductory section of the
Adi Granth. This is a collection of psalms which almost certainly
came from Nanak himself. The following quotations, given for the
most part in the translation of Professor John Clark Archer, will provide a brief indication of the fundamentals of the message of Nanak
in his own words.[28]

> Thinking comprehendeth him not, although there be thoughts by the
> thousands,
> Silence discovers him not, though it be continuous silence;
> Man is persistently hungry, though he eats of tasty abundance;
> Not one of a hundred thousand artful devices avails him!
> How may the truth be attained, the bonds of falsehood be broken?
>   By obeying the will of God as surely recorded, saith Nanak.
>
> The Lord is true, glorious forever, his loving kindness infinite;
> To those who crave and seek he gives, gives with full abandon.
> What indeed must he be offered to throw his court wide open?
> What words must lips be uttering to make his love responsive?
> At deathless dawn give Sat Nam [True Name] thought and glory,
> Put on the garb of deeds—and salvation's way is open!
>   Be sure that he himself is fully true, saith Nanak.
>
> At the place of pilgrimage no bath avails without his favor,
> The whole creation that I see, it came of his exertion,
> Counsel glows like priceless gems, if one harkens to the Guru.
>   Teach me the mystery, O Guru
>   Of the life thou givest—such wisdom may I cherish!
>
> Truth, knowledge and contentment come by harkening,
> By harkening comes the bathing places' merit,

---

[27] Kartarpur was a village on the right bank of the Ravi River, opposite the present
town of Dehra Baba Nanak. Macauliffe, *The Sikh Religion*, I, p.180.

[28] Archer, *The Sikhs*, pp.120-133; see also Sir Jogendra Singh, *Thus Spoke Guru
Nanak, A Collection of the Sayings of Guru Nanak*. 1934.

Honor and the art of reading come by harkening,
And by it the last stage of meditation.

    Devotion leads to happiness, saith Nanak,
    Sins and sorrow are destroyed by harkening.

Wisdom comes and understanding by obedience,
By obedience comes the knowledge of creation,
Slights and slaps are nothing by obedience,
Death's ties are cut asunder by obedience.

The Name is such to him devoid of passion,
Who knows him in his heart by due obedience.

Impressive are the varied forms of beauty,
Who knows the generous bounty of the whole?
How many issues out of one source flowing—
A hundred thousand rivers from one spring.

    What mighty power for man to fix his thought on!
    No self-denial comprehends it all,
    To please thee is a man's best aspiration,
    O thou who art eternal, ever dwelling in repose.

5. THE LATER GURUS

THE adherents of the religion taught by Guru Nanak became known as Sikhs or "learners," and like the founder the following leaders of the church were called Gurus or "teachers." As we have just seen, previous to his death Nanak designated one of the most devoted of his disciples to be his successor, and thus this man, Angad, became the second Guru.

ANGAD

The two chief achievements of Guru Angad (d. A.D. 1552) seem to have been the enlargement of the institution of a public kitchen which Nanak had started, where guests and friends ate with the disciples as a single family regardless of race or religion; and the invention of the Gurmukhi (from Sanskrit *guru*, teacher, and *mukha*, mouth; thus, literally, proceeding from the mouth of the teacher) alphabet in which to write the literature of the faith.[29]

An interesting although perhaps apocryphal story about the same Guru concerns the time when the Emperor Humayun was driven from his throne by Shir Shah. Coming to Lahore, Humayun inquired for some person who could assist him to regain his kingdom. Being told of Angad, the emperor proceeded to the town of Khadur, near Tarn Taran, where the Guru was. Since at the time, however, the Guru was in a trance and his minstrels were playing and singing his hymns, the monarch was kept standing. Angered by such lack of attention, Humayun seized his sword with the intention of striking the Guru, but marvelously enough the weapon would not come out of its sheath. Guru Angad then took notice of the emperor. Addressing him, he reproached him for not having used his sword when he ought against Shir Shah, and then for wishing to draw it against harmless men of religion. "In a cowardly manner hast thou fled from the battle, and now posing as a hero thou wishest to attack a body of men engaged in their devotions." Humayun then expressed his sorrow and begged for the Guru's help. Angad replied: "Hadst thou not put thy hand on the hilt of thy sword, thou shouldst at once have obtained thy kingdom. Thou shalt now proceed for a time to thine own country Persia, and when thou returnest thou shalt recover thy possessions."[30]

[29] Archer, *The Sikhs*, pp.137-139.
[30] Macauliffe, *The Sikh Religion*, II, pp.19f.

AMAR DAS

Guru Angad selected as his successor Guru Amar Das, the latter having been converted to Sikhism through one of his own relatives. Guru Amar Das served as spiritual head of the community from A.D. 1552 until his death in 1574. He made his residence at the village of Goindwal (Govindwal, or Gondwal), in the region of Lahore. He was vigorous in his attacks upon idolatry and polytheism, and also upon the Hindu custom of suttee (*sati*) or widow-burning, which had also continued among the Sikhs.

According to legend, Amar Das, too, had direct contact with the Mughal emperor of his time, in this case none other than Akbar the Great. The story is that the emperor paid a visit of state to the Guru of whose great sanctity he had heard, and brought rich offerings for him. Presenting his gifts, Akbar added, "I will make thee a grant of whatever land thou desirest, and I am ready to perform any other office that may be pleasing to thee." Amar Das, however, replied, "I have obtained lands and rent-free tenures from my Creator. He who cherisheth all existences giveth also unto me. My Sikhs devoutly give me wherewithal to supply my kitchen. Whatever cometh daily is spent daily, and for the morrow my trust is in God." The emperor further urged him to accept the gift of several villages, but the Guru still refused. Akbar then said, "I see thou desirest nothing. From thy treasury and thy kitchen countless beings receive bounties, and I entertain similar hopes. The villages which thou refusest I will grant to thy daughter Bibi Bhani." So the villages were bestowed upon the daughter, and the Guru bade the emperor farewell with appreciation for his pilgrimage.[31]

RAM DAS

Bibi Bhani, the daughter of Amar Das just mentioned, was married to a young man named Jetha who distinguished himself for his devotion and eventually became the fourth Guru under the name Ram Das (d. A.D. 1581). Within the lifetime of Amar Das, Bibi Bhani assigned to her husband the villages she had received from the Emperor Akbar; and Amar Das gave Jetha the following charge: "Search for some place other than Goindwal for the residence of our Sikhs. Go thither, build a great city, and cause it to be inhabited. Thou possessest the lands assigned thee by the emperor. First build a house therein for thyself, and then excavate a pool to the east of it as a place of Sikh pilgrimage."

[31] *ibid.*, p.97.

Jetha found a region some twenty-five miles from Goindwal, built a hut there for himself as did several other people, and began to excavate a pool. Somewhat later Amar Das gave him further instructions: "Cease to construct the rectangular pool thou didst lay out, and on which thou didst perform some work, and give it the name Santokhsar, 'water of joy.' On the low land to the east of it excavate another pool and call it Amritsar, 'water of eternity.' It shall be consolidated with brickwork when there is an opportunity. Go and exert thine efforts to that end."

The location of the Amritsar pool seems to have been on an ancient Hindu property where there was a small sanctuary called Harimandir or "temple of Vishnu." When the new pool was still only partially completed a wonderful occurrence transpired there in the healing of a crippled leper who bathed in its waters. Thereupon he and his faithful wife accepted the Sikh religion and joined in the further efforts toward the completion of the tank.

As the work went on, the hut of Guru Ram Das was enlarged to a better residence, additional accommodations were erected for the laborers as well as for visitors, and eventually a whole city arose. This city was known at first as Ramdaspur, or the city of Ram Das, and later as Amritsar. The residence of Ram Das was called the Guru's Mahal, or palace.[32]

ARJUN

Arjun was the youngest son of Ram Das, and became the fifth Guru, serving as spiritual leader of the Sikhs from A.D. 1581 to 1606. He resided first at Tarn Taran, and then after seven years removed to Amritsar. He did much to make the latter place the real religious capital of the Sikhs. He completed the Santokhsar Pool which had been left unfinished by Ram Das. He rebuilt the former Hindu temple of Harimandir in the midst of the Pool of Amritsar, and renamed it Har Mandir or "everybody's temple." The new Sikh shrine was only a modest structure of burnt brick, but it had doors on all four sides as a symbol of welcome to all worshipers, and when the Adi Granth was compiled the volume was given the central place in the temple. On the bank of the pool he began another shrine, called the Akal Takht or Throne of the Timeless. Also one other pool was excavated by Arjun, its location being in the secluded place where he desired to work on the compilation of the Granth. This pool was called Ramsar.

[32] *ibid.*, pp.141,267-271,276; Archer, *The Sikhs*, pp.141f.

The labor of Arjun in compilation of the Adi Granth has already been described, and this work was doubtless his most important single achievement. Furthermore, under his leadership the organization of Sikhism was much developed, and the movement which had begun as simply the preaching of an inclusive gospel took on more and more the form of a separate church and even of a state. Tithing was instituted to support the Sikh kitchens and sanctuaries and the office of the Guruship, traders were sent as far abroad as Turkestan, and the faith was propagated in an organized way.

A glance at their respective dates will indicate that Guru Arjun was heading the Sikh community during the latter half of the reign of Akbar, which was the time when the emperor was attempting to inaugurate an eclectic religion of his own. As far as we know, however, Akbar took no notice of the proposals of the Sikhs for transcending the differences of Hindus and Muslims, and the two movements went their separate ways. Interestingly enough, while the imperially favored cult perished upon the death of its royal inventor, the humbler and still apparently insignificant church of the Sikhs continued to grow until it became one of India's more important religious groups.

Even if the Sikhs had no connection with Akbar's attempted innovations in religion, they played a relatively prominent part in political affairs immediately after his death. It will be recalled that Jahangir took the throne at that time, but held it only by suppressing a powerful revolt led by his son, Khusrau. In the struggle, Guru Arjun supported Khusrau, making a large financial gift to him and encouraging many of the Sikhs to join the rebel forces. The crucial battle was fought in the region of Lahore, and when Khusrau was defeated Jahangir punished his supporters severely. Guru Arjun was first fined, then apprehended and imprisoned at Lahore where he was tortured and put to death. In the Sikh sources the story is modified to the extent that Arjun is described as walking under prison guard after his tortures to bathe in the Ravi River and there simply disappearing in the waters. Thus he became the first Sikh martyr, and was afterward known as Guru Arjun Deva.[33]

In his time of torture Arjun sent out this message: "I bear all this torture to set an example to the teachers of the True Name, that they may not lose patience or rail at God in affliction. The true test

[33] Macauliffe, *The Sikh Religion*, III; Archer, *The Sikhs*, pp.142-171; Richard Burn in CHI IV, p.157.

of faith is the hour of misery." Before he died he addressed his disciples thus: "I have succeeded in effecting the object of my life. Go to my son the holy Har Gobind, and give him from me ample consolation. Bid him not mourn or indulge in unmanly lamentations but sing God's praises. Let him also restrain from grief the other members of my family. Let him sit fully armed on his throne, and maintain an army to the best of his ability. Let him affix the patch of Guruship to his forehead according to ancient custom, and ever treat his Sikhs with the utmost courtesy. Let him . . . in all respects, except the wearing of arms hereby enjoined, adopt the practices of the preceding Gurus. Cremate not my body, but let it flow on the bosom of this river [the Ravi]."[34]

HAR GOBIND

As intimated in the preceding quotation, from this time on a more and more militant spirit was to come into Sikhism. After the martyrdom of Arjun, there was conscious antagonism between the Sikhs and the Muslims, and the sixth Guru, Har Gobind (A.D. 1606-1645), regularly went about with a large armed guard. Concerning his personal arms the new Guru said, "I wear two swords as emblems of spiritual and temporal authority. In the Guru's house religion and worldly enjoyment shall be combined—the caldron to supply the poor and needy and the scimitar to smite oppressors."[35] The chief building enterprises of Guru Har Gobind were the completion of the Akal Takht or Throne of the Timeless, begun by Arjun, and now dedicated to both peace and war; and the construction of two more pools, Kaulsar and Bibeksar, thus bringing to five[36] the total number of sacred tanks in Amritsar.

HAR RAI

The seventh Guru, Har Rai (A.D. 1645-1661), was the grandson of Guru Har Gobind. In his time both the internal solidarity of the Sikhs and their external antagonism to the Delhi regime were increased. Once again the Sikhs supported the loser in a struggle for the imperial throne. This time it was Dara, eldest son of Shah Jahan, to whom Guru Har Rai lent encouragement. As we already know, it was another son, Aurangzib, who actually obtained the throne. The latter slew Dara, and attempted to arrest Har Rai, but was unsuc-

---

[34] Macauliffe, *The Sikh Religion*, III, pp.94,99.
[35] *ibid.*, IV, p.4.
[36] Santokhsar, Amritsar, Ramsar, Kaulsar, Bibeksar.

cessful in this. Har Rai died in peace, having appointed his own son, Har Kishan, as his successor.[37]

HAR KISHAN

Har Kishan, the eighth Guru, had a relatively brief and uneventful term of leadership of the Sikhs (A.D. 1661-1664). Aurangzib is said to have invited him to Delhi, with a scheme in mind for his destruction. Har Kishan went to the capital, but died there of smallpox rather than by the emperor's intrigue.[38]

TEG BAHADUR

Teg Bahadur, a son of Har Gobind, was the ninth to occupy the exalted but in those days hazardous position of Guru (A.D. 1664-1675). He made his center of residence at Anandpur, a town which he himself founded on the Sutlej River one hundred miles east of Amritsar, but spent much of his time in tours of the surrounding regions. The animosity between the Sikhs and the Muslim government at Delhi continued, and the Guru was eventually arrested and brought to the capital. According to the doubtless apocryphal account of this event, the Emperor Aurangzib said to him: "It is my pleasure that there should be but one religion. Hinduism is false and worthless, and those who profess it will suffer punishment in hell. I pity them and therefore wish to do them a favor. If they of their own accord keep the Id [festival], and fast, and repeat the Muslim creed and prayers, I will reward them with wealth, appointments, land-revenue grants, and lands with irrigating wells. In this case thou, too, shalt have many disciples, and thou shalt become a great priest of Islam. Therefore accept my religion, and thou shalt receive from me whatever thy heart desireth."

To all such invitations Teg Bahadur opposed a steadfast resistance. "Hear, O Aurangzib," he said, "I will never embrace Islam. Thou and I and all creatures are the servants, not the equals of God. The world is subject to him. The prophet of Mecca who originated the religion thou professest, was unable to impose one faith on the world, so how canst thou do so? He was not able to convert even his own uncle to Islam. Of what account art thou? The *aswad* stone [the black stone of Mecca] which the Muslims set up in memory of Adam, and which they call celestial, but which the Hindus call the lingam,

[37] Macauliffe, *The Sikh Religion*, IV, pp.275-314.
[38] *ibid.*, pp.315-330.

is worshiped by Muslim pilgrims. Is it anything more than an idol? When Muhammad drove idolatry out of Mecca, the inhabitants formed a design to assassinate him. When he became aware of this, he made his escape at night to Medina, leaving all his property behind, and never returned. Canst thou justly say that he enjoyed God's special favor? Nay, we are all God's people. God alone is master. He can do what he pleaseth. O Aurangzib, who art thou and what power hast thou to convert the whole world to Islam? The Guru hath said, 'Death laugheth over man's head, but the brute knoweth it not.' O king, through pride thou thinkest not that thou too shalt assuredly die. He who practiceth pride shall be utterly extirpated."[39]

When the emperor heard this reply, the Sikh sources relate, he became enraged and delivered the Guru to torture and at last to death. The execution was by beheading, and the head was taken back by the Guru's followers to Anandpur for cremation.

GOBIND SINGH

Teg Bahadur had designated his son, Gobind Rai, as his successor in the Guruship. When word of his father's martyrdom came to this young man he is said to have uttered these words: "You know, my friends, that my father has been murdered at Delhi. I am left alone, but as long as I live I will never cease to avenge his death; should I die in the attempt, it matters not."[40]

The militant note sounded in these words was characteristic of the adventurous career of the tenth Guru who headed the Sikh movement from A.D. 1675 to 1708. He took for himself the name Singh or "lion," and reorganized his followers into a new military theocracy called the Khalsa. Initiation into the order involved a service of communion and baptism, in which sugar was stirred up in water with a two-edged dagger, and the resulting nectar was both sipped by the new members and also sprinkled upon them. Adherence to the movement was also signified by the utterance of the words, Wah Guruji ka Khalsa, Wah Guruji ki Fatah (Hail the Khalsa of the Guru, Hail the triumph of the Guru); and by the wearing of the five *kakkas* or k's: the *kesh*, uncut hair wound into a topknot; the *kangha*, a hair comb; the *kara*, a steel bracelet; the *kachch*, a pair of shorts; and the *kirpan*, a two-edged dagger.

With the establishment of the Khalsa the second period in the development of Sikhism reached its fulfillment. The first period was

[39] *ibid.*, pp.378,380.
[40] W. L. M'Gregor, *The History of the Sikhs.* 1846, I, p.69.

that from the days of Guru Nanak down to the compilation of the Adi Granth under Guru Arjun when the evolution was essentially peaceful; the second took its rise with the martyrdom of Arjun and was marked by an increasing militancy which came to a climax with the inauguration of the new society of sword-bearing men of religion.[41]

The Khalsa was attacked in military force by Emperor Aurangzib, the sons of Gobind Singh were slain, and he himself was driven into hiding in the deserts of Bhatinda south of Amritsar. There, however, he wrote many of the materials which came to make up the Granth of the Tenth Guru; and despite all of their tribulations his followers were welded together more loyally than ever.

With his own sons slain previously, the personal Guruship came to an end upon the death of Gobind Singh. Before he died, he is supposed to have told his disciples that the work of the Gurus was completed, and that from that time on the Khalsa itself, with the Granth Sahib, would represent their spiritual leadership. "I have entrusted you," he said, "to the immortal God. Ever remain under his protection, and trust to none besides. Wherever there are five Sikhs assembled who abide by the Guru's teachings, know that I am in the midst of them. He who serveth them shall obtain the reward thereof—the fulfillment of all his heart's desires. Read the history of your Gurus from the time of Guru Nanak. Henceforth the Guru shall be the Khalsa [or, in the Khalsa] and the Khalsa the Guru [or, in the Guru]. I have infused my mental and bodily spirit into the Granth Sahib and the Khalsa."[42]

At this point we may consider that the story of the development of Sikhism has been carried far enough to exhibit its chief features as a religious movement. In the later years a sort of confederacy of military bands came into being,[43] and under Maharaja Ranjit Singh[44] (A.D. 1780-1839) so powerful a Sikh army was built up that the subsequent British conquest and annexation of the Punjab was only accomplished with very severe fighting. Into these later political events it is not necessary for us to go.[45]

[41] Indubhusan Banerjee, *Evolution of the Khalsa.* i (1936), pp.3f.

[42] Macauliffe, *The Sikh Religion,* v, pp.243f.; C. H. Payne, *A Short History of the Sikhs,* p.43.

[43] Lajwanti Rama Krishna, *Les Sikhs, origine et développement de la communauté jusqu'à nos jours (1469-1930).* 1933, p.183.

[44] Charles Hügel, *Travels in Kashmir and the Panjab, Containing a Particular Account of the Government and Character of the Sikhs.* 1845.

[45] See J. D. Cunningham, *A History of the Sikhs from the Origin of the Nation to the Battles of the Sutlej* (rev. ed. by H. L. O. Garrett). 1918.

6. THE MONUMENTS OF SIKHISM

AMRITSAR

THE center of the Sikh religion is at Amritsar, the historical importance of which has been apparent in the foregoing narrative. The origin of the chief Sikh shrine at that place has also been indicated. This was the Har Mandir, erected at the end of the sixteenth century by Guru Arjun. In A.D. 1761 this building was demolished by Ahmad Shah (A.D. 1724-1773), Muslim ruler of Afghanistan, on one of his plundering raids into India,[46] but was rebuilt in 1766 on the same site and probably according to the same plan. Finally, when Ranjit Singh took Amritsar in 1802 he adorned and beautified the temple greatly, ornamenting its walls with marble and covering its roof with copper gilt. At this time it became known as the Darbar Sahib or Lordly Court, and now is generally called the Golden Temple.[47]

The Golden Temple (Fig. 256) stands on a small island in the middle of the Pool of Amritsar, a sheet of water perhaps five acres in extent. There are marble pavements around the pool, and from an archway on the west side a marble causeway leads out to the temple. The lower parts of the walls are of white marble, while the upper parts as well as the domes of the roof are encased in gilded copper. There are designs of vines and flowers on the walls, as well as inscribed texts from the Granth Sahib.

On each of the four sides of the building a large doorway, provided with beautiful silver doors, gives access to the interior. In accordance with Sikhism's devotion to one God and opposition to idolatry, there is no idol within. The place of honor is given rather to copies of the sacred Granth.

The archway mentioned above, through which one approaches the causeway to the temple, is part of a larger building which is called the Treasury. Here are kept eight gold doors sometimes used instead of the silver doors on the Darbar Sahib; a jewel-adorned, curved sword of Ranjit Singh; a diadem of diamonds and pearls worn by Ranjit Singh's grandson; ceremonial *chauris* or fly-whisks; and numerous other precious objects used in processions and special observances. A photograph of some of these treasures is reproduced in Fig. 257.

[46] Payne, A Short History of the Sikhs, pp.49-58.
[47] Fergusson, History of Indian and Eastern Architecture, II, pp.162f.

Also on the bank of the pool stands the Akal Takht or Throne of the Timeless (Fig. 258), built originally by Arjun and Har Gobind, and reconstructed by Gobind Singh. It has a gilded dome and two minarets, and within gives the supreme place to the Granth Sahib. Historical treasures likewise are kept here, including a large sword of Gobind Singh.

LAHORE

As we have also seen, Lahore likewise figured prominently in Sikh history and was specially memorable as the place of death of the first martyr, Guru Arjun. It will be recalled that according to Sikh legend his body was carried away in the waters of the Ravi River. Although this river now flows perhaps a mile away to the west, it once washed the city walls. At the northwest corner of the city stands the Shrine of Guru Arjun (Fig. 259), built by Ranjit Singh to mark the place where the body of the great martyr disappeared in the waters. In this sanctuary, too, the place of honor is given to the Adi Granth, over which attendants wave *chauris* in token of reverence.[48]

TARN TARAN

A third important center of Sikhism is Tarn Taran, fifteen miles south of Amritsar. Here Guru Arjun lived for a number of years. The Sikh temple at this place, built by Maharaja Ranjit Singh, is somewhat reminiscent of the Darbar Sahib at Amritsar. It stands on the east side of a magnificent pool of water, which is filled from the near-by Bari Doab Canal. The temple walls are adorned with flower and vine designs, while other outside walls have paintings of gods and goddesses. A corridor runs around the lower room of the temple, and on the south side of this is the Granth, wrapped in silk and fanned by a functionary with a *chauri*. On the temple roof is a small open pavilion and a fine cupola. Panels at either edge of the roof in front are inscribed with the words in Gurmukhi characters, Satinamu (True Name), and Wahiguru (Hail, Guru).[49] A view of the temple and pool is shown in Fig. 260.

[48] *A Handbook for Travellers in India, Burma and Ceylon* (John Murray), p.352.
[49] Archer, *The Sikhs*, p.30.

Index

Abagha, 530
Aban Yasht, 98
'Abbas, al-, 517
'Abbasid, 'Abbasids, 517-521, 526, 530, 532
'Abd Allah, 483, 492, *see also* 'Abdullah
'Abd Allah ibn-Najiyah, 518
'Abd Allah ibn-Yazid, 497
'Abd al-Malik, 498, 511, 512, 513
'Abd al-Muttalib, 495
'Abd al-Rahman I, 526
'Abd al-Rahman III, 526
'Abdullah, 495, *see also* 'Abd Allah
'Abdullah al-Husayn al-Shi'i, 524
abhaya, 284
abhaya mudra, 286
Abhayadeva, 232
Abhayagiri vihara, 297
Abhidhamma, 276, 277
Abhidhammapitaka, 240f.
Abhidhammattha-Sangaha, 242
Abhidharmakośa, 247
Abhinandana, 188, 190
Abikarib Yathi', 476
Abraham, 487, 488
Abu, Mount, 173, 229, 230f.
Abul Kasim Mansur, *see* Firdausi
Abyssinia, 477
Abyssinian, 498; 533
Acalabhrata, 196
Acaranga, 183, *see also* Ayara
Acarangasutra, 193
Acchariyabbhutadhamma Sutta, 250
Accomplished King, *see* Wen
Achaemenes, 73
Achaemenian influence, 474
Achaemenian kings, 121
Achaemenid, Achaemenids, 80, 83, 113
Achaemenid architecture and sculpture, 100-104

Achaemenid inscriptions, 93-100
Achaemenid Period, 73f., 78, 93, 100, 101
Acheulian epoch, 25
Activating Energy, *see* Chi
Adam, 502, 534, 559
Aden, Aden Protectorate, 461, 462, 468, 478
adhan, 498, 499, 508, 514
Adharakhsh, 117
Adharbaijan, *see* Azerbaijan
Adharjushnas, 86, 117
Adi Granth, 541-543, 545, 546, 552, 557, 561, 563
Adiśesha, 228
Aditi, 133
Aditi, sons of, *see* Adityas
Adityas, 132, 133
Admiralty Islands, 21
Admonitions of the Instructress to Court Ladies, 375
Adoration of a Stupa, 269
Adzuchi, 455
Aeshma, 90
Aethiopia, 466, *see also* Ethiopia
Afghan, Afghans, 536f., 538
Afghanistan, 65, 121, 179, 562
Afrasian culture, 123
Africa, 13, 14, 21, 38, 39, 40, 462; North, 511, 522, 523, 528; South, 35, 40; West, 19, 21, 22
Agamas, 164, *see also* Nikayas, Tantras
Agganiya, 183
Aghlabids, 522-525
Aghora, 170
Aglibol, 481
Agni, 129, 132, 162
Agni Purana, 161, 162, 163
Agnibhuti, 196
Agra, 537, 539
Agraeans, 66
Ahab, 463
Ahimsa, 199, 207

Ahmad Shah, 562
Ahmed, *see* Muhammad
Ahriman, 90, *see also* Angra Mainyu
Ahunavaiti, 90
Ahura, Ahuras, 69, 89, 90, 92f., 98
Ahura Mazda, 84, 87, 89, 91, 93, 94, 95, 96, 97, 98, 100, 101, 103
Aibak, *see* Qutbud-din Aibak
Aihole, 164
Ainus, 420, 421, 424, 437
Airan-vej, 85
Airavata, 148
Airyana, *see* Iran
'A'ishah, 497, 498, 499, 506
Ajanta, 224, 290-293, 308, 313, 314
Ajataśatru, 141, 185, 193, 196, 215, 234, 248, 258, 259, 268, 306, 307, 309, *see also* Kunika
Ajita, 188, 190, 191, 204
Ajitavati, 295, *see also* Hiranyavati River
Ajiva, 209
Ajivikas, 218, 256
Ajmir, 173
Aka Manah, 90
Akal Takht, 556, 558, 563
Akal Ustat, 543
Akampita, 196
Akkadian cylinder inscription, 94
Akkadian inscription, 96
Aksum, 477
Alabhika, 195
Alaska, 48
'Ala-ud-din, 537
Albright, William F., 475
Alchemy, Taoist, 393-395
Alexander the Great, 74, 82, 105-107, 109, 110, 141, 142, 147, 276, called "the Ruman," 80, 81
Algonquins, 13
'Ali, 496, 507, 511, 518, 524, 534

[565]

'Athtar, 471, 478, 479, *see also* Astarte
Atiśa, 315
Atlantic Sea, 466
Atman, 136-138
Attainment of the Highest Wisdom, 305
Atthakatha, 236
Atthasalini, 242
Atthinatthippavaya, 183
Atur Gushnasp, 117, 118, *see also* Gushnasp
August-Food-Master, 431
August Pure One, *see* Yu Huang Shang Ti
Auharmazd, *see* Ahura Mazda
Aurangzib, 540, 544, 558, 559, 560, 561
Aurapaccakkhana, 185
Aurignacian epoch, 25, 29, 30
Aus, 484, 497
Australia, 13, 14, 20, 21, 26; Central, 5
avadana, 244, *see also* Apadana
Avadana literature, 244
Avadana-Sataka, 244
Avadhi, 199
Avalokiteśvara, 246, 293, 303, 309, 310, 315, 316, *see also* Kwan-yin, Kwannon
Avalokiteśvara - Gunaka - randa-vyuha, 246
Avamjha, 183
Avanti, 234
Avasarpini, Avasarpinis, 203, 204
Avassaya, 186
avatara, 153, 156
Avesta, Avestan, 75, 81, 85, 88, 99, 105, 110, 113, 120
Avirati, 211
Aviratisamyagdrishtiguna-sthana, 212
aya, 486
Ayagapata, 222, 223
Ayappavaya, 183
Ayara, 183, *see also* Aca-ranga
Ayaradasao, 186
ayat, see aya
Ayodhya, 158

Ayogikevaligunasthana, 213
Ayu karma, 211
Azande, 38, 44-48
Azerbaijan, 69, 85, 86, 88, 116, 117
'Aziz, al-, 525
Azizu, 481

Bab al-'Amma, 520
Bab el-Mandeb, 470, 475
Bab el-Mandeb, Straits of, 463
Baba, *see* Nanak
Babur, 538, *see also* Rai Babur
Babylon, 72, 73, 94, 103, 104, 107, 466, 490
Babylonian elements in the religion of Palmyra, 481
Babylonian ziggurat, 521
Bachhofer, Ludwig, 417
Bactra, 84, 88, *see also* Balkh
Bactria, Bactrian, 84, 85, 104, 107, 147, 148, 151
Bactrian Greeks, 148, 265, 276-281
Bafuka, 47
Bagh, 290
Baghdad, 492, 494, 517, 519, 520, 528, 530
Baghdadi, al-, 517
Bahram I, 115
Bahram V Gor, 116, 118
Bahram Yasht, 111
Bahubali, 226, 227, *see also* Gommata
Bahubali-kevali, 228
Bahuhastika, 269
Bairari, 543
Bakhra, 264
Bakr, Abu, 496, 499, 504, 506, 508
Bakri, al-, 522
Baladevas, 204
Balaq hills, 472
Balban, 537
Balkh, 84, 89, *see also* Bactra
Baluchistan, 65
Bamboo Books, 321, 330, *see also* Annals of the Bamboo Books, Chu Shu Chi Nien
Bandha, 210, 212

Banerji, R. D., 123
Bangkok, 301
Bantu, 13, 14, 15, 21
Baqi, 499
Barabar Hills, 218
Barbarians, Eastern, 438
Bare Willows and Distant Mountains, 417
Barhut, 265-269, 270, 272
Bari Doab Canal, 563
Baroda, 145
Barygaza, 468
Basantu, 543
Basket Makers, 59
Basket of Higher Exposi-tions, *see* Abhidhamma-pitaka
Basra, 509
Basti, 227
Basukund, 193
Batuta, Ibn, 514
Baudhayana, 160
Bavaria, 29
Baybars, 528
Bayon temple, 303
Baysunqur Mirza, 532
Bazugba, 47
Bear, 53
Beas River, 122, 141
Bedouin, Bedouins, 461, 462, 466, 482, 514
Begochiddy, 50, 51
Behistun, Rock of, 73, 94, 103, 110
Behistun inscription, 84, 94, 95, 100
Beindriya jivas, 207
Bel, 481
Belgium, 26
Bell, Robert, 489
Bellary district, 177
Belshamin, 481
Benares, 135, 167, 181, 192, 249, 251, 254, 257, 258, 263, 264, 289, 295, 307, 542, 545, 546, 551
Benedict, Ruth, 60
Bengal, 173, 537, 538, 542
Bengal, Bay of, 42, 121, 122
benge, 46
Beni, 542
Berenice, 467, 468
Berlin, 129
Berossos, 103, 104
Berosus, *see* Berossos
Bertholet, Alfred, 11

Brahmas, 250
Brahmi alphabet, 263
Brave - Swift - Impetuous - Male - Augustness, 428, 429, 430
Breuil, Henri, 31, 32
Bridge of the Separator, *see* Cinvat Bridge
Brihadaranyaka - U p a n i - shad, 139
Brihadratha, 147
Brihatkappa, 186
Brihatkathakośa 216
British conquest of India, 561
British Museum, 254, 286, 375, 383
Broken Hill, 26
Bronze Age, 25, 67, 68, 123, 325, 424
Brown, A. R., 42
Brown, W. Norman, 133
Buddh Gaya, 229, 253, 263, 269-270, 272
B u d d h a, Buddhas, 196, 246, 280, 285, 291, 312, 316, 449; seven last, 273
Buddha, the, 141, 151, 162, 165, 167, 199, 223, 224, 237, 240, 242, 244, 266, 268, 269, 271, 272, 278, 283, 284, 285, 287, 288, 290, 291, 295, 297, 299, 300, 301, 303, 314, 406, 407, 413, 436, 456; Enlightenment of, 269, 272, 305, 307; Great Statue of, 445; Seated, 289; Temptation, 287; *see also* Gautama, Sakyamuni
Buddha of B o u n d l e s s Light, *see* Amitabha
Buddha of Infinite Life, *see* Amitayus
Buddha-charita, 244, 246, 280
Buddhadatta, 241
Buddhadatta's Manuals, 241
Buddhaghosa, 236, 241, 242
Buddhavamsa, 240, 250
Buddhism, 141, 143, 151, 179, 181, 196, 222, 234-316, 364, 370, 372, 377,

380, 400, 403, 404, 405, 406, 407, 409, 412, 425, 436, 437, 442, 444, 445, 451, 453, 456, 458, 530; N o r t h e r n, *see* Mahayana; Shingon Sect, 449; Southern, *see* Hinayana
Buddhist age in Chinese history, 374
Buddhist art, 282-287, 441
Buddhist elements in Manichaeism, 115; in Shinto, 457
B u d d h i s t, Greco-, *see* Gandharan school
Buddhist history, 532
Buddhist influence, 3 7 2, 449f.
Buddhist monastery, 148
Buddhist motifs, 457
Buddhist priests, 412
Buddhist scriptures, 221, 236-247
Buddhist sculpture, 127, 289
Buddhist shrines, 149
Buddhist stupas, 123, 229
B u d d h i s t temples, 444, 447, 455
Buddhists, 159, 198, 223
Buffalo Museum of Science, 21
Buhlul, 537
Bukhari, al-, 492, 493
Bulis, 235, 259
Bundahish, 76, 78, 79, 80, 82, 85, 86, 117
Bundelkhand, 173, 176
Bunzel, Ruth L., 60
Buraq, 496, 533
Buretsu, 434
Burma, 124, 242, 281, 299f., 308
Burnt Island, 467
Burton, Richard F., 506
Bushido, 451
Bushman, Bushmen, 38, 40-42
Butsudo, 437
Byzantines, Byzantine empire, 112, 119, 484, 509

Cairo, 524, 528, 529, *see also* Qahir al-Falak
Cakravartis, 204
Cakreśvari, 232
Calcutta, 163, 266

California, 48, 419
Caliphs, 508-535; Orthodox, 508-510, 522
Cambay, 232
Cambodia, 297, 301-303
Cambyses I, 73
Cambyses II, 73
Cameroons, 22
Campanile, 526
Campo Santo, 525
Cana, 468
Canada, 48
Candala, Candalas, 139, 180
Candapannatti, 185
Candavejjhaya, 185
Cape Comorin, 171
Cape of Good Hope, 40
Capitan, L., 31
Cariyapitaka, 240, 241
Carmel man, 28
Carmel, Mount, 26
Carna, 466, 475, *see also* Ma'in
Carnaites, 467
Carnana, *see* Carna
Caspian plateau, 69
Caspian Sea, 65, 66, 101
Caspians, 65-68
Casteret, Norbert, 34
Catabanei, see Cattabanians, Qatabanians
Cathedral M o s q u e, *see* Great Mosque of Damascus
Cattabanians, 467, 470, *see also* Qatabanians
Catuh-Śataka, 247
Causarana, 185
Cave I at Ajanta, 292, 314
Cave II at Bagh, 290
Cave IV at Bagh, 290
Cave V at Bagh, 290
Caves of the Thousand Buddhas, *see* Ch'ien Fo Tung
Celestial Immortals, 402
C e l e s t i a l Teacher, *see* Chang Tao Ling
Celtic language, 129
Cenozoic epoch, 24
Central Land of Reed-Plains, 428, 429
Ceremonial Records, *see* Li Chi
Ceremonies of Chou, *see* Chou Li

Go-Nishio, 434
Good Thought, see Vohu Manah
gopura, 168, 169
Gorakhpur, 257
Go-Reizei, 434
Go-Saga, 434
Go-Sakuramachi, Empress, 434
Gosala, 218
Go-Sanjo, 434
Go-Shirakawa, 434
Gospel, 488, 502
Go-Suzaku, 434
Gotama, Gotamas, see Gautama, Gautamas
Gotarzes I, 110
Gotarzes II, 110
Gotarzes, the satrap of satrap, see Gotarzes I
Gotarzes, the son of Gew, see Gotarzes II
Go-Toba, 434
Gotra karma, 211
Go-Tsuchi-mikado, 434
Gottama, see Gautama
Go-Uda, 434
Govindwal, see Goindwal
Go-Yojo, 434
Grand-Jewel, 429
Grand Mosque at Delhi, 538
Grande Galerie des Fresques, 32
Granth, 556, see also Adi Granth
Granth of the Tenth Guru, 561, see also Daswan Padshah ka Granth
Granth of the Tenth King, see Daswan Padshah ka Granth
Granth Sahib, 561, 562, 563, see also Adi Granth
grantha, 541
granthi, 541
Great Ascetic, see Samana
Great Bharata, see Mahabharata
Great Bodhisattva, 292
Great Britain, 462
Great Chronicle of Ceylon, see Mahavamsa
Great King of the Wo, see Ta Wo Wang
Great Lake, see Tonle Sap

Great Learning, see Ta Hsüeh
Great Monastery, see Mahavihara
Great-Mountain-Possessor, 431
Great Mosque at Cordova, 526f.
Great Mosque at Damascus, 511, 513-515
Great Mosque at Hama, 509
Great Mosque at Qayrawan, 522-524
Great Mosque at Samarra, 520f.
Great River, see Yangtze Kiang
Great Story, see Mahavastu
Great Stupa at Sanchi, 270
Great Vehicle, 288, 289, 294, 306, see also Mahayana
Great Wall of China, 305, 362, 364, 366, 367
Greater Imperial Palace, 447
Greco-Bactrians, 107, 108, see also Bactrian Greeks
Greco-Buddhist, see Gandharan school
Greco-Persian war, 112
Greece, 111
Greek art, 111, 283
Greek deities, 283
Greek elements in the religion of Palmyra, 481
Greek empire, 88
Greek inscription, 114
Greek language, 129
Greek writings, 517
Greeks, 82, 147, 148, 462, 466
Green Dome, see Golden Gate
Grihya-Sutras, 160
Grimaldi, 29
Grotto of the Garden, see Taq-i-Bustan
Grousset, René, 291
Guardians of the Four Quarters of the World, 309
Guardians of the Religion, see Dharmapalas

Guda, 150
Guhasiva, 299
Guiana, 14
Gujarat, 173, 179, 229, 231, 232, 537
Gujri, 543
Gump's, 301
Gunasthanas, 212
Gundaphorus, see Gondophares
Gupta, Guptas, 152, 306, 308
Gupta Period, 158-164, 224, 288-293, 294, 300
Gupta Temples, 164
Gur, see Firuzabad
Gurbaal, 463
Gurgan, see Astarabad
Gur-i-Mir, 530
Gurjaras, 173
Gurmukhi, 541, 554, 563
Guru, Gurus, 541, 543, 544, 545, 548-553, 554; Later, 554-561
Guru Arjun Deva, see Arjun
Guru's Mahal, 556
Gushasp, 117
Gushtasp, see Vishtaspa
Gwalior, 231, 537
Gyan Parbodh, 544
Gyogi, 449

Habib as-Siyar, 534
Hachiman, 449, 451, 452
Hachiman-no-kami, 444, 449, 451, 452
Hadad, 481
Hades, 401, 404
Hadhramaut, 461, 470, see also Hadramyta
Hadhramautians, 466, 471, 473-475, see also Chatramotitae
Hadith, 492f., 494, 518
Hadramyta, 470, 473, see also Hadhramaut
Hagar, 495
Hagmatana, 72, see also Hamadan
Hahjeenah-dinneh, 51
Hai-den, 456
Hair, al-, 520
Hajar, al-, 471
hajj, 500
Hakam, al- II, 526

laksha, 191, *see also* lakh
Lakshamana, 168
Lakshmi, 162, 545
Lalita-vistara, 243, 244, 303, 304
Lamaism, 315
Lan Ts'ai Ho, 402
Land of Beautiful Mountains, *see* Koryo
Land of the Morning Cool, *see* Tjoson
Lanka, *see* Ceylon
Lankavatara, 245, 247, *see also* Saddharma-Lanka-vatara-Sutra
Lan-ling, 359
Lao Lai Tzu, 382
Lao Tzu, 343, 344, 353, 372, 380-387, 388, 389, 390, 400, 401, 403, 406, 407, 409, 412, 413, 414, 458
Laos, 301
Larkana, 123
Lascaux, 34, 36
Last Day, 503
Late Stone Age, 122
Later Han Annals, *see* Hou Han Shu
Latin, 129
Laufer, Berthold, 334
Laugerie-Basse rock shelter, 29
Lauriya-Araraj, 263
Lauriya-Nandangarh, 263, 264
Lavanasamudra, 203
Law Books, *see* Dharma-Sutras
Legend of the Jetavana Garden, 267
lei, 325
Leng Yen, 406
Lesser Vehicle, 288, *see also* Hinayana Buddhism
Lhasa, 315
li (measurement), 289
Li (name), 332, 380
Li (Ultimate Reason), 378
li (vessel), 318, 319, 325
Li Chi, 338, 340, 365
Li Ch'üan-hsien, 374
Li Erh, *see* Lao Tzu
Li Hexagram, 336
Li, Mount, 368

Li Ssu, 359, 361, 365
Li Tan, *see* Lao Tzu
Li T'ieh-kuai, 402
Li Yung Shih, 376
Liang, 333, 356, 358, 389, *see also* Wei
Liao-tung, Gulf of, 362
Licchavi, Licchavis, 193, 235, 259
Lie, *see* Druj
Lieh Tzu, 395
Lieh Yü-k'ou, *see* Lieh Tzu
Lieh-tzu, 395f.
Li-hsiang, 380
Lihyanite inscriptions, 482f.
Ling Pao T'ien Tsun, *see* Tao Chün
Lingaraja, 176
Lin-t'ao, 362
li-ting, 325
Little Gandak River, 258
Little Vehicle, 294, 295, 306, *see also* Hinayana Buddhism
Liu Pang, 364, 396
Liu Shao, 370
Lively, 159
Lloyd, Lucy C., 40
Lodi, 537, 538
Logavindusara, 183
Lohans, 312, *see also* Arhats
Lohrasp, 89
Lokeśvara, 303
lokottara, 243
Lokottaravadins, 243, 279, 280
Lonaśobhika, 223
London, 286, 548
Long River, *see* Yangtze Kiang
Lop Nor, 306
Lord of the Dance, *see* Nataraja
Lord who looks down, *see* Avalokiteśvara
Lot, 502
Lotus of the True Law, *see* Saddharma-punda-rika
Lower Aurignacian Period, 25
Lower Magdalenian epoch, 35

Loyang, 331, 332, 337, 344, 364, 376, 382
Lu, 333, 338, 343, 344, 345, 346, 347, 348, 353, 356
Lü Tung-pin, *see* Lü Yen
Lü Yen, 402, 405
Lucknow Museum, 223
Luebo, 38
Luis Alameida, 443f.
Lumbini, 249, 250, 263, 289, *see also* Lummini
Lummini, 249, *see also* Lumbini
Lun Yü, 339f., 349, 350, 365
Lung Shan culture, 324
Lung Shan Hsien, 319
Luqman ibn-'Ad, 473
Luristan, 67
Lut, 65
Luxuriant-Jewel-Princess, 431
Lu-yi, 382
Lydda, 513

Ma, 99
Ma Lin, 417
Ma Yüan, 416, 417
Ma'an, 475
Macedonia, 74
Madabum, 474, *see also* Hureidha
Madain Salih, 481
ma'dhana, 499, 508
Madhyamika, 246, 247
Madhyamika-Sastra, 246
Madja, ibn-, 492f.
Madras, 122, 150, 177, 286
Madras Presidency, 174
madrasa, 509
Magadha, 141, 142, 143, 147, 159, 196, 217, 234, 235, 236, 241, 249, 253, 257, 259, 260, 263, 290, 307, 315
Magadhan culture, 143
Magadhi canon, 243
Magadhi language, 236
Magdalenian epoch, 25, 29, 36
Magi, Magians, 73, 85, 86, 88, 95, 100, 117
Mahabharata, 152, 153f., 156, 162
Mahanama, 241, 242

Mahaniddesa, 240
Mahanisiha, 185
Mahapaccakkhana, 185
Mahapadana Suttanta, 250, 254
Mahaparinibbana Suttanta, 248, 252, 258, 259
Maha-Prajña-Paramita-Sastra 246
Mahasena, 241
Mahasihanada Sutta, 252
Mahasthamaprapta, 310
Maha-Tat, 300, 301
Mahavagga, 237, 243, 253, 271
Mahavamsa, 218, 236, 242, 248, 297
Mahavihara, 297
Mahavira, 141, 182, 185, 186, 190, 192, 193-201, 202, 204, 214, 218, 224, 226, 232, 233
Mahayana Buddhism, 243, 244, 245, 246, 247, 279-281, 283, 297, 302, 304, 305, 309, 409, 445
Mahayana-Sutras, 244, 246
Mahdi, 518
Mahendra, 188, 297, see also Mahinda, Śakra
Maheśvara, see Śiva
Mahinda, 297, see also Mahendra
Mahmud, 179, 181, 536
Mahmud ibn al-Husayn, 491
Mahuvastu, 243
Maidhyo-maungha, 87
Ma'in, 475, 476, see also Carna
Main Shrine, see Hon-den
Maisur, 167, see also Mysore
Maitreya, 247, 309
Majh, 543
Majjhima Nikaya, 198, 238
Majumdar, N. G., 124
Malak-bel, 481
Malar, 543
Malay Peninsula, 42, 301
Malay, proto-, see proto-Malay
Male-Who-Invites, see Izanagi-no-kami
Malichas, 467

Maligaura, 543
Malik Bakhshi, 533
Malikite college, see Sharabishiya, ash-
Malinowski, Bronislaw, 18
Mallas, 235, 258, 259
Malli, 189, 190, 205
Malwa, 173, 270
Malwiya, 521
Mamali, 466, 470, see also Minea
Mamluk, Mamluks, 524, 528f.
Ma'mun, al-, 512
Man, kingdom of, 68
mana, 12, 15, 19, 20, 21
mana, "to mete out," 483
Manat, 482, 483, 484, 496
Manchus, 379
mandala, mandalas, 129, 316
mandapam, mandapams, 169, 226, 230
Manditaputra, 196
Mani, 115, 534
Manichean sect, 118
Manichean theory of evil, 76
Manicheism, 373
manitou, 13
Manjuin Temple, 454
Manjuśri, 245, 309, 316
Mansabra, 263
Manu, 160, 161, 162, 228
Manushkihar, 76, 80, 86; Epistles of, 76
maqsurah, 523
Mara, 287, 305, 307, 316; Daughters of, 287
Maracanda, see Samarkand
Maragha, 117
Marananda, 311
Maras, 250
Marasinha II, 225
Mardana, 551
Marduk, 94, 103
Marett, R. R., 19, 24
Margiana, 107
Marhaya, see Mashya
Marhiyoih, see Mashyoi
Mariaba, 467
Marib, 470, 471, 473, 475, 476, 482
Marquis Ts'ai, see Ts'ai Lun
Mars, 524

Marshall, Sir John, 128, 149
Marsiaba, see Marib
Maru, 543
Maruts, 132, 134
Maruyama Okyo, 458
Mary, 494, 502
Masa-ka-a-katsu-kachi-hayabi-ame-no-oshi-ho-mimi-no-mikoto, 430
mashhad, 512
Mashya, 79
Mashyoi, 79
masjid, 508, 512
Masjid al-Haram, 506, 512, see also Sacred Mosque
Masjid al-Nebi, 506, 507
Masjid-i-Jami', 530
Masjid of the Holy City, 512, see also Dome of the Rock
Master Mo, see Mo Tzu
Master-of-the-August-Center-of-Heaven, 426
Master of the Great-Land, see Oho-kuni-nushi-no-kami
Master of Heaven, see Chang Tao Ling
Master of Secrets, see Sang-dui
Masudi, 84
Mat, 151
Mathura, 151, 222f., 224, 286, 288, 542, see also Muttra
Mathura Museum, 222
Matsuno-o-no-jinja, 449
Maudgalyayana, 257, see also Moggallana
Mauer, 26
Maurya dynasty, 272
Maurya empire, 147
Maurya Period, 142-146, 216-221, 260-264
Mauryaputra, 196
maya, 172
Maya, 228, 250, 267, 307, 316
mayura, 272
Mazda, 90, 91, 92, 93, see also Ahura Mazda
Mazdaean, 150
Mazdak, 118
Mazdayasnian, see Ardashir I

Sage of the Sakyas, *see* Sakyamuni
Saheth-Maheth, 257, *see also* Śravasti
sahih, 495
Sahl Bishr ibn-Ahmad ibn-Bashshar al-Isfara'ini, Abu, 517f.
sahn, 521
Sahure, 462
Sa'id, Abu, 530
Sailendra dynasty, 304
Saimei, 434
St. Petersburg Public Library, 491
Saint Thomas, Mount, 150
Sainu, 542, 546
Śaivism, 144, 176
Śaivite, Hinduism, 229, 315
Śaka Era, 197
Sakaki tree, 429
Sakala, 159
Sakas, 107, 147, 220
Saketa, 234, 258
Sakhra, as-, 511, 512, *see also* Dome of the Rock
Sakiyans, 249
Sakiyas, 235, *see also* Sakyas
Sakka, 267
Śakra, 188, 193, *see also* Indra
Śakti, Śaktis, 127, 164, 315, 316
Śaktism, 127
Sakuramachi, 434
Sakyamuni, 249, 313, 314, *see also* Buddha
Sakyans, 197
Sakyas, 235, 249, 259
Sal, 542
salat, 499
Saleśi, 208
Salhin, 471, 472
Salih, 502
Salmah, Abu, 518
Salt Sea, *see* Lavanasamudra
Salt Woman, *see* Asheen-as-sun
Sama, 481
Sama-Veda, 129
Samadhi, 205, 284, *see also dhyana*
Samadhiraja, 245
Samaga, 195

Samagama, 197
Samana, Samanas, 194, 271, 272, *see also* Śramanas
Samantabhadra, 245, 309
Samarkand, 106, 491, 530, 533
Samarkand Kufic Qur'an, 491
Samarra, 518, 520-521, 531
Samavaya, 183
Samayasara, 187
Sambat, 548, 552
Sambhal, 537, 538
Sambhava, 188, 190
sambhoga-kaya, 280
Samkarshana, 145
Sammeta, Mount, 193, *see also* Parasnath Mountain
Samprati, 219, 220
Samsara, 139f., 178, 181, 188, 195, 207
Samsari, 207
Samsi, 463
Samthara, 185
Samvara, 205, 210, 316
Samudragupta, 158
Samyutta Nikaya, 238, 258, 268
San Francisco, 22, 301
San Huang Ti, 361
San Juan, valley of the, 59
San'a, 469, 475, 477
Sanchi, 269, 270-273, 274, 292
Sandrocottus, 142, *see also* Chandragupta
Sang-dui, 316
Sangha, 216, 257
sangharama, 274
Sanjo, 434
Śankara, 136, 161, 171f., 178, 247, 294
Śankhaśataka, 196
Sanskrit, 75, 121, 129, 131, 183, 241, 517
Sanskrit writings of Buddhism, 242-247
Santander, 30
Śanti, 190, 226
Śantibhattaraka, 226
Śantinatha, 189
Santinatha Temple, 232, *see also* Nagin Das
Santokhsar, 556

Saphar, 468, 476, *see also* Raidan, Zafar
Sarang, 543
Saranyu, 133
Sarasvati, 204, 220, 232
Sardis, 104
Sargon II, 72, 463, 470
Śariputra, 257, *see also* Sariputta
Sariputta, 257, 316, *see also* Śariputra
Sarnath, 264, 289f.
Sarnath Museum of Archaeology at Benares, 289
Sarvanubhuti, 205
Sarvartha, 206
Sarvarthasiddha, 206
Sarvastivada, 243, 244, 247
Sarvastivadins, 243, 279
Sasaki Ujisato, 457, *see also* Sawada Gennai
Sasan, 112
Śasanadevata, 204, *see also* Yakshi
Sasanian art, 306
Sasanian empire, 152
Sasanian Pahlavi, 114
Sasanian Period, 112-120
Sasanians, 67, 80
Sasanid rock reliefs, 368
Saśvasadanagunasthana, 212
Sat, 133, 134
Sat Nam, 552
Śatakirti, 205
Satan, 496
Śatapatha-Brahmana, 163
sati, 555
Satinamu, 563
Satisfied Gods, *see* Tushita
Satna, 266
Satrapes, 481
Śatrunjaya, 229f.
Satta, 212
Saua, 468
Saud, 462
Saudi Arabia, 462
Saumya, 193
Savatthi, 234, 257, 258, *see also* Śravasti
Savignac, Père, 476
Sawada Gennai, 457
Sawdah, 497
sawm, 500

ILLUSTRATIONS

187. Haniwa of the Dolmen Period

188. A Facsimile Page of the Kojiki

189. The Great Shrine of Izumo

190. The Great Ise Shrine, Seen through the Trees

191. Entrance to the Great Ise Shrine

192. The Kasuga Shrine in an Ancient Picture Scroll

193. Praying in Seclusion at the Kasuga Shrine

194. The Kasuga Shrine

195. The Kitano Shrine

197. Shinto Goddess

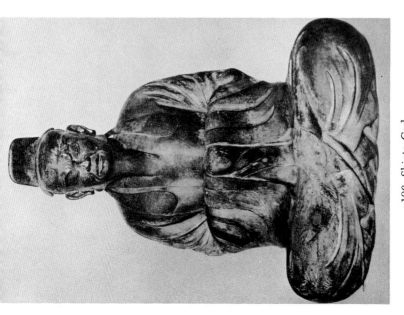

196. Shinto God

200. The Shrine of Hachiman

201. Tamayori-hime

203. Winter Landscape, by Sesshu

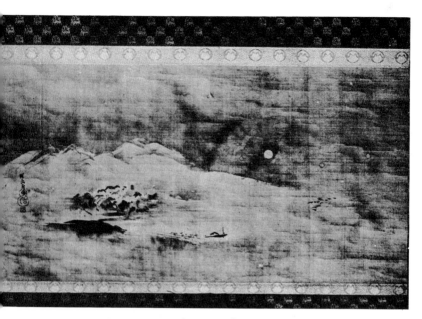

205. Moon upon the Snow, by Kano Tanyu

みのふる はるか
をかの 高根いる
ふきの人々
いそかるらむ

壬辰仲秋寫
應挙

206. Mount Fuji, by Okyo

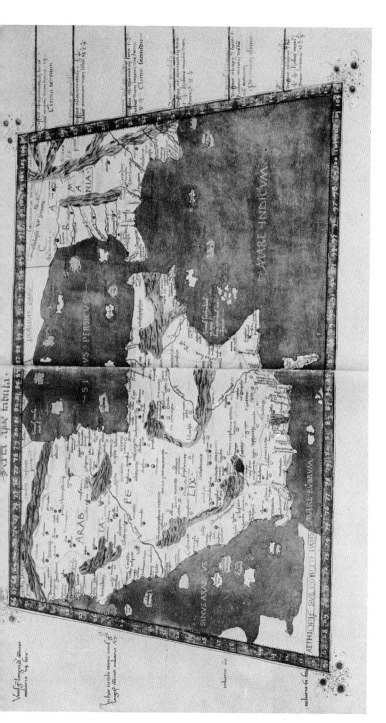

208. Arabia as Shown on the "Sixth Map of Asia" in Ptolemy's *Geography*

209. Baetyl in the Moon Temple
at Hureidha

210. Image in the Moon Te
at Hureidha

211. Minean Inscription from al-'Ula

212. Mask of Kaddat

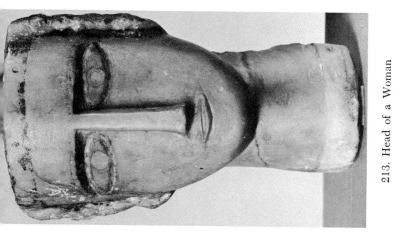

213. Head of a Woman

214. Statuette of 'Ammyada

215. Stela of ʿIgli

217. Amulet of Ilza'adi and Hillqahi

216. Fragment of a Funeral Stela

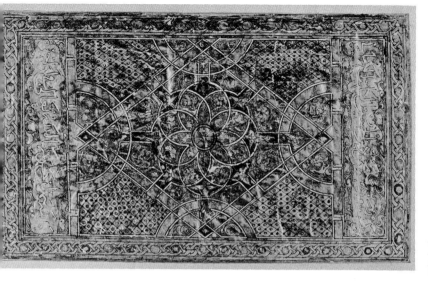

220. A Page in the Samarkand Kufic Qur'an

221. Colophon Page
in a Persian Qur'an

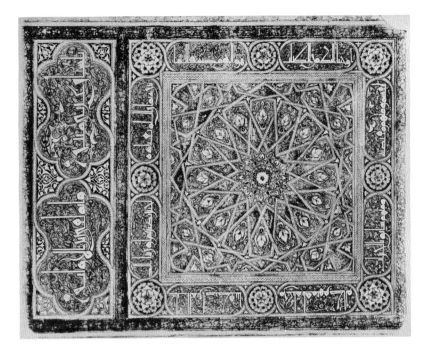

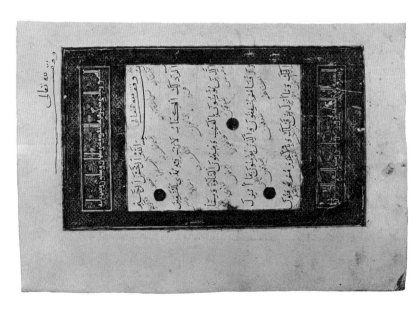

224. Mecca and the Sacred Mosque

225. The Ka'bah at Mecca

226. The Mosque of the Prophet at Medina

Inside the Dome
of the Rock

228. The Great Mosque at Damascus (*From Creswell, "Early Muslim Architecture," Clarendon Press*)

229. Qusayr 'Amra from the Air (*From Creswell, "Early Muslim Architecture," Clarendon Press*)

230. Carved Tower of Mshatta (*From Creswell, "Early Muslim Architecture," Clarendon Press*)

231. The Ruins of the Great Mosque at Samarra (*From Creswell, "Early Muslim Architecture," Clarendon Press*)

232. The Great Mosque of Qayrawan (*From Creswell, "Early Muslim Architecture," Clarendon Press*)

233. Inside the Great Mosque of Qayrawan (*From Creswell, "Early Muslim Architecture," Clarendon Press*)

234. The Pulpit in the Great Mosque of Qayrawan (*From Creswell, "Early Muslim Architecture," Clarendon Press*)

235. The Mosque of ibn-Tulun (*From Creswell, "Early Muslim Architecture," Clarendon Press*)

236. In the Sanctuary of the Mosque of ibn-Tulun (*From Creswell, "Early Muslim Architecture," Clarendon Press*)

237. The Mosque of al-Azhar

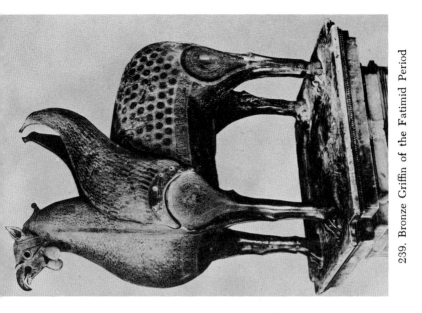

239. Bronze Griffin of the Fatimid Period

238. Fatimid Ewer of Carved Rock Crystal

242. Inside the Mosque of Qa'it-bay

241. The Mosque of Qa'it-bay

243. The Mosque
at Varamin

244. The Tomb of
Timur at Samarkand

245. Muhammad Preaching His Farewell Sermon

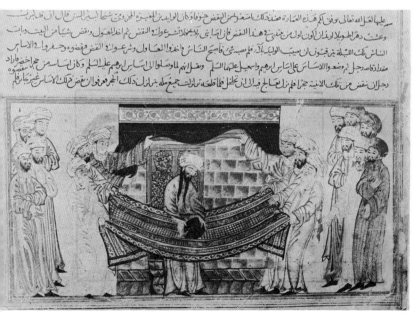

246. Muhammad Replacing the Black Stone in the Ka'bah

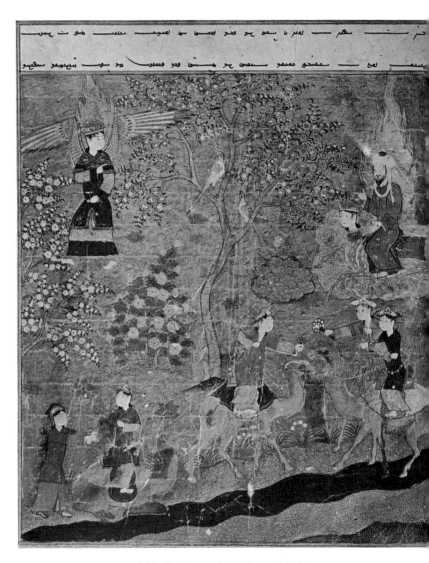

247. Muhammad's Visit to Paradise

248. Muhammad Seated among His Companions

249. Dancing Dervishes

250. Tower of Mahmud at Ghazni

251. The Qutb Minar, Delhi

252. Entrance Gateway of Akbar's Tomb at Sikandra

253. The Taj Mahal, Agra (*Copyright reserved by the Archaeological Survey of India*)

254. A Page in an Early Janamsakhi

255. An Illuminated Janamsakhi Manuscript

256. The Darbar Sahib at Amritsar

257. In the Treasury at Amritsar

258. The Akal Takht at Amritsar

259. The Shrine of Guru Arjun at Lahore